P9-CKR-102

A Being So Gentle

THE FRONTIER LOVE STORY OF RACHEL AND ANDREW JACKSON

Patricia Brady

palgrave
macmillan

For Michael, with love

A BEING SO GENTLE
Copyright © Patricia Brady, 2011.

All rights reserved.

First published in 2011 by
PALGRAVE MACMILLAN®
in the United States—a division of St. Martin's Press LLC,
175 Fifth Avenue, New York, NY 10010.

Where this book is distributed in the UK, Europe, and the rest of the world,
this is by Palgrave Macmillan, a division of Macmillan Publishers Limited,
registered in England, company number 785998, of Houndmills,
Basingstoke, Hampshire RG21 6XS.

Palgrave Macmillan is the global academic imprint of the above companies
and has companies and representatives throughout the world.

Palgrave® and Macmillan® are registered trademarks in the United States, the
United Kingdom, Europe, and other countries.

ISBN: 978–0–230–60950–1

Library of Congress Cataloging-in-Publication Data

Brady, Patricia, 1943–
    A being so gentle: the frontier love story of Rachel and Andrew Jackson /
Patricia Brady.
        p. cm.
        Summary: "The dramatic story—from adulterous beginning to tragic
    end—of the passionate relationship between Andrew Jackson and his wife
    Rachel"—Provided by publisher.
        ISBN 978–0–230–60950–1 (hardback)
        1. Jackson, Andrew, 1767–1845. 2. Jackson, Andrew, 1767–1845—
    Marriage. 3. Jackson, Rachel, 1767–1828. 4. Jackson, Rachel, 1767–1828—
    Marriage. 5. Presidents—United States—Biography. 6. Presidents'
    spouses—United States—Biography. 7. United States—Politics and
    government—1829–1837. I. Title. II. Title: A being so gentle.

E382.B825 2010
973.5′6092—dc22   2010029014

A catalogue record of the book is available from the British Library.

Design by Newgen Imaging Systems (P) Ltd., Chennai, India.

First edition: January 2011

10 9 8 7 6 5 4 3 2 1

Printed in the United States of America.

CONTENTS

Two eight-page photo inserts appear between pages 74 and 75
and between pages 170 and 171.

The Jacksons' Three Homes

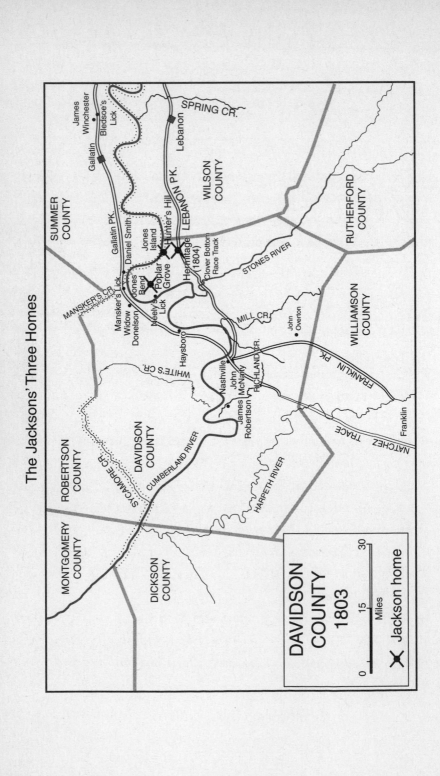

DAVIDSON COUNTY 1803

Miles
0   15   30

✕ Jackson home

MONTGOMERY COUNTY

ROBERTSON COUNTY

DICKSON COUNTY

DAVIDSON COUNTY

SUMMER COUNTY

WILSON COUNTY

RUTHERFORD COUNTY

WILLIAMSON COUNTY

SYCAMORE CR.

MANSKER'S CR.

CUMBERLAND RIVER

WHITE'S CR.

HARPETH RIVER

STONES RIVER

MILL CR.

RICHLAND CR.

SPRING CR.

Gallatin PK.

LEBANON PK.

Hunter's Hill

FRANKLIN PK.

NATCHEZ TRACE

James Winchester

Bledsoe's Lick

Gallatin

Lebanon

Daniel Smith

Jones Island

Hermitage (1804)

Clover Bottom Race Track

Mansker's Lick

Widow Donelson

Jones Bend

Poplar Grove

Neely's Lick

Haysboro

Nashville

John McNairy

James Robertson

John Overton

Franklin

ACKNOWLEDGMENTS

My heartfelt thanks go to the Ladies' Hermitage Association, which has preserved and maintained the Jacksons' Hermitage since 1889. From the beginning, they have been committed to returning portraits, furniture, decorative arts, clothing, and other artifacts to the property and in the process amassing a very significant material-culture collection. The Hermitage is a model historic site. Its mission includes not just property preservation but the preservation of historical memory through educational and interpretative programs, extensive archaeological investigations, support of the *Papers of Andrew Jackson*, and the accumulation of extensive study files of information about the lives of Rachel and Andrew Jackson that are difficult to find elsewhere. Howard Kittell, president and chief executive officer of the Hermitage, generously encourages all studies of the Jacksons. Marsha Mullen, vice president for museum services and chief curator, and Anthony Guzzi, vice president for preservation and site operations, shared their combined years of knowledge, guided me through the Hermitage collections, and answered numerous catch-up questions. Thanks also to Sarah Antczak, an intern from Harding University, for her assistance.

At the Tennessee State Library and Archives, archivists Dr. Tom Kanon and Susan L. Gordon were most helpful, and Dr. Wayne Moore, assistant state archivist, expedited last-minute requests for illustrations.

At the Williams Research Center of the Historic New Orleans Collection, which houses an outstanding collection related to the Battle of New Orleans, Jason Wiese, assistant director, Mary Lou Eichhorn, research associate, and Daniel Hammer, head of reader services, assisted my research. Director Priscilla Lawrence continues to make researchers' needs central to the Collection's operation, as she did during our many years of working together.

Susan Larson was as inspiring and helpful with this book as she was with my earlier biography of Martha Washington. Susan, Michael Ledet, and Jane Brady read drafts of the manuscript, critiquing it with kindness and letting me know when something didn't make sense. My family and friends suffered through a year of neglect with a minimum of complaints.

At Palgrave, Alessandra Bastagli, executive editor, had faith from the beginning that the love story of Rachel and Andrew Jackson should be retold for a contemporary audience. Her thoughtful editing is much appreciated. Special thanks go to Colleen Lawrie, assistant editor, and Erica Warren, associate production editor, for their care and patience. Georgia Maas was an alert and eagle-eyed copy editor. They all improved this book enormously. Any remaining mistakes and infelicities are my own.

Lisa Adams of the Garamond Agency is just what an author's agent should be. She edits, advocates, nurtures, and protects. Her support made the completion of this book possible.

PROLOGUE

The People's President

The presidential election of 1828 turned the American political world topsy-turvy. General Andrew Jackson, political outsider, westerner, and military chieftain (as his enemies referred to him, meaning potential dictator), crushed the incumbent John Quincy Adams, son of a founding father, government insider, and intellectual. Supporters on each side had fought harder and more viciously than in any of the young nation's previous ten elections.

Mountains of paper and rivers of ink had been expended on newspapers and broadsides, each more partisan than the next. Scurrilous charges and indignant rebuttals, more scurrilous countercharges and even more indignant rebuttals had flown. The candidates had been accused variously of corruption, incompetence, dishonesty, violence, pimping, and even murder. For the first time in the Republic, their wives had been fair game as well. Rachel Jackson was called an adulteress, a bigamist, and a whore, and declared unworthy to grace the presidential mansion.

Crowds at political meetings cheered impassioned oratory, devoured herds of barbecued hogs, and knocked back uncounted barrels of liquor. Twice as many voters participated in this election as in any previous election in American history, and the people's choice of the man to be the seventh president was overwhelming: Andrew Jackson.

For the first forty years under the Constitution, the presidents of the United States had been members of the gentry, men of financial substance, education, and dignified manners. All of them had been born and bred on the Atlantic seaboard, the two Adamses in Massachusetts, the other four in Virginia with its self-conscious traditions of gentility and well-defined class distinctions. Only George Washington had much in common with Jackson. He too had been largely self-educated, a military hero who had experienced the West firsthand.

Washington's successors knew the frontier merely by report, much of it negative. Now, political power had shifted westward with the waves of settlers who had gone over the mountains, swelling the white population to nearly 2.5 million. Of the twenty-four states in the Union, nine lay west of the Appalachians, and their voters were Jacksonian almost to a man.[1]

Washington, D.C., was agog with anticipation and suspense. Ever since 1800, when Thomas Jefferson defeated the incumbent John Adams, the presidential succession had been entirely predictable. The party of republicans organized by Jefferson and James Madison to overwhelm the Federalists soon became the Republican Party with a capital "R." From Jefferson onward, Republican followed Republican. Each president chose as secretary of state the man anointed to follow him in office—and so those men did, with clockwork regularity. But the political machine had been fractured with the rancorous opposition to John Quincy Adams within the Republican Party in 1824 and had completely broken down in 1828. A great expansion of the suffrage, changes in the way candidates were nominated, and the emergence of powerful new political factions had changed the game board.

By December 1828 it was known that Jackson would be the next president. That meant changes in the capital, but no one knew how far-reaching they would be. In a city of fewer than 40,000 people, "society," that is, upper- and upper-middle-class adults, probably consisted of fewer than a thousand people—and they all knew or knew about each other. Congressmen came and went, sometimes remaining in office for years, often resurfacing as cabinet members; upper-echelon government employees had been retained in office through administration after administration so that they seemed like permanent fixtures.

Andrew Jackson would naturally name new cabinet members, but government appointees could be a different matter. He had made it clear during the campaign that he believed in rotation in office, but did that mean a wholesale firing of competent, experienced men? Even some of his supporters in Washington regretted the prospect of losing acquaintances who would have to leave the city if they lost their jobs; others were excited by their own ambitions. Margaret Bayard Smith, a writer who kept a sharp eye on the capital's social and political life, remarked on "the hopes and fears of the expectants and the fearers—both tremblingly alive to what may happen." Tension was almost palpable in the air of the capital.[2]

Despite his deep disappointment and disgust at the electoral outcome and an ongoing physical malaise, President Adams kept up appearances, attending public events and greeting guests at his wife's receptions. Begun by Martha Washington, these so-called drawing rooms were large affairs at the presidential mansion, where the first ladies entertained both ladies and gentlemen. An acute observer remarked, "How strange it is, that every individual of the administration, should be ill."[3] Indeed, perhaps as a response to the intensity and bitterness of the contest, Adams's four closest adherents in the cabinet were quite ill, and all were gloomy, giving up their rented houses, selling their furniture, and arranging to go back to their home states immediately after the inauguration. All the Adams men dreaded the public hoopla that would attend the arrival of their nemesis.

But Jackson surprised supporters and opponents alike. Plans for mass celebrations along his route from Tennessee and a grand parade to greet him in the capital were declined by the president-elect. In fact, he avoided any reception at all in Washington. The death of his beloved wife, Rachel, just before Christmas had plunged him into profound sorrow. Escorted by some ten horsemen, veterans of the American Revolution who had requested the honor, the single coach carrying Jackson and his party rolled into Washington early on Wednesday morning, February 11. Arriving four hours earlier than expected, they eluded the welcoming committee and went directly to the elegant Gadsby's National Hotel on Pennsylvania Avenue, conveniently located about halfway between the presidential mansion and the Capitol. Jackson was in town for hours before anyone knew he was there.[4]

February 11 was the date appointed for the joint houses of Congress to count the votes of the Electoral College. Even though the results had been known since the fall, this ceremony was important. Snow, rain, slush, muddy streets—the weather was terrible, but it didn't dim the spirits of Jackson's admirers. Margaret Smith remained snugly at home, but she could hear the "cannons firing, drums beating, and hurrahing" that greeted the official announcement of the election of their hero.[5]

In the three weeks between the count and the inauguration, society was dullness itself. Adams's supporters were too depressed for parties, and Jackson and his family declined any invitation that hinted at gaiety. The general met privately with his closest advisers, forming a cabinet during those weeks. He was also besieged by aspiring officeholders at "the Wigwam," as Washingtonians mockingly referred to Gadsby's. One traditional duty he refused to perform: The incoming president was expected to call on the incumbent at the presidential mansion to pay his respects, but because of the vicious attacks on his marriage by the Adams press during the election, Jackson pointedly omitted that courtesy call.

The suspense was nearly unbearable. Inauguration day was Wednesday, March 4, and Jacksonians by the thousands flooded the city in the days beforehand. Jackson's opponents were floored by the turnout and its political implications. "I never saw such a crowd here before," Senator Daniel Webster wrote. "Persons have come five hundred miles [then a great distance] to see General Jackson, *and they really seem to think that the country is rescued from some dreadful danger.*"[6]

A journalist and political observer wrote: "It was like the inundation of the northern barbarians into Rome...you might tell a 'Jackson man' almost as far as you could see him. Their every motion seemed to cry out 'victory!' Strange faces filled every public place, and every face seemed to bear defiance on its brow." Whatever their politics, the capital's permanent residents were bemused to see the city so full of strangers "who have flocked here from the East, the West, the North, and the South," as Margaret Smith put it. The city's hotels, inns, taverns, and boardinghouses were packed to bursting, several men to a room; latecomers had to move out to Georgetown or Alexandria; there wasn't a bed anywhere to be had by the inaugural eve.[7]

Although one snowstorm had followed on the heels of another throughout February with temperatures so bone-chilling that the Potomac River had frozen over, in perfect symbolism, March 4 dawned bright, sunny, and warm. Everyone had assumed that Jackson, like his predecessors, would ride to his inauguration in a carriage with mounted escorts. Instead, he announced that he would walk down Pennsylvania Avenue from Gadsby's to the Capitol, the first president to do so since Thomas Jefferson. The city's grandest avenue was unpaved and muddy, but it was flanked by wide, paved sidewalks. Because of the immense throng in the city, the inaugural ceremony was moved from the Senate chamber outside to the East Portico.

The morning of March 4 opened with "a national salute," twenty-four rounds of cannon fire in honor of the twenty-four states of the Union. By 10:00 AM, the Capitol grounds were thronged with an immense crowd, as were the surrounding streets. Admirers even swarmed up the portico steps so that a ship's cable had to be stretched across the steps to hold them back. It was an American festival of liberty.

Andrew Jackson left his hotel at 11:00 AM, escorted by a few military veterans and his Washington committee. He was dressed all in mourning black—suit, tie, hat, and long overcoat—dignity itself. Pennsylvania Avenue was clogged with vehicles of every description—carriages, hacks, gigs, sulkies, wagons, carts—as well as horsemen and pedestrians, all straining to see him, cheering every step of the way. At the Capitol, he and his escorts pushed through the crowd to witness the swearing-in of the vice president, John C. Calhoun, in the Senate chamber. Unlike previous presidents, John Quincy Adams absented himself from the ceremony, piqued at Jackson's refusal to call on him.

At noon, Jackson strode out onto the portico where the waiting crowd, estimated at fifteen, twenty, even thirty thousand people, burst into frenzied huzzahs at his appearance, and he responded with a bow. Tall, thin, black-clad, Jackson was recognizable even from a distance by his upstanding cockscomb of white hair. Among the observers, Francis Scott Key, author of "The Star Spangled Banner," kept exclaiming, "It is beautiful, it is sublime!" And his companion, Margaret Smith, wrote, "the shout that rent the air, still resounds in my ears."[8]

Facing the crowd, few of whom could actually hear him, Jackson delivered his inaugural address, a brief and succinct statement of his reform plans. Only when the speech was published in the newspapers the next day did most people learn what he had said. But little did they care. They knew what he stood for, and he was their champion.

After the address, Chief Justice John Marshall, who had sworn in every president since his appointment by George Washington, administered the oath to Jackson. The new president kissed the Bible, then bowed again to the people. They went wild. Cheering, they surged forward, breaking the hawser barring their way, to congratulate and shake the hand of the man they had elected. At last, urged by his friends, Jackson left the Capitol through another door, mounted a white horse provided for him, and rode up the avenue to his new home, the presidential mansion, which had been vacated by Adams the previous night.[9]

Flowing along behind, beside, and even in front of their hero, the crowd headed for the mansion as well. And what a crowd! As Margaret Smith observed, the wealthy and socially prominent were in the minority, while "country men, farmers…boys, women and children, black and white" were rampant. Afoot, on horseback, in a wild assortment of carriages and carts, the celebrants pursued their quarry. It took nearly an hour for the pavements to clear as they moved determinedly forward.[10]

Following previous inaugurations, a sedate group of friends and supporters had visited the president at his residence, congratulating him and taking modest refreshments. The staff had made similar preparations with punch, wine, cakes, and ice cream ready for the new president's guests. Imagine their astonishment when a considerable portion of the thousands who had attended the inauguration began to push their way in. Even before Jackson arrived, the rooms on the lower floor were crammed with a wild assortment of humanity, tracking mud over all the carpets. As orange punch was brought out, thirsty celebrants lunged for drinks, breaking cups and upsetting trays. "The reign of King 'Mob' seemed triumphant," a conservative judge lamented. "I was glad to escape from the scene as soon as possible."[11]

The crowd was determined to shake the hand of their hero and congratulate him and themselves on the victory of a new sort of politician, a new sort of president. Jackson was so besieged by devotees that he kept retreating until he was pressed against a wall. His friends surrounded him, making a barrier of their bodies to prevent his admirers from crushing him. Men who couldn't get close enough jumped up on the satin damask chairs in their muddy boots, craning for a sight of the man. Women fainted, and men angered by the pushing and shoving bloodied one another's noses. The pressure of unwashed bodies was so great that the staff threw open the windows leading out to the gardens and carried tubs of punch and buckets of liquor outside. The president finally slipped away to Gadsby's to rest. He had, of course, declined to attend the inaugural ball. Instead, he dined privately at the hotel that evening with his vice president and a few friends, retiring early.

Waiting until the crowd had cleared out somewhat, Margaret Smith and her friends arrived after the president's departure. "The *Majesty of the People* had disappeared," and in their place was "a rabble, a mob...scrambling, fighting, romping. What a pity what a pity!" As she pointed out, only ladies and gentlemen had been expected, as in the past, not this multitude. But, she mused, "it was the People's day, and the People's President and the People would rule." Breakage and damages ran to several thousand dollars.[12]

Traditionalists were shocked by the melee, but Jackson's adherents thought the whole affair went off very well. Neither then nor later did the president apologize for the exuberance and rowdiness of that party. He had come much further than they, but these were his people, and he stood for them. Never would he turn his back on these republicans of a free nation. He understood that they were merely celebrating the new day dawning in government. After the excitement of the inauguration, that very night the Jacksonian strangers to the capital began leaving for home. By the following afternoon,

Washington had emptied out, as though the people's festival had never been.

Andrew Jackson had won a huge victory for himself and his constituency, but that triumph had turned to ashes with the death of his wife. Rachel Donelson Jackson had been his life's partner, the woman who had been everything to him for nearly forty years. Beneath his mourning attire, he wore her miniature suspended by a cord. Without Rachel, his emotional life was a desert.

Struck down by a heart attack at sixty-one, she had been buried in the garden at their home outside Nashville on Christmas Eve. Instead of dancing at the inaugural ball in the white satin gown she had chosen, she had worn that gown to the grave. Jackson would live on for another sixteen years, transforming the American political scene. But every day of those sixteen years, he would remember and grieve for Rachel. Their love was the stuff of fables. This is their story.

CHAPTER 1

The Tennessee Frontier

West of the Appalachian Mountains lay the wilderness of Kentucky and Tennessee, the backcountry of the colonies of Virginia and North Carolina. For several competing Indian nations, they were traditional hunting grounds. For white explorers and hunters who began coming over the mountains from the East as early as the 1740s, these were lands waiting to be claimed. The beauties of the untouched wilderness—a land of hills, rivers, and vast forests, teeming with game—called out to them. They would return time and again. Within two decades, they would be followed by permanent settlers, their numbers swelling into the thousands, until they made it their own.

In the eighteenth century, the Tennessee country was the site of only a few Indian towns despite earlier, denser habitation by Native Americans in that region. The two most important Indian claimants to dominion and hunting rights in middle Tennessee were the Cherokees to the east, largely living in North Carolina and Georgia, and the Chickasaws of Mississippi to the west. The Shawnees to the north had once claimed the Cumberland Valley area, but had been driven out by the Cherokees and Chickasaws. Still, there were conflicting claims by all three nations along the Cumberland.

The first whites to come out to that frontier were the long hunters, following trails trodden out over hundreds of years by wild animals and then by Indians. Armed with rifles, they came singly or in small groups on horseback leading packhorses for the deer hides and beaver pelts they expected to amass as they hunted. Staying several months or even a year or two (hence "long" hunters), they lived off the land. In such a large territory crisscrossed only occasionally by roving bands of Indians, the long hunters frequently made it back east without encountering adversaries, making a tidy profit and raving about the paradise they had seen. At other times, their luck ended with an encounter with an Indian hunting party. Sometimes they were killed, but more frequently the affronted Indians merely confiscated all their hides and guns and sent them home sadder and poorer.

Speculators were sure to follow the hunters' paths as land was the bonanza of America. In Europe, land was owned by aristocrats and rented to tenants. There were some independent yeoman farmers, but hardly anyone could hope to acquire land except through inheritance. In America, land seemed endless. Indian patterns of use didn't approach anything whites could recognize as settlement. Speculation—buying or claiming large tracts—and then making a profit by installing tenants or selling small sections at greatly increased prices was a time-honored American pastime.

In 1750 the Cumberland Gap, the largest and most accessible pass through the mountains from Virginia to Kentucky, was explored by Dr. Thomas Walker, a Virginia physician and speculator. In 1769

Daniel Boone, North Carolina farmer and hunter, went on a long hunt in the Kentucky country, coming home broke (after a losing encounter with Shawnees) but inspired. Another land speculator, Judge Richard Henderson of North Carolina, hired Boone in 1775 to arrange a meeting with Cherokee elders. They sold Henderson land in Kentucky to which they had no claim and in Tennessee, including the Cumberland Valley, to which they did. Boone then led an expedition through the Cumberland Gap with a group of muscular axmen, following Indian trails and cutting a road through the forests into Kentucky that became known as the Wilderness Road.

They built a settlement called Fort Boone or Boonesborough, where Boone brought his extended family to live. An ever-growing flood of white settlers followed the Wilderness Road to Boonesborough or to neighboring Harrodsburg, founded at about the same time. Steep, winding, rocky, and clogged with tree stumps, the road west wasn't for the cowardly. Kentucky was the first of the trans-Appalachian areas to be heavily settled by whites, but the area to the south, Tennessee, soon followed.

Rachel Donelson was the ninth of eleven children of one of the founding white families of middle Tennessee. Her father, John Donelson, was an educated surveyor, planter, and land speculator of Scottish-Welsh heritage. Born in Maryland in 1718, a third-generation American, as a young man he moved to Virginia, where he met and married Rachel Stockley in 1744. She was a native Virginian of Ulster Scottish-English stock. The groom was twenty-six, the bride only fourteen. They moved westward in Virginia to frontier

Pittsylvania County in the foothills of the Appalachians, where their fourth and last daughter, a brown-eyed baby girl with curly black hair, called Rachel after her mother, was born in 1769.

Donelson acquired an iron foundry and a plantation, worked by some thirty slaves. He was appointed county surveyor in 1767, represented Pittsylvania in the House of Burgesses for five years, and joined the county militia as colonel at the outbreak of the American Revolution in 1775. The Donelsons were prosperous and well-respected minor gentry and might have lived out their lives in Virginia if John Donelson had not gone over the mountains to survey western lands.

As colonies, both Virginia and North Carolina were bounded by the Atlantic Ocean on the east, with northern and southern borders designated carefully by latitude. But their western boundaries were theoretically almost limitless. The grants ran from sea to sea, and no one had a notion how far away the western sea might lie. With a surveying crew, Donelson trekked through the Cumberland River area of middle Tennessee with its broad bottomlands, navigable rivers and streams, and abundant salt licks. On the frontier, it seemed that ambitious and industrious men could better themselves with claims to fertile bottomlands like the early planters on the Atlantic coast. Going west embodied the American dream of wealth and freedom.

In 1779 Richard Henderson contracted with John Donelson and James Robertson to lead settlers to the Cumberland. Henderson's earlier purchase of Cherokee lands in Kentucky had run into trouble, but he still had hopes for Tennessee. Like Henderson, Robertson was a North Carolinian. In 1769 he had established a claim in the upper Holston Valley near the Watauga River of Tennessee. There he settled his family and several neighbors; they formed a government known as the Watauga Association in 1772. But, like John Donelson, Robertson became entranced by the Cumberland while on a surveying trip. A few settlers already lived at French Lick on the Cumberland River, the site of present-day Nashville. Salt licks or salt springs were very much sought after because imported salt was expensive and cumbersome to transport. Naturally occurring salt attracted game and was easily processed for human consumption.

Robertson and Donelson planned a joint expedition to French Lick in company with their extended families, neighbors, friends, and a few slaves—more than one hundred people altogether. The larger the group, the safer they would be from hostile Indians and the more mutual assistance they could count on in clearing land, planting, harvesting, and building.

After the fall harvest of 1779, the Donelsons sold their land and the furniture they couldn't bring along. John and Rachel Donelson, their eleven children, in-laws, slaves, and neighbors mounted their horses and rode up the rocky trail into the mountains. Because of the snow and sleet, they all wore several layers of clothes, further wrapping themselves in quilts, the hats on their heads tied down with shawls against the angry wind. They were accompanied by a train of packhorses loaded with barrels, baskets, boxes, and saddle bags filled with the necessities for frontier life. At last they reached the defensive blockhouse on the far side of the mountains and turned south on the trail to Fort Patrick Henry, built at the beginning of the American Revolution as protection against the British and the Cherokees and manned throughout the war.

At the settlement outside the fort on the Holston River, they met the Robertson party. There they divided forces, most of the men going with Robertson on horseback, driving all the cattle, horses, hogs, and sheep before them, chivvied along by their dogs. They rode back up to the blockhouse, then turned westward to the Cumberland Gap and on down the Wilderness Road to Kentucky. On the road to French Lick, they met a group of families heading for Harrodsburg and convinced them to go to Tennessee instead. They arrived at their destination during Christmas week of 1779. The Cumberland River was frozen solid, and they completed their 400-mile journey by driving their large herd across the ice to their new home on Christmas Day.

Back at Fort Patrick Henry, the Donelsons and the rest of their party were confronted with one of the coldest winters ever known in those parts. Suffering from hands and feet swollen and ulcerated with chilblains and in danger of frostbite, they built the boats that would take them on their epic journey. At least timber was readily available in the heavily forested valley. The Donelsons' large flatboat, christened the *Adventure* by its proud owners, was about a hundred feet long and twenty feet wide. There were probably a dozen or more flatboats capable of transporting large families in their flotilla, as well as assorted smaller boats, including canoes and dugouts, bringing the total to about thirty vessels. Their route— down the Holston River, to the Tennessee, continuing onward to the Ohio for a short stretch before ascending the Cumberland River to French Lick—was more than a thousand dangerous miles long, what with Indians, shoals, rapids, and the very real prospect of running out of supplies. By road today, the distance between the fort, now Kingsport, and Nashville is about 285 miles. But back then it was a wilderness so impenetrable to large parties that the long, long river journey was a reasonable option.

John Donelson kept an illuminating journal of the voyage, which he described as "intended by God's permission." He made brief, fairly regular entries, writing more extended accounts of dangers and hardships. He never mentioned his twelve-year-old daughter Rachel or any other family member. That omission indicated how well the Donelsons fared on their trip. The people Donelson mentioned by name were those who suffered some catastrophe—shipwreck, Indian attack, illness, death, or separation from the party.[1]

On December 22, 1779, the boats departed the fort, floating down the Holston River. They didn't get very far. Just a few miles down, they reached the mouth of Reedy Creek, where they were marooned by severe frost and the falling level of the river, no longer sufficient to float their crafts. Camping there for nearly two months, they suffered severely from the cold and low spirits.

In February, they were able to float a few more miles before fetching up at the mouth of Cloud's Creek on February 20. There they lay for another week and then sailed again, now in company with vessels that had just come down from the fort. But that very day, the *Adventure* and two other boats struck the Poor Valley Shoal, where they lay stuck all afternoon and overnight in what Donelson described as "much distress."

The following morning, the river rose a bit, and, after offloading about thirty passengers, they were able to get off the shoal. They sailed during the day and tied up at night to avoid running into shoals or other obstructions in the dark. The next few days were miserably rainy. On March 2, one of the boats was driven onto an island by the force of the current and sank. All the party put ashore to help, bailing out the swamped boat and refloating it.

Although everyone had brought barrels of salted meat and bags of cornmeal, as well as dried and pickled fruits and vegetables, provisions were already running low because of their two-month delay. Hunting in the woods along the river was essential to feeding the party. The day the boat sank, a young man went hunting in the thick forest and didn't return. To guide him home, Donelson fired the cannon on the *Adventure,* and the others shot their guns; several men went into the woods looking for him without success. So the following day they set off again, leaving behind the boats of the boy's distraught parents and some of their friends to continue the search. Unexpectedly, the main party came upon him several miles down the river where he had wandered and took him aboard.

After entering the Tennessee River, the fleet arrived at a deserted Chickamauga town on March 7. The Chickamaugas were a breakaway group of Cherokees who had settled in several towns along the southern bank of the Tennessee. Their leader was a chief called Dragging Canoe. Incensed at the sale of Cherokee lands to the east and determined to turn back the white tide, the Chickamaugas were ferocious enemies of the settlers. Although they had deserted some of their towns because of militia attacks that spring, the Indians still maintained a strong presence along the river.

The next day, the boats came to a town that was very much populated. Upon spying the Donelson party, the Indians made signs of friendship and called them brothers. Donelson's son and another man started paddling toward shore in a canoe when they were warned off by a boatload of Indians. Among them was Archy Coody, described by Donelson as a "half-Breed," who advised them that they were in danger and should continue on downstream. After some confused negotiations, the whites saw a number of Indians embarking in their canoes, armed, and painted red and black. They outran that group, then came upon another town, where one young man of their party was shot and killed when his boat ran too near the shore.

Later that day, still more shocking to the voyagers was the "tragical misfortune," as John Donelson called it, of the Stuart family and their friends—twenty-eight in all. Part of the expedition since the beginning, several family members had come down with smallpox, one of the most virulent and contagious illnesses of the day. The leaders of the main party and Mr. Stuart agreed that their boat should be quarantined, lagging some distance to the rear to keep the infection from spreading and camping separately each night. The increasing numbers of Indians marching along the shore, shadowing the travelers, took note of the isolation and helplessness of the trailing boat. They struck at once, out of sight of the flotilla. But the main party could hear the agonized screams and cries of the Stuarts and their friends as they were killed or taken prisoner.

Fearing for their own lives and not daring to pause, the convoy kept an anxious watch on the Chickamaugas, who continued to keep pace with them. When the Cumberland Mountains narrowed on both sides of the Tennessee River, the Indians could no longer continue along the banks, but the rapids through this gorge were dangerous enough. Going through the choppy upper portion, called the "boiling Pot," a large canoe was overturned. Everyone landed at a level spot to help rescue its cargo. To their horror, the Indians reappeared atop the cliffs and started firing down at them, wounding four people slightly. They immediately pushed off and headed into another trial, a place where the river rushed so rapidly over rocks that it created a powerful whirlpool called the Suck or the Whirl.

As they caromed through the Suck to the wide and peaceful current on the other side of the gorge, one boat ran aground on a large rock. Unable to approach safely, the others abandoned the hapless passengers to drown or be taken by Indians. The boat belonged to Jonathan Jennings and his family, like the Stuarts part of the original expedition. Terrified to stop, the other boats continued on throughout the night and the next day. Finally at midnight, they believed they were beyond the reach of the Chickamaugas and set up camp on shore.

At four o'clock the next morning, March 10, however, they were awakened by cries of "help poor Jennings," coming from upriver. To their surprise, some of the Jennings family had caught up with them, their boat riddled with bullet holes, battered by rocks, and practically useless. Floating downriver, they had found their companions by the light of their campfires.

Their survival was the stuff of legend. Trapped on the rock and under blistering fire from the Indians, they had started throwing goods overboard to lighten the boat so it could float free. Their son, a male passenger, and a male slave went overboard, possibly wounded, to be captured or killed by their attackers.

Jonathan Jennings, an excellent marksman, fired back while his wife, a black slave woman, and their passenger, the wife of Ephraim Peyton, one of the men who had gone overland with James Robertson, continued tossing the cargo. Mrs. Peyton was particularly valiant since she had given birth only the night before. Mrs. Jennings finally got out and shoved, nearly getting left behind when the boat suddenly slipped off the rock. In all the hurry and confusion, the day-old Peyton baby was killed, perhaps going overboard. Donelson remarked that all their clothes, particularly those of Mrs. Jennings, were "very much cut with bullets."

After redistributing the Jenningses and Mrs. Peyton among the other boats, the party floated on. On March 12, they arrived at Muscle Shoals (in present-day Alabama), a fearful danger in their path. The roar of high water running at a great speed over rocks could be heard for miles. But they had hopes of ending their river journey without attempting these rapids. It had been agreed that Captain Robertson would explore an overland route from French Lick to the Tennessee River above Muscle Shoals, leaving signs that they could debark and finish their journey on land. To their intense disappointment, there were no signs, so they had to run the shoals.

The current of the river ran in every direction. The boats frequently dragged the bottom, and they feared being dashed to pieces. Donelson had been told that the shoals were twenty-five or thirty miles long. Since they passed through them in about three hours, he guessed that they had descended at great speed. As soon as they got through—all alive—they camped and rested for the night. Their last days on the Tennessee were mostly peaceful, free from natural obstacles and disturbed by only one Indian attack.

On March 15 they arrived at the mighty Ohio River, in full spring flood with a racing current. After all this time gliding downstream, the party now had to pole their very unwieldy boats upstream against the current, several men on each side. Some of the party lost their nerve in the face of such hard going and turned their boats downstream, deciding to follow the Ohio to the Mississippi as far as Natchez.

Besides the exhausting labor of poling the boats against a strong current all day while making scant headway, everybody was weak from hunger. Their food supplies were gone, and they were entirely dependent on whatever wild game they could kill. After nine weary days on the Ohio, on the afternoon of March 24 they came to the mouth of a small river that John Donelson hoped was the Cumberland. Others doubted, but he was right. Although still poling upstream, they were now upon a much smaller river with a gentler current. As the boats continued along slowly for the next month, the men frequently killed buffalo and once a swan, which they found delicious. They also gathered green herbs, called by some Shawnee Salad, in the river's bottomlands.

They were nearly worn to the bone with the fatigue of moving their boats upstream when, on April 24, after four months of grueling adventures, the party (minus those killed by Indians, disease, accident, or drowning, and those who had chosen to go a different way) arrived at their destination. Donelson concluded his journal, "This day we arrived at our journey's end." At French Lick they were delighted to find the James Robertson party, reuniting family members who by this time had almost despaired of seeing each other again. The wives and daughters from the river trip, including Charlotte Robertson, James's wife, and both Rachel Donelsons were among the first white women in Tennessee.

Colonel Richard Henderson, who had been responsible for the Robertson-Donelson expeditions, appeared soon after the flotilla of boats landed at French Lick, having arranged for the welcome delivery of a load of cornmeal. He insisted on a name change for the fledgling settlement, choosing Nashborough in honor of a Revolutionary commander. He also led the other men in setting up an interim government under the Cumberland Compact until East Coast institutions could reach them.

The Cumberland seemed a new Eden to the Donelsons and the other settlers. Rich soil, abundant timber for building, a profusion of game, moderate weather, easy access to the Mississippi River down the Cumberland and the Ohio, and a beautiful situation—soon they had surveyed and bought their acreage, built cabins, and put in crops.

After building shelters, getting a crop of corn into the ground was essential to life on the frontier. All settlers brought a leather pouch of seed corn, but most had to clear the land before they could plant. Trees held no beauty for pioneers. They were useful for building houses, boats, fences, wagons, furniture, bowls, utensils, and a thousand other things. But they were huge obstacles in the way of cleared fields, not to speak of providing shelter and hiding places for reconnoitering enemies. Chopping down smaller trees, girdling the larger ones, grubbing up roots as best they could—all were necessary tasks in the process of creating fields to plow and plant.

John Donelson, however, was astute in the land he claimed—a clover bottom. This was a low-lying field of clover with very few trees alongside a river. Clover Bottom, as they called their place, was on the Stones River, a few miles east of the new town. Without the heavy labor of clearing a forest, Donelson, his many sons, and enslaved blacks were able to plant fields of corn and the first cotton in Tennessee.

Away from the riverbanks, the new settlers found themselves in a howling wilderness, delightful to hunters, but fearsome to farmers and their wives. A dark virgin forest of huge trees stretched on endlessly. To their ears, the wilderness literally howled—with storm winds, the calls of birds and animals, the screams of attacking Indians. Perhaps in response to these frightening noises, much like whistling when passing a graveyard, the pioneers were noticeably fond of their own voices, except when stalking game, of course. They talked all the time, spinning tales, rhyming, riddling, trying out tongue twisters, imitating animals, arguing, and challenging one another. Whistling and singing made almost any job go faster and contributed to their evening's entertainment as well. The Donelsons were known as especially good talkers.

That spring, the settlers had to make almost everything from scratch. The most valuable items for their new lives they brought with them—all the manufactured metal implements that they couldn't make themselves. Rifles were essential, both to kill game and to protect against enemies. The favored gun was a long-barreled lightweight model developed by arms makers in Pennsylvania. These so-called American, later Kentucky, rifles were easy to carry, accurate at long distance, silent in loading with a hickory rod, and so small-bored that a pound of lead was sufficient to make sixty to seventy bullets in the molds that all pioneers owned. They also brought knives, tomahawks, axes, adzes, hoes, froes, mauls, needles, thimbles, and pins.

A few log cabins and lean-tos had been built by the advance party before the voyagers arrived, but there were many more to raise, as well as a fort and blockhouses against Indian attacks. Trees felled, logs shaped and notched, chinking cut, pegs carved, shakes adzed, clay and mud brought up wet for daubing: building even a simple cabin was backbreaking work.

Theoretically, the tasks of men and women fell into familiar gender-based divisions. Men were primarily responsible for building houses and fences, tending stock, plowing, planting, hunting, and defense. Women were primarily responsible for cooking, processing food, spinning and weaving cloth, sewing, mending, and child-rearing. But that word "primarily" says it all. On the frontier, there was tremendous blurring of responsibility. A woman who couldn't shoot a gun or wield an axe in defense of her family didn't amount to much, and when crops had to be planted or harvested, everyone turned to. But a man who scorned to sew a ripped shirt or cook up a pot of buffalo stew was considered equally useless.

When they discovered a new white settlement smack in the middle of their hunting grounds, the Chickasaws of northern Mississippi were outraged. A group of Cherokees might have sold their own rights, but they had no authority to dispose of land claimed by the Chickasaws. They were joined by the Chickamaugas under Chief Dragging Canoe's leadership. Here was the very incursion onto Indian lands that he had foreseen when he opposed the sale of Cherokee lands to Henderson and other land speculators. Because of them, he had moved his people west, and now white settlers had followed.

Soon, the Indians began a constant stream of attacks on farms, houses, and even the fort, with hit-and-run raids that resulted in houses in flames, settlers killed or taken prisoner, horses and other livestock driven away. Working in the fields, picking berries, going to the stream for water, milking the cows, visiting a friend—any daily activity could become a death sentence if Indians were in the area. The settlers responded with equally deadly violence as posses tracked the raiders back to their towns. Methods of warfare on both sides were swift and deadly—lightning in-and-out raids, destruction of homes and crops, killing women and children without mercy. Scalping, stealing horses, and taking plunder from dead enemies were commonplace among both whites and Indians.

Besides the fort at Nashborough, earlier settlers had built sturdy blockhouses, homes that were very fort-like. The Donelsons withdrew to the fortified station of Kaspar Mansker, a German immigrant and former long hunter. In addition to the constant Indian attacks that prevented them from tending their crops, the Stones River flooded, swallowing up the fruits of their labor. When the water went down, some of the men went to Clover Bottom to harvest and were attacked by Indians.

By the end of 1780 it began to seem that the Chickasaw-Chickamauga strategy would succeed, and the Nashborough settlement was doomed. Many of the residents went back east over the mountains to Virginia or North Carolina. Others, like the Robertsons, determined to stay, generally living "forted up," as they called their situation. All the neighborhood crowded into the fort or blockhouses, and armed men went along to protect anyone working the fields or doing chores.

Although they believed, quite incorrectly, that James Henderson's negotiations with the Cherokees had given them a valid claim to the land, John and Rachel Donelson chose to make a strategic retreat to Kentucky. They intended to return to Clover Bottom when the Indians were less "troublesome," the term commonly used by settlers for a barrage of raids. Longer settled and more heavily populated, the Kentucky heartland was more secure from Indian raids than the Cumberland settlement. In late 1780, after less than a year in Tennessee, the large Donelson clan, including thirteen-year-old Rachel, saddled up and headed north up the trace to Kentucky.

CHAPTER 2

A Marriage Made in Hell

*I*n 1780 John Donelson claimed more than 2,000 acres of land near Davies Station outside Crab Orchard, a small settlement on the Wilderness Road to Harrodsburg, the first town permanently settled in the Kentucky territory. The family might have lived on the land (though this is unlikely, given the fear of Indian attacks), in Crab Orchard, or in Harrodsburg, the most comfortable and secure of their options with a fort overlooking the town. Unlike most frontier towns, where the cabins were thrown up higgledy-piggledy, the ten or fifteen log cabins of Harrodsburg were laid out on a grid plan with wide streets. Residents operated some commercial enterprises, including gristmills to grind corn, replacing the laborious hand mills used by the earliest settlers. Only ten miles from the Kentucky River, the town had a busy little port called Harrods

Landing, where immigrants landed and goods were shipped out. Both tobacco and hemp had become viable exports.[1]

John Donelson frequently traveled on business, looking after his farming, surveying, and land speculation interests. He was in an area with easy (for the period) access to Virginia and North Carolina via the Wilderness Road, to Natchez and New Orleans by way of the Kentucky, Ohio, and Mississippi rivers, and to Nashborough (soon renamed Nashville) down a well-trodden trace.

Although the Harrodsburg neighborhood was safer than the Cumberland, the American Revolution was a time of ferocious battles between British-led or -instigated forces of Indians and white settlers in Kentucky. From their main fort at Detroit and their smaller outposts throughout the Ohio country, the British rained death and destruction on American frontier settlements. Supplying hostile Shawnees and their allies with weapons, ammunition, and trade goods, the British cemented the Indians' allegiance to their cause with the promise to help drive all white settlers out of the natives' traditional hunting grounds. But young George Rogers Clark had led Kentucky's militia against the British and the Indians in the Ohio country throughout the Revolution. By 1780, both Crab Orchard and Harrodsburg were generally peaceful.

The Donelsons soon made friends in Kentucky. They were members of the frontier gentry who could move from place to place with relative ease. Not by any means members of the upper tier of great landowners, they nevertheless had enough money to buy a few thousand acres of land to be worked by their slaves. John Donelson's prestigious military and political appointments in Virginia brought respect from his peers. The title of colonel went far on the frontier. He was fairly well educated, as were his children. America had a social mobility unknown in Britain, and people had a habit of defining and redefining themselves. Because the Donelsons defined themselves as gentry according to their understanding of British standards, they were perceived as such by their fellow citizens. They followed basic rules of civility and, given the stringencies of frontier life, incorporated proper standards of dress and decor. In the Harrodsburg area, they would have been perceived immediately as members of the upper class.

Social and economic differences among frontiersmen were immediately obvious. Housing was a clear giveaway even though most people still lived in log cabins. The poor and new arrivals often lacked the time or expertise to build snug log cabins and threw up ramshackle sheds with dirt floors and slanting roofs, leaving one side open with only a cloth drape to keep out the weather. One traveler was amazed to see several people living in a huge hollow sycamore tree, entering and leaving via a hole in one side and making their fire outside. Others failed to caulk the spaces between the logs of their cabins, leaving the interiors open to the wind and cold, making for a nice airy quality, according to a pioneer reminiscing with rose-colored glasses. All of these poorer cabins had but one room for an entire family and any visitors to carry out their daily activities. An open loft reached by a rough ladder occasionally provided more sleeping space. They used a big wooden spoon to dip into the communal bowls. Men, women, and children were armed with sharp knives to use for daily tasks or defense, but they also ate with their knives, spearing hunks of meat from the frying pan and poking them into their mouths.

Those with higher standards—and more money—lived in finished cabins with more than one room, with fireplaces, puncheon floors, wooden doors on hinges, and sometimes even glass windows; most important, cracks between the logs had been caulked and made airtight. They also daubed and whitewashed the interior walls. People like the Donelsons had more and better homemade furnishings than most of their neighbors; and sometimes they had even managed to haul a few professionally made pieces of furniture over the mountains with them.

Cleanliness was very much a class signifier. The poor, who were intent on clearing fields and scratching out a living, put little time or effort into cleaning themselves or their houses. Water for bathing, washing clothes, or scrubbing the house had to be hauled laboriously from the nearest stream. Travelers commented on how dirty these westerners were; their filthy cabins were infested with fleas, lice, and other pests. This was hardly surprising, considering that the entrances to their cabins seldom had doors, and children, hens, dogs, and hogs tracked dirt inside all day long.

At thirteen, Rachel Donelson had already spent years helping her mother and older sisters with chores in the house, the garden, the dairy, and the chicken coops, learning as she worked. Although her family owned slaves, most of them would have been employed as farm laborers in the fields, with stock, and at the million and one tasks needed to start a new plantation. At most, one or two enslaved women might have been spared for household work—hauling water, washing clothes, tending the garden, and cooking under Mrs. Donelson's direction.

By 1780 Rachel's two oldest sisters were married with their own households to care for. Only she and Jane, still unmarried in her late twenties, were left at home to help care for a large household of active men. Of her five older brothers, ranging in age from twenty-one to thirty-one, only one was married. Some or all of them probably lived with their parents. Even those who might have lived in a separate cabin probably depended on their mother and sisters for meals, laundry, clothing, and medical care. The Donelson household was completed by their father and two little brothers of seven and three.

Rachel was thus trained to be a careful and economical housewife by her mid-teens, adept at all the myriad tasks required of a woman before she was considered marriageable. A list of all the responsibilities of frontier women to their families is overwhelming. First came food—not just cooking, but growing and preserving in a world without refrigeration. Men provided the meat by tending herds or hunting in the forest, but women produced the rest of the family diet. They tended the vegetable garden, the orchard, the fowls, and the dairy. They preserved fruits and vegetables for winter meals by pickling, salting, sugaring, or drying; kept track of brooding hens, gathering eggs and candling them to decide which to eat and which to return to the nest; boiled and skimmed the sap of the sugar maple for hours to make crystallized sugar or a form of molasses; dried and purified salt brought from the salt springs; and searched the nearby forest for plants and herbs to concoct home remedies. They also processed whatever meat couldn't be eaten fresh by smoking, salting, or jerking over a slow fire Indian fashion.

Women were also expected to clothe their families with decency. They retted, pounded, and wove hemp; carded, spun, and wove wool, sometimes in combination with hemp or linen to make the pioneer's staple cloth, linsey-woolsey; colored the cloth with natural dyes from the forest in a range of soft golds, tans, and browns; hand sewed all the family's clothes, including hunting shirts, breeches, leggings, dresses, aprons, and sunbonnets; knitted socks, stockings, scarves, hats, and mittens; made soap, washing vast cauldrons of filthy clothes; patched, mended, and darned; and quilted, often with groups of neighborhood friends. And with their extra time, they could collect firewood, find and herd stock, and generally help the men with their chores. All the while keeping a rifle and knives at the ready and an alert eye out for attacking Indians.

It's amazing that the Donelsons or any frontier woman found time for socializing, but they did and treasured every minute of it. Visiting friends and relatives and helping out those in need were important marks of a caring woman. They carried food and remedies to the sick; gathered around at births, marriages, and deaths; helped newcomers get settled in; and worked together at quilting or sewing bees.

Singing and making music, usually with a fiddle, was the centerpiece of most social gatherings, and the Donelsons were a very sociable lot. Rachel had a clear, pleasant voice and became a stylish, untiring dancer, a great addition to any party. The dances favored on the frontier tended to be vigorous romps, like the reel and the jig. She also loved to talk to anyone and everyone. Friendly and outgoing, she made quite an impression as a teenage flirt in Kentucky.

By 1784, when she turned seventeen, Rachel had received a basic education in reading, writing, and figuring, although she never became adept enough at writing to enjoy it. Her spelling and grammar ranged all over the place, as did most people's in the eighteenth century, but she was not illiterate and was in fact better educated than the majority of western women of her day. Frontier cabins didn't run to books, other than the Bible, almanacs, and home medical texts, and Rachel was more active than introspective. Only in later life, with more leisure, did she broaden her reading tastes.

Now was the time for Rachel and her family to look about among the Kentucky gentry for a likely husband. We don't know who her suitors were, but a newcomer from Virginia moved to the Harrodsburg area in 1784. When Lewis Robards caught sight of the brown-eyed girl who tossed her black curls so saucily while she danced, he fell hard for the last woman on earth he should have married and began a determined courtship. Rachel Donelson reciprocated his interest and consented to marry the last man on earth she should have married.

Captain Lewis Robards was twenty-six when he, his widowed mother, and younger brothers and sisters moved permanently to Kentucky. In 1782 and 1783, he and three brothers had already spent time clearing land for cultivation on the Cane Run a few miles from Harrodsburg. The Robards family was more socially prominent than the Donelsons, but their Virginia plantation land had been left to the children of their father's first marriage. Lewis was the eldest child of a second marriage. He had served in the Virginia Regiment, Continental Line, rising to the rank of captain before mustering out after Washington's victory at Yorktown. When he moved to Kentucky, he owned 1,800 acres and two slaves. His siblings were similarly provided for, and, moving as a family, they multiplied their chances of success by living together, combining their efforts, and sharing the labors of their slaves.[2]

In 1785 John Donelson decided that Tennessee was safe enough from Indian attacks for the family to return to the Cumberland. The young people's courtship had progressed far enough by then that Lewis Robards requested her father's permission to marry seventeen-year-old Rachel. On February 9, Donelson gave his permission to the county clerk to issue a marriage license. On March 1, Lewis Robards signed a marriage bond, ensuring that the intended marriage would shortly take place.[3] The couple was duly married in Harrodsburg—we don't know the circumstances of the ceremony—and moved in with the widowed Elizabeth Lewis Robards, several siblings, and their boarders. It was just the sort of large, extended family that Rachel had grown up in. Mrs. Robards took to the pretty young girl and welcomed her warmly. Satisfied that their youngest daughter was settled, the rest of the Donelson family moved south to Tennessee soon afterward.

Everything seemed to be in place for a happy marriage—families of the same social class, money on both sides, an established husband, a charming wife, a welcoming family. Unfortunately, the qualities that had first attracted Lewis to Rachel were the very things that began to drive an intensely jealous and possessive husband mad. With seven brothers, Rachel enjoyed the company of men, and they reciprocated. Her beauty, sociability, and warmth became triggers for anger, reproach, and scenes. She remained open, approachable, and friendly with everyone, and he couldn't bear it.

Robards did well in Kentucky, becoming a militia captain, developing his acreage, and apparently setting up as a merchant with some success. But there were also signs of financial irresponsibility as men turned to the law to collect money he owed them. His younger brother, George, had been named executor of his father's will, instead of Lewis, the eldest son, who would have been the more usual choice. It seems that the father might have had doubts about Lewis's financial acumen or character. The brothers quarreled constantly over money and land until they became completely estranged. Money was surely important in the breach, but so was Lewis's jealousy that his brother had taken the place in the family that he thought should be his. The desire for undisputed possession created recurring dramas in his life.

Meanwhile, Rachel, who loved her mother-in-law, was probably having doubts about her husband. A girl of spirit, she was not accustomed to being treated with unkindness and suspicion. The Donelsons were an exceptionally close family, and Rachel's position as the cosseted and adored baby daughter had not prepared her for disapproval and disharmony. She missed her family's company, particularly when her father was murdered in mysterious circumstances later in 1785.

After two years, Rachel was certainly fed up with her husband. When a well-to-do Virginian named Peyton Short came to live at the Robardses' house as a boarder in 1787, there were months of jealous scenes and accusations. Lewis had someone to fix his free-floating suspicions on. He must have sensed that his wife no longer loved him. A man of his temperament couldn't believe that his own behavior had altered her feelings: an outsider must be to blame for the change. There is no doubt that Short was smitten with Rachel and sympathetic to her plight in an unhappy marriage, but there is no reason to believe that she encouraged his love. Short dashed home to Virginia, planning to gather the necessary funds to carry her away. He sent her a very indiscreet letter, proposing that they elope. She had clearly been unaware of his plans until then.

As might be expected from such a suspicious man, Robards intercepted and read the letter. He followed Short to Virginia intent on revenge. There the astute Short offered Robards the satisfaction of a duel or a payment of $1,000, perhaps knowing that Robards had debts. Robards took the money and returned home, but he must have felt keenly the humiliation of accepting his rival's money. His treatment of his wife worsened, probably aggravated by his own shame. Rachel was not one to accept unwarranted criticism without defending herself, and their marriage deteriorated further. One of Lewis's sisters-in-law later charged that he was violent toward Rachel, and that he frequently visited the slave quarters at night, cajoling or forcing sex from enslaved black women.[4]

In the late summer of 1788, after only three years of marriage, Rachel's favorite brother, Samuel, came to fetch her home to Nashville. Sources differ on the circumstances of this separation. Members of the Robards family later claimed that she had merely gone for a visit, and that the couple at first had every intention of reuniting. On the other hand, the Donelsons claimed that Robards had written to Rachel's mother, telling her that he would no longer live with her daughter and directing her to send an escort to take Rachel away. During the summer of 1788, Robards purchased considerable acreage in the Cumberland area, indicating that he intended to give the marriage another try, regardless of what Rachel's plans might have been.

He did indeed follow her to Nashville later in the year, moving into her mother's house and Rachel's bed. But such an ill-assorted pair continued to make each other miserable. At twenty-one, she was still lovely, sprightly, friendly to men, and admired by them. At thirty, he was as jealous, touchy, and suspicious as ever. And he had an admirable object for suspicion—Mrs. Donelson's new boarder, a lawyer named Andrew Jackson, newly arrived from North Carolina.

Jackson had been drawn to Nashville by the opportunities it offered for a single young man determined to move up in the world. After years of violence between Indians and whites—raids, attacks, counterattacks, frightful atrocities on both sides, treaties and purchases both duplicitous and honest—the balance of power had swung in favor of the whites, even though frontier violence would continue to ebb and flow until the turn of the century. Hundreds of thousands of acres of former Indian lands had been opened to white settlement, usually without their acquiescence, and thousands of land-hungry families swarmed over the Appalachians. The growth of Tennessee towns like Nashville, Knoxville, and Jonesborough, along with the organization of judicial systems and district militias, opened the door to both professional success and military honor for an ambitious young lawyer.

Andrew Jackson was far from the social or economic equal of the Donelsons. He was the son of Scots who emigrated in 1765 from the poverty and despair of Ulster in northern Ireland to the backwoods Waxhaw area, which straddled North and South Carolina. Andrew and Elizabeth Hutchinson Jackson took up a life of labor on a subsistence farm. In 1767, Andrew Jackson dropped dead, leaving two small sons and a very pregnant wife behind. This baby, called Andrew after his father, was born at an aunt's house in South Carolina. Throughout his childhood, the Jacksons lived with their uncle and aunt, his mother serving as the housekeeper, the family treated as poor relations.

Elizabeth Jackson had hoped that her youngest son would become a minister—Presbyterian, naturally—and saw that he received a better education than his brothers. But that education was still sketchy at best, because of both the inadequacies of backwoods schools and Andrew's own resistance to learning. His hair-trigger temper made the ministry an unlikely career for the mischievous, athletic boy. When the British attacked South Carolina in 1780, all three Jackson boys joined the patriots even though they were just teenagers. Andrew's two older brothers died, and his own health was severely damaged by imprisonment, starvation, and smallpox. Recovering at home, he lost his mother to cholera in British-controlled Charleston, where she had gone to aid her imprisoned nephews.

At fourteen, Andrew Jackson was a veteran of the Revolution, a lifelong enemy of the British, and an orphan without prospects. Depressed and hopeless, he fell in with a group of wild young men and became as much a ne'er-do-well as the rest. At odds with his relatives, Andrew went to Charleston in late 1782, where he wasted a small inheritance from his grandfather and got deeply into debt. Through a lucky gamble, he cleared his debts and headed home. At seventeen, he went to Salisbury, North Carolina, where he studied law with Spruce McCay, a distinguished attorney. Never a very serious student, he learned enough to satisfy the less than stringent requirements of the day, while paying much more attention to the dancing lessons so essential for an elegant social life. Mostly he partied—partied very hard indeed. He and his friends drank, gambled, womanized, rollicked, and roistered about the town. They could be seen at cockfights, horse races, and brothels, but were also popular enough to be invited to respectable dances and social occasions. Boys, after all, will be boys, seemed to be the attitude of Salisbury society.

After being admitted to the bar, he practiced desultorily and not very successfully in North Carolina, adrift and seemingly without purpose. Then John McNairy, a law studies friend who had been named Superior Court judge for the Western District of North Carolina, that is, western Tennessee, offered him the position of public prosecutor for that district. At last, a chance to make something of himself. McNairy, Jackson, and other lawyers selected to bring justice to the West set out on horseback down the Wilderness Road for the newly named Mero District in the summer of 1788.

Jackson was determined, fearless, and charismatic, possessing that spark that made other men follow him. Until he arrived in

Tennessee, however, he had wasted his gifts of character and personality, sowing acres of wild oats with other rowdy young men. Going west was an important step in his reinvention of himself as a gentleman, notwithstanding his parents' poverty and his own scanty education. On the frontier, a gentleman was whoever claimed that status and was able to maintain it in the face of the world.

After their grueling trek through the 200 miles of wilderness between North Carolina and Jonesborough, the easternmost town of Tennessee, Jackson, John McNairy, and the rest of their party arrived in August and stopped to spend the fall there. They had another 200 miles of rough country to struggle through before they could reach Nashville and set a spring court session.

But money was a constant problem for the impecunious Jackson. Since boyhood he had loved and worked with horses. A passionate devotee of horseracing, he went to work at a local stable as a trainer. He also presented himself to the community as a lawyer, accepting the few civil cases that came his way.

Eager as he was to rise in the world, Jackson's insecurity about his social and professional position showed in an early foray into a Jonesborough courtroom on August 11. In this case, opposing counsel was Waightstill Avery, a noted attorney and law teacher with whom Jackson had unsuccessfully applied to study in North Carolina. Put on his mettle before someone he admired, Jackson failed very publicly indeed. His preparation was inadequate and his arguments ill-conceived. Avery was dismissive of the entire performance, his rebuttal delivered sarcastically. Enraged and embarrassed, Jackson ripped a blank page from a law book and dashed off a challenge to a duel. When Avery refused to take the matter seriously, Jackson wrote a letter the next day reiterating his challenge and demanding a meeting after court adjourned.

His letter almost quivered with passion: "My character you have Injured; and further you have Insulted me in the presence of a court and a larg audianc [*sic*]."[5] Although Avery had no use for dueling, he knew that refusing a challenge would damn him forever as a coward on the frontier.

Both men hastily found seconds. Like most duels, this meeting was acted out by gentlemen for the benefit of the community. Unlike the rougher sort, who took after each other with eye-gouging, ear-biting, alcohol-enhanced fury, gentlemen followed an established dueling code in which their seconds agreed beforehand on place, time, distance, and weapons.

On the evening of August 12 a little after sundown, Avery and Jackson met in a hollow north of town, paced off the agreed-upon distance (usually ten to twenty paces), and leveled their pistols. Then in an anticlimax that was a feature of many duels, they both deloped, that is, deliberately fired into the air to bring the conflict to an end without wounding or killing an opponent.[6] According to the thinking of the time, Jackson's honor was satisfied merely by meeting Avery. Later, this Avery affair would be pointed out as the beginning of a life of violence. At the time, however, it created little comment.

When the group arrived in Nashville in the fall, they found a town of a few hundred residents living in houses and cabins, as well as a courthouse, two stores, two taverns, and a distillery. Jackson took lodgings with Mrs. Donelson, who lived in a protective block-house ten miles outside of town, along with her daughter, her newly arrived son-in-law, and several sons. He moved into one of the cabins included in the Donelson compound.

At twenty-one, just Rachel's age, Andrew had at last found his place and his future. Never handsome, he was nonetheless very striking in appearance, seeming to be a "somebody," as Virginians phrased it, long before he was anybody. Tall, skinny, pale-skinned, he looked a typical Scot with his lantern jaw, thick sandy red hair, and piercing blue eyes. Never again would he return to his favored haunts of taverns and brothels. Now serious about his career, he soon became serious about Rachel Robards as well.

Throughout his life, Andrew Jackson had a reputation for violence, sometimes exaggerated but basically true. Jackson was willing to fight and to kill in defense of his honor and his sense of righteousness. He was also innately chivalrous toward women, enjoying their company, sensitive to their rights and wrongs, and flaming into anger at the suggestion of any mistreatment. The Robardses' situation could not have been more calculated to arouse his best and worst instincts. A lovely and charming woman, a member of a close-knit and admirable family, was being falsely accused and berated by a cowardly and despicable husband, who even had the nerve to accuse Andrew of wrongdoing.

Thus, Andrew Jackson was moved to defend Rachel and to remonstrate with Lewis Robards. Suspicious of the attraction, all too real, between Rachel and Andrew, Lewis forbade them to speak to each other and then was enraged at finding them in the most mundane conversation. He harped on his doubts, interrogating his wife about her every movement and action, despite her and her mother's tears and denials. Their home became as unhappy as the Robards place had been in Kentucky.

The Donelsons started to turn against Lewis, as tired of him as Rachel was. They were an exceptionally close-knit family—parents, siblings, in-laws, nieces, and nephews, living close to one another, socializing, joining each other in business ventures, helping each other in times of need. "Little Rachel," as her family still called her, was a much beloved member of the Donelson clan. Lewis Robards had seemed an acceptable husband for the Donelsons' baby sister in 1785, but four years later their mistake was clear.

The public scenes he created were an embarrassment to the entire family. As Lewis's obsessive distrust of his wife became fixed on Mrs. Donelson's popular lodger as her lover, Andrew was forced to move. At his friend John Overton's urging, he moved to lodgings at Mansker's Station to calm the tense situation.

Unlike Robards, Jackson did have the ability to make friends easily. The Donelsons had taken very kindly to the charming, outgoing Jackson, who treated their sister and mother with such courtliness. Neither then nor later would there be anything but friendship and mutual trust between the family and Jackson.

A couple of incidents that occurred during 1789, recounted by John Overton during the 1828 presidential campaign, illustrate the dynamic between Jackson and Robards.[7] Once, near the orchard fence, Jackson approached Robards to reason with him about the injustice he was doing his wife, as well as himself. Robards became violently angry, threatening to whip Jackson and making a show of doing so. When Jackson offered to duel with him instead, Robards withdrew but declared that he had no use for Jackson or for Rachel. Any man looking into those blazing eyes knew that, neither then nor later, would Jackson hesitate to shoot to kill if he were sufficiently offended.

Robards couldn't seem to stop talking about his grievances, real or imaginary. One day, he went with a group of women, presumably the Donelsons, to pick blackberries. They were accompanied by armed men on guard against Indian attacks. Robards told the men that Jackson was too intimate with his wife. Lewis Robards was not popular with other men; Jackson was. After some of the men repeated the story to him, Jackson confronted Robards and threatened to cut his ears off (a common western mode of assault) if he continued to make such remarks. Robards left the scene to swear out a peace warrant against his tormentor. Such a warrant would have forbidden Jackson to trouble Robards further under penalty of the law.

When Jackson was arrested by several armed men, Robards accompanied them to see the magistrate. Subsequent events give some hint of frontier opinion of a husband who went to court instead of a dueling field with the man he suspected of seducing his wife. Jackson asked one of the men to lend him his large knife. After being assured that he would do no harm with it, the man obligingly handed it over. Jackson began playing with the knife point and edge, looking menacingly at his accuser. Robards lost his nerve and ran, pursued by Jackson, plunging into a thick canebrake and out of sight. The others continued to the magistrate's office, where, the plaintiff not being present, the charges were dismissed.

Whether or not every detail of these stories is true, it is clear that Jackson stood up for the mistreated Rachel, that Robards was convinced of their guilt, and that he was terrified of Jackson. In the end, Robards stormed off back to Kentucky, vowing never again to live with his faithless wife.

By this time, the summer of 1789, it had no doubt become clear to both Rachel and Andrew that they were in love. For her, reconciling with her husband was no longer possible, and, even if she could have, Andrew could not have borne it. What were they to do? The chance of their ever being legally married and living together in respectable society was as much a long shot as any of the gambles of Jackson's wild youth.

CHAPTER 3

The Elopement

arriage and divorce were not taken lightly on the frontier in the 1780s. But they were considered to be the purview of the fiercely independent residents themselves, not of authorities far away over the Appalachians. Self-marriage and self-divorce were important western concepts. Before there were sufficient ministers or legal authorities, couples simply declared themselves married. Equally, marriages with serious defects were dissolved by the couples themselves. The ultimate test of any such marriage or divorce was its acceptance by the family and community. Rachel could no longer live with Lewis Robards, and Andrew could no longer live without her.

As members of the gentry, the Donelsons preferred to observe the legalities because of inheritance and property rights. They were still westerners enough, however, to see no reason why Rachel should be trapped in an unhappy marriage, nor be forbidden to remarry.

Unlike England, where divorce was overseen by Parliament, bound by the rules of the Church of England, and thus almost impossible to obtain, parts of the United States had considerably loosened matrimonial bonds. There were no federal statutes governing divorce: each state had its own rules and procedures. South Carolina, for example, did not allow divorce on any grounds. Connecticut's rules, at the other extreme, were so lax that preachers attacked that state for encouraging prostitution and adultery.[1]

It is extremely doubtful that Rachel ever considered filing for divorce herself. By the standards of the day, she simply had no grounds. In 1789 North Carolina (Tennessee was still part of that state when her marriage broke up), the grounds for divorce were quite specific and limited—adultery, desertion, and extreme cruelty. The legislature granted fewer than half of the petitions brought before it, and was generally more favorably inclined toward men than women. The few divorces granted were legal separations that did not allow the parties to remarry.

To try to prove any of the three permitted grounds against Lewis Robards would have been ludicrous. Although Lewis Robards's estranged sister-in-law, as well as a boarder in his mother's house, avowed many years later that he had been in the regular habit of visiting his slave quarters for sex, southern courts seldom construed such behavior as adultery. Only in the few cases where a husband set a black mistress over his white wife would the wife be allowed a divorce. Such decisions were made to maintain social conventions of white power and black helplessness, rather than granting power to wronged wives.

Desertion would have been even more far-fetched. Lewis Robards had left his Kentucky house to move to Nashville and attempt to reconcile with his young wife. Even cruelty was out of the question.

Although he quarreled with Rachel incessantly, accusing her of impropriety and adultery, there is no credible evidence of physical battery. In any case, of all the permitted grounds for seeking divorce, cruelty was the least likely to succeed. Southern legislators saw nothing amiss with a man's chastising his wife, even hitting her now and then when provoked, in order to maintain proper masculine order and authority in his household.

Self-divorce was still a viable option on the frontier, but it left open the possibility of Lewis's dragging his wife to Kentucky or of making demands on her property. Married women were considered *femes covert* in every state; that is, they had no separate legal existence. Husband and wife were considered one entity before the law with men acting for their wives. Husbands controlled joint property, including inheritance. Men could use or dispose of their wives' property as they saw fit. Even in the case of divorce, husbands usually retained their wives' property, giving the women only an allowance. Two of the more famous of such cases involved Eliza Custis, George Washington's step-granddaughter, and Frances Wright, the radical writer and reformer, both of whose properties remained in the hands of vengeful husbands.

Rachel could not realistically seek a divorce, nor could she and Andrew count on living peacefully together in Nashville. Only two options remained to the young couple—relinquish their relationship or elope. They couldn't face permanent separation, so they started planning their elopement. To achieve their aim of living together, they needed to go to a territory that was beyond the reach of American law and either stay there permanently or return after the discarded husband had given up hope of reconciliation.

In midsummer 1789, probably after Robards had gone back to Kentucky, Jackson went downriver to Natchez, Mississippi, in

Spanish territory. Natchez was an important mercantile center, a way station for trade between Kentucky and Tennessee and the port of New Orleans with its access to overseas trade. It was the closest town outside American territory that offered a chance for an ambitious man like Jackson to make a living. A number of Americans had taken up residence near Natchez, trading, planting, or both. Robards could not interfere there with the new life together that Rachel and Andrew were planning.

On July 15, 1789, Andrew Jackson swore allegiance to the king of Spain, a necessity for any foreigner seeking land grants in the territory. Although not essential for trading privileges, most American merchants in Natchez had sworn the same oath as a matter of course. The eventual fate of the western lands of Kentucky and Tennessee was still in doubt—would they be American, independent, or part of the Spanish empire? There was no shame or taint of treason in taking such an oath, either in Natchez or in New Orleans.

Going down to Natchez by flatboat, Jackson brought cotton, furs, swan skins and feathers, lime, pork, beef, and slaves to sell, sometimes on his own account or at the behest of friends or clients. Through his friendship with the Donelson family, he became acquainted with important Anglo merchants in the town. Thomas Green, a longtime friend of the Donelsons, welcomed Jackson and gave him a power of attorney to act for him in Davidson County, Tennessee, the seat of which was Nashville. Personal contacts were key to doing business on the frontier.

On his return to Nashville in time for the fall 1789 court session, Andrew was reunited with Rachel and her family. Travelers between Nashville and Harrodsburg were as regular as the news and gossip they brought with them, and Rachel and Andrew soon heard bad news. Lewis Robards planned to make one last try at making his marriage work. According to their sources, his mood was angry and vengeful. He planned to return to Nashville, retrieve Rachel, and take her back to Kentucky with him, far from Andrew Jackson and the disobliging Donelsons. He would certainly be well within his legal rights, whatever the lady or her family thought of the plan.

In December 1789, Rachel Robards and Andrew Jackson boarded a flatboat on the Cumberland River and sailed down the Mississippi to Natchez. This was the biggest town the unsophisticated Rachel had ever seen. Perched on a high bluff overlooking the river were the houses of Spanish gentry and Anglo traders and their businesses. When flatboats landed at the city's docks, the more fastidious travelers averted their eyes from the squalor of Natchez-under-the-hill, the town's riverfront that was home to saloons, gambling dens, and brothels. Their goods loaded onto waiting wagons by stevedores, they climbed aboard and ascended a steep roadway to the city proper.

What they told their friends in the Natchez area about their appearance together there is unknown. At this time, Rachel was still indisputably married to Lewis Robards. Although they later claimed to have been married in Natchez, such a claim is surely untrue. No record whatsoever exists of such a marriage in any archive. Catholic priests were the only clergy allowed to perform religious rites in Mississippi, and they surely would have refused to marry Protestants. A wandering Protestant clergyman would have had no legal right to perform a ceremony in Spanish territory.

A story exists that they were married by Thomas Green's father, Colonel Thomas Green, at Springfield, his plantation outside Natchez. Although he was a former magistrate in Georgia, Colonel

Green had no legal standing in Natchez, and a marriage performed by him would have been null. Nor did the Jacksons themselves name him then or later. The most likely scenario is that they simply announced themselves as a married couple, visited among their friends, and settled into a house at Bayou Pierre, a small community a few miles north of Natchez. There is no record of any property purchase by either of them, so presumably they rented the house and land.

The regard in which the couple was held by the Natchez community is shown by the continued trust shown to Jackson in business matters by prominent Natchez merchants. A letter to him from one of these men, George Cochran, in October 1791, dealt primarily with debts and other business. But at the end, he addressed himself to Mrs. Jackson, "the most pleasing part" of his letter. He declared his happiness at hearing of her good health since he looked on her as a friend "in the nearest light of a sister." He remembered with pleasure "the agreeable hours I have past in your friendly retreat at Bayou Pierre." Several years after the Jacksons' sojourn in the Natchez area, in April 1797, he lacked "terms suitably expressive of my respect & esteem for Mrs. Jackson," wishing to have her again as a "Neighbor and friend." Never did he indicate that he knew her as a single woman.[2]

The Jacksons remained in Bayou Pierre until the summer of 1790. Andrew made trips back and forth between Natchez and Nashville to discharge his legal responsibilities in Tennessee, to trade, to carry news between Rachel and her family, and to keep his ears open for rumors of Robards's response to their elopement. During the spring of 1790, Jackson kept an account with a Natchez merchant, Melling Woolley, for items delivered to Bayou Pierre. Itemized are such items as a tea tray—hardly a purchase for a single man—as well as pots, knives, one-half yard of muslin, and two and one-half yards of cloth, all presumably meant for their household or for Rachel.[3]

In no way were they in hiding. They lived openly together, entertaining friends and taking part in the community's social life. Despite the fact that she was still legally married to Lewis Robards, Rachel had determined that their marriage was over and had committed herself completely to Andrew Jackson. Since Robards seemed to have quit Nashville for good, in July 1790 Rachel and Andrew joined an armed party riding back to the Cumberland along the Natchez Trace. Like most of the roads traveled in the West, it began as a game trail and then became an Indian hunting trail. Connecting two major trading towns, it had been used regularly by white traders, hunters, and boatmen going upriver. Such heavy use had widened and deepened the Trace, and wagons had worn deep ruts into the soil. As it wound northward through heavy forest and into ever hillier territory, in some places the roadbed was four or five feet lower than the surrounding land. The sunken road, overhung by huge trees and underbrush, was the perfect place for an ambush. The Trace was no place for a couple to venture alone. Many travelers who hadn't found a group to join paid with their lives when they were attacked by Indians or by outlaws.

Rachel was a dashing horsewoman who could keep up with any man on the Trace. In the event of an attack, she was perfectly capable of riding hell for leather to escape. But their trip didn't include the excitement of an attack, probably because their group was large enough to ward off danger. They rode long days before camping in tents beside streams or staying at one of the primitive stations that had sprung up along the road.

The trip did include an unexpected, but probably fortuitous, danger. Traveling with their party was Hugh McGary, a respected military man from Mercer County, Kentucky, where Lewis Robards lived. On his return home, he told Robards of the open relationship between Rachel and Andrew. His report that they were "bedding together" was the solid evidence the affronted husband needed to set in motion an action for divorce in the fall of 1790. Since Kentucky was still part of Virginia, Robards's petition had to be submitted to the Virginia General Assembly.[4]

Legal divorce was still a very rare thing in Virginia and was unknown in Kentucky or Tennessee. Only one bill of divorcement had previously been passed by the assembly. Luckily for Robards, his brother-in-law, Jack Jouett, represented the Kentucky District in the Virginia legislature and sponsored his petition. On December 20, 1790, an act was passed giving Lewis Robards permission to sue Rachel Robards for divorce out of the office of the supreme court of the district of Kentucky. Such an act did not constitute a divorce but merely gave the plaintiff permission to bring suit and have the case tried before a jury.[5]

Robards's failure to bring suit immediately gave rise later to much debate and speculation. His next step should have been to apply for a writ against Rachel in Kentucky, to publish the nature of the case for eight successive weeks in the *Kentucky Gazette,* and to have depositions taken and witnesses subpoenaed. After this, a jury would be summoned, and Rachel would have the right to defend herself. If the jury found that she had indeed deserted her husband "and lived with another man since such desertion," then the marriage between them would be totally dissolved. In that case, both would have the right to remarry.[6]

As Lewis well knew, Rachel was eager to be shed of him and to marry Andrew. He certainly had every reason to disoblige his wife and her lover, but monetary considerations were probably paramount in his delay. The estate of Rachel's father had not yet been settled, and, under the laws of coverture, Lewis had every right to claim his wife's share. His earlier actions had indicated a certain greediness—his arguments and estrangement with his brother over their father's estate and his acceptance of $1,000 from Rachel's would-be suitor Peyton Short.

Almost as soon as he received notice of the success of his petition in Richmond, Lewis wrote to Rachel's brother-in-law, Robert Hays, on January 9, 1791. Apparently, he had no doubt either of his rights or of their being upheld by another male, even though he was part of the Donelson clan. He asked for a number of favors. Apparently Hays had sold Robards's corn for a horse after his departure for Kentucky. He asked for the horse to be sent to him and for Hays to look into selling his Cumberland land for $250 with long credit. He was willing to take half the amount in Negroes if they were young and good workers. As an option to sale, he would be willing to accept several families on his land as tenant farmers.[7]

But the crux of the letter was the opening of John Donelson's succession. Oddly enough, Robards asserted his confidence in Hays and John Overton, Andrew Jackson's confidential friend, to see that no advantage was taken of him because of his absence from the Cumberland. Overton knew the Robards family from his earlier residence in Harrodsburg and was considered by them a friend, but Lewis clearly had no idea that Rachel's family and Jackson's friends had turned against him and supported the eloping couple.

Meanwhile the Jacksons had settled quietly in the Nashville area, probably in Mrs. Donelson's compound, embraced by family and friends as a married couple. It is not known whether or how Robert Hays answered Robards's demands on John Donelson's estate. But it is clear that the Donelsons had discarded him from their calculations and welcomed Andrew Jackson as Rachel's husband. On January 28, 1791, the inventory, appraisal, and division of her father's estate was begun without reference to Lewis Robards or his rights; it was subsequently extended to the April term and completed on April 15. Rachel's brother William was administrator of the estate; the three trustees included John Overton. Throughout the document, she is referred to as Rachel Jackson.

With a widow and eleven children as heirs, the trustees worked hard to effect an equal division of the estate. The twenty-nine slaves were divided into twelve lots grouped apparently by value and seemingly also by family units. Then lots were drawn on behalf of the heirs by an unnamed "unexceptionable person." Rachel received the slaves George and Moll, whose combined value was appraised at 333 1/3 "hard dollars," that is, specie, not paper money. Part of the calculation in dividing the estate involved the "advancements" made by John Donelson to three daughters and three sons during his lifetime. Rachel had received by far the greatest share, a bed and furniture (bed curtains, spread, and perhaps a tester), a mare, a cow and calf, and an iron pot, valued altogether at $97. Beds were quite valuable pieces of furniture and were often given to children, especially girls, on their marriages.[8]

Probably the reason that Rachel's advance was so much greater than the others was that the family left her behind in Kentucky after her marriage, and gifts sent from Tennessee would have caused transportation problems. It may be also that Lewis Robards had bargained for the items as a sort of dowry. In any case, she had left everything behind when she left Kentucky, except perhaps for the mare.

Nashville was a small enough town that everyone knew about the Jacksons' elopement and Robards's act of divorcement, though whether everyone understood that an actual divorce had not yet been granted is unclear. On the western frontier, where conversation was one of people's main pleasures, gossip ran as fast as galloping horses. Gossip about sexual misdoings, particularly involving the gentry, was a great treat. That meant that their affairs were discussed throughout Tennessee and Kentucky.

Most people followed the Donelsons' lead in their treatment of Jackson. As a member of one of the most important families of the Cumberland, he gained in prestige and frequently joined his in-laws in business ventures. He began to accumulate acreage as private clients sometimes paid his legal fees in land when they lacked sufficient cash. In late 1789, North Carolina had ceded its western land, that is, Tennessee, to the new federal government, which created the Southwest Territory the following spring.

After serving as public prosecutor and attorney general for the Mero District for two years, Jackson had established his reputation as a hardworking and successful official, impressing the territory's new governor, William Blount, a debonair North Carolinian. Blount had lobbied hard for the governorship, largely because he had accumulated hundreds of thousands of acres of western land and wanted to keep an eye on his investment. The governor reappointed Jackson as attorney general for the district in February 1791 to serve "during his good behavior," in the formal words of an appointment for a position without a fixed term. Apparently Jackson's marital misadventures did not constitute bad behavior to one of the most powerful men in Tennessee politics. That year, Jackson was also elected to the board of the prestigious Davidson Academy in Nashville. In September 1792, Governor Blount next appointed him judge advocate of the Davidson County cavalry regiment, not coincidentally commanded by Robert Hays. Jackson was clearly a man on the rise.

More than thirty years later, the Jacksons claimed that they had no idea that Robards had not divorced Rachel in 1790 and that they were not legally married. Times had changed by then, particularly beliefs about divorce, elopement, and remarriage. It is most unlikely, however, that an attorney would be so uninformed about the laws regulating divorce or that Jackson had never checked into the matter in the two years they lived as husband and wife in Nashville. The suspense about when Lewis Robards would call for a trial must have been nerve-racking.

Finally, in January 1792, Robards approached the court of Mercer County, Kentucky (still part of Virginia), with his legislative decree and a public writ for a trial. The timing of his action is interesting. He had been excluded from any share of the Donelson estate in April of the previous year, and he probably wanted to remarry. During the months of February and March 1792, he placed the required advertisements in the *Kentucky Gazette,* summoning "Rachel Robards" to court "to answer a charge of adultery" against her.[9] As the first newspaper in the West, the *Gazette* was surely readily available in Nashville. It is impossible that the Jacksons had no clue that the process was under way. They continued their policy of living as they chose, in February 1792 buying a small plantation on the Cumberland River where they built their first home, Poplar Grove.

Politics, however, intervened in the completion of the Robards divorce. After several attempts to win its independence from Virginia,

Kentucky was finally admitted as the fifteenth state on June 1, 1792. Matters pending before the courts had to wait for the installation of new state officials and institutions. Robards, however, went ahead and bigamously married his intended, Hannah Wynn, in December 1792 in Jefferson County while the divorce was still up in the air. Finally, in August and September 1793, Lewis Robards appeared in court with U.S. Senator John Brown as his attorney; Hugh McGary appeared as a witness to his allegations about the behavior of the Jacksons in July 1790. Neither Rachel nor Andrew appeared. By this time, their adultery was indisputable, and they definitely wanted the divorce to go through. The jury found for the plaintiff, and, on September 27, he was granted a complete dissolution of his marriage on the grounds that his wife had deserted him and "hath and doth Still live in adultery with another man."[10]

In November 1793, Lewis and Hannah married again in Mercer County, legally this time; they continued to live quietly there with their children for the rest of their lives. In the meantime, Rachel and Andrew were in a quandary. With the divorce now completely legal, they were free to marry. But by doing so, did they admit to desertion and adultery? Finally, on January 17, 1794, Andrew Jackson, John Overton, and Robert Hays posted bond for the marriage of Andrew Jackson and Rachel Donelson "Alias Rachel Roberts" if there was no lawful cause preventing their marriage.[11] In his capacity of justice of the peace, Hays married the lovers on January 28, 1794.

CHAPTER 4

Making a Life Together

Once they settled down outside Nashville, the Jacksons entered into what might be considered the second act of their lives together, a long peaceful lull in the 1790s after the drama of their elopement. Surrounded by friends and family, Rachel enjoyed the good reputation and respect accorded any married woman. The unhappiness of her first marriage and the scandal of her separation, it seemed, could be buried at last. Safely remarried back in Kentucky, Lewis Robards had sold his land in the Cumberland area. Apparently he never returned to Nashville and certainly didn't further trouble Rachel's serenity.

Andrew brought Rachel love, thoughtfulness, and respect. Besides her answering love and constant attention to his needs, Rachel provided Andrew with a large family who embraced him, supported his ambitions, and loved him as one of their own. As an orphan and poor relation, Andrew had been a pitiable individual—his few relatives hadn't taken much interest in him as a youth.

Masculine honor in the South rested on personal courage but also demanded a foundation of kinship. A man of honor protected his family members, and, in return, they stood up for him. Lack of family meant helplessness and loneliness, and, though beyond an individual's control, being kinless was considered somehow disreputable. Jackson's violent touchiness about his reputation and gentility has been attributed to his early losses and lack of a family network. Only when the Donelson clan enfolded him did Andrew really begin to come into his own.[1]

When Rachel's marriage to Lewis Robards came to a crisis, her family had chosen Andrew Jackson over the offended husband. Certainly her brothers and brothers-in-law could have forcibly prevented her elopement or run Jackson out of town had they chosen to do so. Instead, they allowed the two to depart for Natchez and recognized them as a married couple on their return. Some six weeks after Robert Hays married them in 1794, Andrew wrote a letter to Rachel's brother Stockley Donelson in Knoxville, offering his friendship and hospitality at their home. Stockley responded with enthusiasm, averring that "Nothing has for a long time given me more real Satisfaction than your expressions of Friendship" and "also My little Rachel."[2]

In every possible way, the Donelsons made it clear that Jackson was one of them. Eventually, eight of Rachel's siblings produced nearly sixty nieces and nephews, many of whom had similarly large families. Wherever the Jacksons lived, there was always a parade of children on short or long visits. Andrew was delighted to be part of such a large clan, furthering the careers of several of Rachel's nephews whom he considered his own. Only fourteen when his own mother died, he became deeply attached to his mother-in-law. In one early letter to Rachel after their marriage, he sent his compliments to "my good old Mother Mrs. Donelson, that best of friends." He asked Rachel to tell her "with what pain I reflect upon leaving home without shaking her by the hand and asking her blessing."[3]

In all the important business of a man's life in eighteenth-century Tennessee—lending and borrowing money; acquiring and defending land claims; business partnerships; slave acquisition and discipline; co-signing notes or standing bond for one another's actions—a man with resolute family members willing to help out or to be helped trumped a single man every time. It's no wonder that so many settlers who moved west brought their large extended families. For Jackson, becoming part of a family as respected as the Donelsons also meant joining a greater circle of family friends, united by affection, business, and politics. Jackson was transformed by his marriage from a young bachelor scuffling for a living as a lawyer into a man of family with extensive resources that he could call upon.

After he met Rachel in 1788, Jackson buckled down and began to grow up. Back east, acquaintances would have been amazed at the ambition and energy he put into making a career, building up an estate, and looking after his wife. The power of love can certainly be exaggerated, but the change in Jackson's life after he and Rachel became a couple is impressive. Despite his sometimes rough ways with other men, he was a romantic who idolized his wife and fretted about her when they were apart. He began his letters: "My Dearest Heart" or "My Love."

The first surviving letter from Andrew to Rachel was written May 9, 1796. They were both twenty-nine and had been a couple for seven years, but his letter reads as though they were in the early stages of romance. It is worth quoting in its entirety for the light it sheds on the passion and depth of his feelings.

> *My Dearest Heart*
> *It is with the greatest pleasure I sit down to write you. Tho I am absent My heart rests with you. With what pleasing hopes I view the future period when I shall be restored to your arms there to spend My days in Domestic Sweetness with you the Dear Companion of my life, never to be separated from you again during this Transitory and fluctuating life.*
>
> *I mean to retire from the Buss [business] of publick life, and Spend My Time with you alone in Sweet Retirement, which is My only ambition and ultimate wish.*
>
> *I have this moment finished My business here which I have got in good Train and hope to wind it up this Touer [tour], and will leave this tomorrow Morning for Jonesborough where I hope to finish it, and tho it is now half after ten o'clock, could not think of going to bed without writing you. May it give you pleasure to Receive it. May it add to your Contentment until I return. May you be blessed with health. May the Goddess of Slumber every evening light on your eyebrows and gently lull you to sleep, and conduct you through the night with pleasing thoughts and pleasant dreams. Could I only know you were contented and enjoyed Peace of Mind, what satisfaction it would afford me whilst travelling the loanly and tiresome road. It would relieve My anxious breast and shorten the way—May the great "I am" bless and protect you until that happy and wished for moment arrives when I am restored to your sweet embrace which is the Nightly prayer of your affectionate husband, Andrew Jackson.*[4]

Although in fact he never retired from the business of public life to spend his time with Rachel in "Sweet Retirement," he imagined it as an ideal. For someone as ambitious for public acclaim as he, such retirement would have been impossible. For her, it would have been heaven. Such was the deep difference between them.

For all the drama of its beginning, the Jacksons' marriage was typical of the nineteenth century. Their division of gender roles was completely conventional. He worked at his profession, entered politics, and traveled on business. He oversaw the plantation, and when employees, like the overseer or craftsmen, or slaves were disobedient, he saw to their chastisement. She kept house, gardened, maintained a closely knit web of family and friends, and arranged their entertaining and social life. Unlike some patriarchal husbands, he also depended on Rachel completely and trusted her to make decisions about money, the plantation, and any other matters of importance during his frequent absences from home.

Theirs was a harmonious partnership of opposites. He wanted to contend with other men and triumph, to become a leader, to travel, to mix in grand affairs. She didn't. She was a person who lived in the place she loved and wanted to stay there. She missed him terribly during the weeks and sometimes months when he was away.

During the 1790s Jackson began his rise to political prominence under the guidance of his new friend, Governor William Blount of the Southwest Territory. In Andrew Jackson, Blount had seen the kind of ambitious, loyal young man he liked to surround himself with. Jackson worked hard as both a public and private attorney, riding a circuit around the Cumberland and as far east as Jonesborough, with almost half of each year spent traveling and appearing in log courthouses.[5] As attorney general, he most commonly prosecuted defaulting debtors. His private practice usually dealt with disputed land claims or assault and battery.

Since no salary had been agreed upon by the government for his services as attorney general, Jackson was forced to petition for payment, sometimes successfully, sometimes not. He also had trouble getting paid by his private clients. Hard currency was almost impossible to come by on the frontier, so he might be paid with notes of hand, as promissory notes were then known, or with commodities, bushels of cornmeal, say, or livestock, or best yet, with land.

Hand in hand with political power, land, acres upon acres of productive land, was essential to maintain "the character of a gentleman," as class-conscious Americans phrased that desirable status. Few professional men—be they attorneys or doctors—planned to spend their lives employed by others. The ultimate goal of ambitious men in the southwest was to become planters, men of wealth and importance in their communities.

The more land Jackson could accumulate, the more likely he was to become wealthy when he sold acreage at greatly inflated prices to latecomers in Tennessee. In fact, he went into the land speculation business with his friend John Overton, putting together parcels of land that seemed likely sites for future townships. Most of their purchases were made on credit as they gambled on the growth of Tennessee.

Most things went well for the young couple at Poplar Grove. By 1795, through Rachel's inheritance and Andrew's purchases, they owned several slaves to work the land and serve in the house. Their neighbors were close relatives and friends, including Rachel's mother and brothers and her sister Jane and brother-in-law Robert Hays.[6] Besides their interwoven social life and mutual business dealings, they were all loyal supporters of William Blount in politics. Visiting, dining, telling stories, dancing (a fiddler was required for any evening entertainment), the Jacksons enjoyed their lives. The men added drinking, gambling, cockfighting, gossiping, and horseracing to their joint activities while the women got together to trade household advice and family news, gossip, care for children and the sick, and sew for their large families.

By 1795, American negotiations with Spain resulting in Pinckney's Treaty had brought a considerable degree of peace to the frontier. Although the treaty was not officially ratified until the following year, the agreement had immediate effects with Spain's agreement to stop arming and encouraging Indians to attack American settlers. Settler raids and reprisals had also forced the Chickamaugas, their fiercest opponents in the Cumberland, back to their Cherokee homeland in the East.

Now when the Jacksons rode into Nashville, they delighted in all the signs of civilization. It was the prototype of frontier towns to come. Surveyors had laid out the town as a long rectangular grid of streets at right angles to each other. A public square in the center of town was situated on the crest of the bluff near the riverfront. This square boasted a one-room log courthouse, a log jail, and a pillory. A business district surrounded the square, including two taverns, a distillery, a dry goods store, and a blacksmith shop. The Methodists had built a log chapel, and the Presbyterians had broken ground for a stone church.

Population in the territory had soared, and by the end of the decade Nashville boasted sixty to eighty family homes, mostly log or frame, but including one brick building. With the improvement of roads, coaches and carriages were brought west from Philadelphia. Mail service between Nashville and the rest of the United States through Knoxville had been established. River traffic on the Cumberland had skyrocketed as the port of New Orleans was opened to American trade. The pirogues, canoes, and keelboats of earlier days were joined by increasing numbers of flatboats, huge floating boxes that could carry 200 to 300 tons of goods. Boats came down to Nashville from Pittsburgh with manufactured goods—guns, ammunition, metal tools, fine fabrics, hats, furniture, books, and whatever else Tennesseans could afford to buy. At Nashville, boats loaded cotton, tobacco, pelts, whiskey, lime, and bacon for the journey down the Mississippi to Natchez and New Orleans.[7]

In 1795, Andrew joined Rachel's brother Sam in opening a dry goods store. Able to buy goods wholesale for their store, the Jacksons and Donelsons were among their own best customers for luxury goods from the East. Rachel and Andrew bought a carpet for their house, thirty pounds of coffee, combs, two cases of "segars," vellum, linen, ribbon, scissors, pins and needles, ladies' gloves, pocket handkerchiefs, both corded and clouded muslin, striped woolen durant, silk hose, calico, paper, sugar, wine, chocolate, and tea.

These goods give a sense of the elegance with which the Jacksons and other gentry families were beginning to live: cigars in place of chewing tobacco, refined cane sugar instead of maple sugar or honey, wine instead of home-brewed whiskey. The luxuries of chocolate and tea had previously been unobtainable on the frontier. Rachel had given up the homespun of her girlhood and now wore dresses made of fashionable and expensive fabrics imported from Europe. She bought material for both winter and summer dresses with heavy woolen durant contrasting with cool cottons— gaily printed calicos and delicate pastel muslins. Gloves and silk hose completed a genteel picture, along with ribbons to trim her bonnets.[8]

All Andrew's friends felt warm affection and admiration for Rachel and sometimes expressed it by sending her gifts of dress fabrics or jewelry to suit her newly fashionable tastes. During these years, for example, Alexander Outlaw, a prominent politician, sent her five and a half yards of black cassimere, a soft-textured wool, for a dress; a yard of white muslin for trim; and a necklace. William

C. C. Claiborne, later governor of Louisiana, had taken one of Rachel's rings to Philadelphia to be repaired and in the process had a miniature likeness of Washington placed in the setting atop the ring. In his letter to Andrew, he requested, "Will you inform your Lady, Sir, that I took much pleasure, in having her Ring repaired, and request her, to accept of it as a small but sincere token of my Respect and Esteem."[9]

One of the Jacksons' purchases, however, is a key to the greatest sorrow of their young married life. In August 1795, they acquired Alexander Hamilton's *On Female Complaints,* bought by Andrew in Philadelphia. Hamilton was a distinguished specialist on gynecology from the University of Edinburgh, the leading medical school in the English-speaking world. There was a steady market for his book, which went through at least seven printings and was still being cited by specialists at the end of the nineteenth century.[10]

Still under thirty and a member of a very fertile family, Rachel had not yet given birth. Nor is there any evidence that she had ever been pregnant in her two marriages spanning ten years altogether. Clearly, she suspected that something was amiss. *On Female Complaints* was a mine of the latest scientific thought on menstrual cycle dysfunction and the causes of and possible cures for sterility.

Whatever information they may have gleaned from the book and whatever remedies they may have tried, Rachel never became pregnant. It was a terrible misfortune for both of them. American men desired sons to carry on their names, to assist in their endeavors, to inherit property, and to care for the family. Men naturally assumed, often falsely, that the failure to have children was the result of some defect in their wives. In this case, it seems likely to have been so since Lewis Robards had many children with his second wife.

Childlessness in women, like kinlessness, was pitiable and even contemptible depending on the observers' sense of charity. Barren women were seen as a disappointment to their husbands and families, incomplete, and failures in their primary roles as women.[11] Surrounded by her flocks of nieces and nephews, Rachel must have suffered bitterly as, month by month, then year by year, her hopes of having a child receded.

By 1795, waves of migration and a booming birthrate had provided Tennessee with many more than the 60,000 inhabitants required to apply for statehood in the United States. Even before Congress voted to admit the latest western applicant (Kentucky had become a state in 1792), Governor Blount called a convention to write the new state constitution in January 1796. Andrew Jackson served as one of the delegates, writing what Thomas Jefferson considered a model democratic constitution.

Even as he was practicing high-level statecraft, Jackson was rushing around staving off bankruptcy. Earlier in 1795, when preparing to open the store with Sam Donelson, Jackson had gone for the first time to Philadelphia, the nation's capital, commercial center, and largest city. There, he made the foolish mistake of taking unsecured notes in return for more than 50,000 acres of land from one of William Blount's associates, David Allison. More disastrously, he signed over the notes to a city firm in return for merchandise for the store. After he returned home and opened the store, he was stunned by a letter informing him that Allison had defaulted and that he himself was now liable for full payment of those of Allison's debts covered by the notes. Only by selling the store and a great deal of land at bargain prices did Jackson stay afloat.

Still solvent, though barely, Jackson bought a new plantation in the spring of 1796. Rather than the usual log house, Hunter's Hill was an impressive two-story frame house. Oddly enough, the land had been purchased by Lewis Robards when he hoped to live there with Rachel. He had sold it after her elopement, and the subsequent owner had built the house.

The years 1796 and 1797 marked the debut of Andrew Jackson in national politics, longer absences from Nashville, and Rachel's increasing unhappiness. In May and June 1796, he returned to Philadelphia to sell land, buy merchandise for a new store, and try to deal with the Allison mess. Back home, he was elected to the U.S. House of Representatives, where he served respectably in Philadelphia from December 1796 through March 1797.

Rachel was more than capable of keeping everything afloat while her husband was gone, but she didn't like the necessity. Neither at this time nor later did she see why Andrew should travel far and wide, leaving her alone. At each farewell, she objected bitterly and dissolved into tears, causing her tenderhearted husband extreme distress.

On December 6, 1796, the first day of the congressional session, Andrew wrote the ever-reliable Robert Hays about politics and business, but included two requests to care for Rachel. He wrote, "I beg of you to amuse Mrs. Jackson let her not fret If possible." Then three paragraphs later, he returned to the theme, "I will thank you to see Mrs. Jackson as often as you Can with Convenience, I am Distressed in mind about her." Still in Philadelphia, Jackson wrote to Hays again in January 1797. It was a long letter about politics, but he enclosed a letter for Rachel, asking him to "Deliver the enclosed letter and take care of my little Rachel until I return."[12]

The end of his term as representative heartened her, but the following autumn he was selected a U.S. senator by the state legislature; senators were not elected by popular vote until the twentieth century. The new position again required him to leave home for some months. The scene at the doorstep on this departure must have been truly upsetting. On the way to Philadelphia, he met a friend in Knoxville and took the opportunity to send a letter for Hays. On November 2, 1797, he wrote:

> *I must now beg of you to try to amuse Mrs. Jackson and prevent her from fretting. the situation in which I left her—(Bathed in Tears) fills me with woe. Indeed, Sir, It has given me more pain than any Event of my life—but I trust she will not remain long in her dolefull mood, but will again be Cheerfull.*[13]

Why didn't she go with him if she missed him so? Primarily because she didn't want to live in a boardinghouse in a big city, far from home and family, where everything would be foreign to her. In general, very few congressmen brought their wives to Philadelphia. Life there was very expensive compared to the rest of the nation, and congressmen lived in boardinghouses with other temporarily single men, "clubbing" together to take their meals. There was not as yet a social political community in which wives could be comfortable.

The Jacksons might well have gone broke without Rachel's constant attention to the plantation and other business matters. She was the stable force at home, dealing with creditors and debtors, buyers and sellers, overseers and slaves. Throughout his absences, she was particularly attentive to saving money.

During his tenure in the Senate, Jackson seldom spoke and contributed little. At this time, he got wind of a spectacular land fraud, orchestrated by some of the leading men of North Carolina and Tennessee, including John Sevier, a Revolutionary War hero and a political enemy of William Blount. Shocked by the brazenness of the scheme, he began gathering evidence to use later back home.

In the spring of 1798, recognizing his own ineffectiveness, the rivalries with political enemies in Tennessee, and homesickness, Jackson resigned his position. He also had the chance of another employment that would suit both him and Rachel better. Later in the year, he was elected by the state legislature to the Tennessee Superior Court, where he would serve with distinction and forcefulness for the next six years. The salary was decent enough—$600 annually, surpassed only by the governor's $750. Although he would still be away for weeks when he held court in other towns, it was better than spending months in Philadelphia. Being based in Nashville also meant that he could continue his land and mercantile ventures part-time in association with a series of partners.

Although records of the court's decisions were not kept at that time, Jackson was considered effective, impressive, and fair. He attended punctually to his circuit of towns and villages, clearing dockets in record time. Most of the state's politicians and private citizens who encountered Judge Jackson admired his methods and wanted him to remain on the bench.

When necessary, he would use the threat of violence to keep wild backwoodsmen in order. A famous story of his grit is recounted in a couple of variants by an early biographer, James Parton, who conducted extensive interviews with old-timers who had seen Jackson in action. Russell Bean, a big gunsmith of great strength and irascibility, had been imprisoned for cutting the ears off a baby not his own who had been borne by his wife while he was away on a very long trip. He broke out of jail the very first night and defied anyone to take him back. The sheriff and his deputies tried unsuccessfully. Then, seeing Jackson coming down the street to take him in, Bean immediately surrendered to the one man he feared.

More colorfully, newspapers reported that Bean, armed to the teeth, disturbed a court session by blustering and cursing outside in the street. Neither sheriff nor posse dared lay hands on the violent giant to arrest him for contempt of court. Jackson then adjourned court for ten minutes and walked up to Bean and a crowd of ruffians gathered about him as he swore defiance.

Pistols in hand, Jackson walked into the center of the group and said, "Now, surrender, you infernal villain, this very instant, or I'll blow you through!" Bean looked for a moment into the judge's blazing eyes and then gave up, allowing the sheriff to lead him away.

A few days later, when asked why he allowed one man to cow him when he had defied an entire posse, he replied, "Why, when he came up, I looked him in the eye, and I saw shoot, and there wasn't shoot in nary other eye in the crowd; and so I says to myself, says I, hoss, it's about time to sing small, and so I did."[14]

Stories about Jackson's steely determination and his willingness to use violence when he felt it necessary were rife in Tennessee. Based at least loosely on the truth, they were a measure of the respect and admiration his fellow citizens felt for him. They were also the reason for Rachel's fears that he would go too far and be killed.

In the Jacksons' correspondence, it is striking how often he, Rachel, and their correspondents wrote about bad health, symptoms, and treatments. In 1800, at thirty-three, they were already beginning to suffer from chronic complaints. As a teenage messenger for the rebels during the American Revolution, Andrew had been slashed with a sword by a British officer for refusing to clean his boots. In an abominably crowded British prison, he had contracted smallpox and malaria. He emerged with scars, light pock marks, and recurrent bouts of ague, that is, chills and fever. Malaria was endemic on the frontier, so the chances are that Rachel also suffered from it. Almost everyone did.

From a lifetime of long, strenuous rides over rough terrain, Andrew already had "the rheumaticks," as he called arthritis. His knees were especially bad, exacerbated by a fall on the Philadelphia ice. Both of the Jacksons frequently contracted heavy colds that settled in their lungs. Such colds were worrisome because they feared pneumonia, a deadly killer before the discovery of antibiotics. Headaches, stomachaches, and diarrhea were painful in themselves, but were also feared as the harbinger of something more serious. Rachel suffered from recurrent "female complaints." Living in a world where neither the cause nor cure of diseases was known, they were often fearful and anxious about their health.

In July 1800, for the first time in their lives, the Jacksons took a trip not connected with Andrew's career. Combining a serious purpose with pleasure, they traveled to the health resort of Warm

Springs in Bath County, Virginia. With them in their coach they took Rachel Hays, one of Rachel's seven namesakes among her nieces. The daughter of Jane and Robert Hays, little Rachel was about seven and behaved, according to Andrew, "more like a Woman of mature age, than anything Else."[15]

Up in the mountains of today's West Virginia, they rented a small cabin, which they had to furnish, took the mineral waters, enjoyed the air, admired the scenery, ate well, and took pleasure in "a genteel Society." They spent a month there and felt their health much improved. Unfortunately, on the trip home, everyone had to get out of the coach to ease the horses' burden while they went up "a tremendous mountain" in a very hard rain. Rachel caught a "violent" cold, which left her feeling quite ill.[16]

On April 1, 1802, Jackson achieved a longtime goal when he was commissioned major general of the Tennessee militia. Like all westerners, Jackson craved military command. Nothing set the seal on a man's gentility like a military title, and all those militia captains, majors, colonels, and generals were addressed by their titles for the rest of their lives, however short or undistinguished their service may have been. Although he had no experience to speak of, Jackson believed fervently that he was born to command.

For years he had been working toward that goal, quietly politicking among the state's officers. When the position opened up, these officers put his name forward "unsolicited." In Tennessee, militia officers were elected, and Jackson was widely admired and imitated by the younger men. Even running against John Sevier, Jackson

James Madison (Library of Congress)

JAMES MADISON.
President of the United States.

Dolley Madison (Library of Congress)

James Monroe (Library of Congress)

Elizabeth Monroe (Library of Congress)

John Quincy Adams (author's collection)

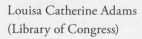

Louisa Catherine Adams (Library of Congress)

Religious revival on the Frontier (Courtesy of the Tennessee State Library and Archives)

PIONEERS ON THE OHIO

[112]

Flatboat on the Ohio (Library of Congress)

Andrew Jackson by Ralph E. W. Earl, with a view of the first and second Hermitages in the background (The Hermitage: Home of President Andrew Jackson, Nashville, Tennessee)

Andrew Jackson by Ralph E. W. Earl (The Hermitage: Home of President Andrew Jackson, Nashville, Tennessee)

Rachel Jackson miniature by Mary Catherine Strobel (The Hermitage: Home of President Andrew Jackson, Nashville, Tennessee)

Rachel Jackson by Ralph E. W. Earl (The Hermitage: Home of President Andrew Jackson, Nashville, Tennessee)

William Harris Crawford (Library of Congress)

Thomas Hart Benton (author's collection)

Henry Clay (author's collection)

achieved a tie. Fortunately for him, the new governor was Archibald Roane, William Blount's partisan and his own good friend. Roane broke the tie in his favor, and Andrew Jackson was commissioned as the top military officer in the state.[17]

Everything seemed to be going Andrew's way. Rachel was contented. He had received the appointment of his dreams. They had a lovely house and enough money to maintain their position. No longer forced to struggle for respect and position, Andrew Jackson had become a true Tennessee gentleman.

CHAPTER 5

The Hermitage

Snatching the command of the Tennessee militia from the outstretched hands of John Sevier, longtime adversary of the Blount political faction, was a great pleasure in itself for a man as competitive as Andrew Jackson. Becoming a major general in 1802 both enhanced Jackson's reputation and eventually opened the way to the military fame he craved. He enjoyed the privilege of being addressed as "General" by all the world.

Sevier was a Tennessee titan. An early settler in the eastern Watauga area, he had the military experience that Jackson so clearly lacked. As a commander in the North Carolina militia, he had won the only major frontier battle of the American Revolution, at King's Mountain in 1780, turning the British away from the West. He was widely admired by white Tennesseans as an Indian fighter and skilled treaty negotiator.

With such a background, Sevier had been elected the first governor of the new state of Tennessee in 1796 and served three consecutive two-year terms. The state constitution stipulated that no one could serve a fourth consecutive term. Sevier had planned to command the militia during the two-year interval before he was eligible to return to the governorship.

Imagine his surprise and fury when Andrew Jackson, an inexperienced young upstart, nipped in and carried off the appointment, furthering his offense by attacking the hero's honesty as well. Sevier was nearly twenty-five years older than Jackson, experienced and admired. As far as he could see, Jackson was only good at politicking.

Despite his political opposition to Sevier, Jackson had remained on civil terms until their rivalry for command erupted. When Jackson prevailed in the militia election, he was primed to bring Sevier down politically as well. At about the same time that he was commissioned in April 1802, Jackson provided the new governor, Archibald Roane, with documentary evidence of massive land frauds orchestrated by Sevier and other Tennesseans in collaboration with James Glasgow, secretary of state for North Carolina. Himself rigidly honest, Jackson was outraged by the deals. He had begun gathering information in 1797 while he was serving in the U.S. Senate.

As politically crafty as he was honest, however, Jackson had saved the unveiling of the evidence until a propitious moment. He fully expected that exposure of the charges would ruin Sevier and his friends, perhaps sending them to prison, and certainly blocking any political future. He and Roane waited more than a year to see what Sevier's next move would be.

When Sevier announced his intention to run against Roane in 1803, the incumbent governor disclosed the evidence of land fraud. Jackson followed up with an account in the *Knoxville Gazette* of July 27, 1803, charging Sevier with bribery and fraud, and laying out his proof. Sevier responded, as he had to earlier queries in North Carolina, in the paper and by letter, claiming that all his documented payments to Glasgow were merely generous fees, not bribes. Furthermore, he claimed that Roane and Jackson had trumped up the charges to smear him on the eve of the election. Scandal and rumor rocked Tennessee.

Andrew Jackson had seriously miscalculated. Destroying John Sevier proved to be far beyond his powers. Some land grants were rescinded, and several of the smaller players were ruined financially, but Sevier survived unscathed. Most Tennesseans couldn't believe, or didn't choose to, that the state's hero could be guilty. His followers took violent exception to the charges. In their eyes, Andrew Jackson was a lying scandalmonger, and he deserved a taste of rough frontier justice!

Rachel was terrified for her husband's safety. As a judge riding circuit, he was required to travel regularly through eastern Tennessee, Sevier's stronghold. Despite her pleas in person and by letter, he went about his business as usual. While on the road to Jonesborough shortly after the exchange in the *Gazette,* Jackson fell ill with a very high fever. When he arrived in town, he went straight to bed at his hotel. Already alerted that Sevier's supporters planned to "mob him" at the first opportunity, Jackson was hardly surprised when a friend ran into the bedroom to warn him that a group of rowdies under the command of a Colonel Harrison had gathered in the street out front. They planned to tar and feather him—rough frontier justice indeed.

Rather than locking the door as his friend begged, Jackson leaped out of bed and threw the bedroom door open. He sent the man down to deliver a message: "Give my compliments to Colonel Harrison, and tell him my door is open to receive him and his regiment whenever they choose to wait upon me; and that I hope the colonel's chivalry will induce him to lead his men, and not follow them."[1] Dismayed by the threat of violence from their intended victim, the group dispersed without entering the hotel. Once again, Jackson had faced down opponents by sheer bravado and unbending will.

The contest between Jackson and Sevier had unexpected consequences for Rachel's reputation, however, keeping the memory of her elopement and divorce alive throughout the state. It was only a matter of time before the principals would run into each other. That time came on October 1, 1803, in Knoxville, where Sevier was ensconced as the newly reelected fourth-term governor. In the capital to preside over local cases, Jackson unexpectedly encountered Sevier in the town square in front of the courthouse. Jackson was carrying a cane and Sevier a sword when they came upon one another. Sevier began screaming at Jackson in his fury. How dare a mere pettifogging lawyer defame him, challenge him, and attempt to humiliate Tennessee's leader. Caught off balance, Jackson haltingly began to defend his own services to the state.

Deriding Jackson's lack of military or any other combat experience, Sevier went even further. "Services?" he sneered. "I know of no great service you rendered the country, except taking a trip to Natchez with another man's wife."[2]

The crowd in the square was shocked. Sevier had probably not meant to go so far, but had been carried away by his fury. Jackson was now as enraged as his attacker. He thundered, "Great God! Do you mention her sacred name?"[3] As usual in a frontier fracas, pistols were drawn by many of those present, shots were fired, a bystander was grazed, and friends of the men separated them before the square could be engulfed by a fatal brawl. The Glasgow affair was almost forgotten as the original reason for all the bitter words.

The next day, Jackson wrote Sevier a sizzling challenge:

> *Sir*
>
> *The ungentlemanly Expressions, and gasconading conduct, of yours relative to me on yesterday was in true charactor of your self, and unmask you to the world, and plainly shews that they were the ebulutions of a base mind goaded with stubborn prooffs of fraud, and flowing from a source devoid of every refined sentiment, or delicate sensation. But sir the Voce [Voice] of the people has made you a Governor. this alone makes you worthy of my notice or the notice of any Gentleman. To the office I bear respect, to the Voice of the people who placed it on you I pay respect, and as such I only deign to notice you, and call upon you for that satisfaction and explanation that your ungentlemanly conduct & expressions require, for this purpose I request an interview, and my friend who will hand you this will point out the time and place, when and where I shall Expect to see you with your friend and no other person, my friend and myself will be armed with pistols. you cannot mistake me, or my meaning. I am &c &c*
>
> *Andrew Jackson*[4]

Sevier answered with equal provocation—indeed in almost the same words and phrases, "ungentlemanly," "gasconading" (a useful frontier word that meant bragging without the ability to back up one's claims), "unmasked yourself." He offered to meet Jackson in Georgia, Virginia, or North Carolina. As governor, he refused to meet in Tennessee since the legislature had outlawed dueling in 1801.[5] What seemed destined to become a fatal encounter, however, soon descended into farce as insulting missives were delivered back and forth, sometimes daily, by the men's friends during the next several days. Every proposal for a place or time for the encounter was rejected with counterproposals. Each letter was filled with insults as they labeled each other cowards, blackguards, and paltroons [poltroons].[6]

Jackson continued to rage at the insult to Rachel, which was actually more pointedly aimed at him. The implication of Sevier's remark was that Jackson was a seducer and an enticer, who had interfered in another man's family and with his legal right to his wife and her possessions. Nonetheless, he wrote to Sevier that "in the Publick Streets of Knoxville…you ransacked the Vocabulary of Vulgarity for insulting and blackguard Expressions. You without provocation made the attack, and in an ungentlemanly manner took the Sacred name of a lady in your poleuted lips."[7]

Sevier, apparently not wanting to push the matter over the edge, never mentioned Rachel again although he continued to insult Jackson. One comment must have stung, as the soldier wrote the lawyer: "As to answering all your Jargon of pretended bravery, I deem it perfectly beneath my character, having never heard of any you ever exhibited."[8] Truly, with his reputation for heroism secure and with eighteen children to provide for, Sevier had nothing to gain by a duel. Without actually backing down, he made a meeting all but impossible, driving his enemy into a frenzy. Finally, Jackson posted a notice in the *Knoxville Gazette* on October 10, reiterating the circumstances of the initial quarrel and charging in the stylized language of honor that Sevier was "a base coward and paltroon. he will basely insult, but has not courage to repair the wound."[9]

Sevier finally seemed to agree to a morning meeting two days thence, at South West Point in Indian territory to the east of Knoxville. Jackson and his second, Captain Andrew White, immediately rode to the destination and waited—and waited. When Sevier did not appear, they rode back to Knoxville, swearing revenge. On the road, they encountered a group of men riding toward them, led by Sevier and one of his sons. The encounter was a travesty of the gentlemanly ideal of a duel.

Both waving a pair of pistols, Jackson and Sevier dismounted and faced each other, shouting and cursing at the tops of their lungs. In a ludicrous series of events, they holstered their guns, and Sevier's horse ran away with his pistols. When Jackson drew a bead on him, Sevier sheltered behind a tree as his son aimed at Jackson, and Andrew White covered the son. The other men present finally convinced the protagonists that the situation had gone beyond the ridiculous. Anticlimactically, everyone went home without firing a shot. Although Jackson and Sevier remained political enemies, they never met on the field of honor or burst out into further public quarrels. Of the two, Jackson's reputation was much harder hit.

What with regular travel and newspaper delivery between Knoxville and Nashville, Rachel certainly knew about the quarrel and the intended duel before Andrew returned home. The embarrassment of having the circumstances of their marriage talked about publicly and the danger of losing her beloved husband made her miserable and suspicious of Andrew's intentions when he next set off for Knoxville on his way to Philadelphia. His temper and touchiness were bywords, and she found it hard to believe that such a monstrous clash would simply fade away.

Andrew, too, was doubtful that his quarrel with Sevier was over. In February 1804, he wrote to his friend John Coffee asking Coffee to meet him in Knoxville the following month. Stating that "I fear not the Hellish crew, or any act they can do to me," he nonetheless wanted a supporter at his side in case a fight broke out because "a trusty friend on those occasions is important."[10]

Rachel tried to prevent his leaving, suspecting that further violence might be in the wind, and then sent letters after him begging him to return home. She continued to fret until her nephew, Jack Hutchings, one of her husband's business partners, showed her a copy of a letter from Knoxville dated March 17. In it, Jackson assured him that the "Severites is all quiet." It was not until the end of the month that Hutchings returned to Nashville and read the letter and showed it to his aunt. He reported to Jackson that the letter eased her mind, since "She had Taken up the Idia that mr. Coffee was going on Dueling Bisness." She knew her husband all too well. He was concerned enough about her peace of mind to lie to her about his apprehensions and intentions, blithely trusting that things would turn out well in the end.[11]

Of course, Jackson *had* anticipated a possible duel, but now he wrote to Rachel, pretending that there had never been a hint of danger. He argued reasonably enough that it would give him real pleasure "to return to your arms [to] dispel those clouds that hover around you," but "the question occurs, would it bring contentment to my love, or might it not involve us in all the calamity of poverty—an event that brings every horror to my mind."[12] He had written by every post since leaving Nashville and would continue to do so in order to assure her that he was safe. Rachel was needed at home (not that she wanted to leave) as he depended on her to keep a watchful eye on spring planting, oversee their various businesses, arrange for the storage of newly purchased trade goods, and make on-the-spot decisions essential to their financial well-being.

Not yet recovered financially from the 1795 Allison debacle, the Jacksons worked together to recoup their losses. Besides the plantation and stores, they owned at various times cotton gins, distilleries, a racetrack, and a boatyard. But everything was subject to the vicissitudes of nature and the economy. During this time, the still at Hunter's Hill burned to the ground, destroying 300 gallons of whiskey along with its expensive equipment. The Louisiana Purchase of 1803, which made the port of New Orleans an American possession, had encouraged them to plant cotton. They no longer had to fear having their downriver shipments blocked by Spanish authorities. Prices for produce swung wildly, and they had no way of knowing in advance what price their own crops and those they purchased from others would bring. Sometimes bales weren't properly packed, water seeped in, and the cotton rotted. Jackson tried without success to acquire a salt lick for a salt-making business. He had also angled for the governorship of the new territory of Orleans in 1803, but it went instead to his friend, William C. C. Claiborne.

The basic problem with all these business enterprises was the lack of currency circulating in the West. Everyone bartered, trading what they had for what they needed. But it was an uncertain business of complicated calculations. How many hogs was a gelding worth, how did bushels of corn compare to tanned deer hides, how much should a cotton gin charge for de-seeding neighbors' crops? Notes of hand were traded like currency, but that too was tricky as debtors often defaulted. In one instance, Jackson declined to accept a note on one of Rachel's brothers-in-law from a third party. He doubted that it would be paid, and "I have formed a resolution never to sue a relation if I can avoid it."[13]

Rachel continued to be the court of last resort at Hunter's Hill, except in the discipline of their enslaved workers. That she hated to do, leaving any problems to their overseers or to Jackson. The area she chose as her own was gardening and planting. Nearly twenty-five years earlier, when the Donelsons came to Tennessee from Virginia, they had carried leather pouches of the carefully gathered seeds of their favorite plants. For all the early settlers, seeds were the source of living memories. Everyone traded the seeds and slips of plants.

By the turn of the century, there were still neither seed catalogues nor well-established nurseries, so seeds were bought as they happened to become available. In eastern Tennessee, Jackson purchased a great variety of garden seeds, as many of each as he could get. He sent them back to Nashville by an acquaintance and requested that Rachel share any extra seeds. At about the same time she oversaw the planting of 500 apple trees and ten rows of peach trees.

Poor health—agues, dysentery, flu, and a host of other ailments, as well as accidents—continued to plague Rachel and Andrew, and every letter was filled with inquiries and reports on their well-being. Once while Jackson was in Jonesborough, three stables caught fire in the night, burning to the ground along with four horses. He ran out into the cold air without a jacket, going into the stables three times before he could force his maddened horse to go outside. He saved the horse, but contracted a very bad cough and accompanying chest pain. No wonder Rachel feared letting him leave home since he always seemed to run into trouble or get sick.

On his return, Andrew found not only that was Rachel ailing, but that Sam Donelson, his wife Polly, and their little boys were in residence at Hunter's Hill because Sam was very sick. Rachel's brother died that summer of 1804, leaving a young widow and three sons who became Jackson's wards.

Bereft at the loss of her favorite brother, Rachel also had to help her husband face the need for additional financial retrenchment. Despite their best efforts, they needed to sell their handsome home, its extensive plantings, the store, and 640 acres in order to settle all debts and achieve economic stability. In July 1804 they sold Hunter's Hill and bought the adjacent 425-acre tract. Jackson also resigned as judge so that he could spend more time at home and devote himself to business.

Not only was the acreage smaller on their new plantation, but they moved into a log house, clearly a step down from Hunter's Hill. Fortunately, they found log houses perfectly acceptable. Only four years old, the house had been solidly constructed of top-quality materials by a master carpenter and stonemason. Although they first called the new property Rural Retreat, they almost immediately changed the name to the Hermitage.

The property had a feature that especially endeared it to Rachel. Behind the house in a ravine ran the Sinking Creek, which joined the Gravelly Spring 300 yards behind the house before continuing on to the Stones River. The spring produced clear, drinkable water all year long, sufficient for everyone at the Hermitage. Once a spring house was built, butter, eggs, and milk could be kept cool there, lasting for days without turning.

The Hermitage was a two-story log building with a limestone chimney. Its three-room plan, known as a Penn plan, was very common all over the West. The ground floor was one large room (24' x 26') with sturdy paneled front and back doors, flanked by double-hung sash windows with glass panes. The walls were of well-finished beaded board, the floor made of wide boards. On one side wall was a huge open fireplace; on the other an enclosed corner stair-case. The room served as a sitting room, parlor, dining room, and kitchen (until they built a separate kitchen and slave quarters behind the house in 1805). In the middle of the room was a long dining table, which could easily seat twelve to fourteen people. At Andrew's request, it was always set, ready to entertain their many guests at a moment's notice.

Upstairs, the staircase opened onto a square hall with two doors, one leading to a small bedroom and the other to the Jacksons' bed-room, a spacious room running the length of the house and warmed by a fireplace. The hall also contained a handsome black walnut ladder leading to the unfinished attic, used for storage and perhaps as a small sleeping area.[14]

Because the purchaser of Hunter's Hill was anxious to move in, the Jacksons had moved into the Hermitage at once even though they were in the middle of improving their new home. In July Andrew hired a French dancing master from Nashville, who was clearly something of an artist as well, to dress up the house. Charles Loumier painted and applied faux graining to the doors, stairs, banisters, and other woodwork. He also installed expensive hand-painted French wallpaper in the bedrooms—all for the princely sum of $37. They put down carpets and bought comfortable furniture, some imported from Philadelphia and some made by local crafts-men. This would be their home for the next seventeen years, where they would happily entertain all sorts of dignitaries, including an American president and vice president. The next spring, they built a distillery, a separate kitchen, and other outbuildings, as well as put-ting more land under cultivation and building split-rail fences.

In later life, both Sarah Childress Polk, wife of President James K. Polk, and Jefferson Davis, president of the Confederacy, recalled with pleasure childhood visits to this log house. Both described it as roomy and comfortable. Davis, whose family stayed for several weeks, wrote movingly of Rachel, whom he remembered as "the kind and tender wife who presided over his [Jackson's] house."[15]

Phasing out his Hunter's Hill enterprises, Andrew also became involved with a number of businesses at Clover Bottom, a stop for stagecoaches on the way to Nashville. He had a general store, a tavern and inn, and a racetrack. He rode over every day to tend to his affairs there.

Their financial setback meant that Andrew generally stayed close to home, conforming to Rachel's ideal of married life. The Hermitage was a part-time home to a crowd of little boys who came to live with them for months at a time, sleeping like puppies in a heap in a shared bedstead or on pallets on the floor, depending on the number of adults in the house. Rachel's brother Sam's three— John Samuel, Andrew Jackson, and Daniel Smith Donelson, boys of seven, five, and three—were often there. Eventually, Andrew's namesake lived there full-time, attending school and becoming a surrogate son. Andrew had also become guardian for the four children of his friend Edward Butler, one of the five fighting Butlers of Revolutionary War fame, who died in 1803. The children's mothers were living, but public opinion called for a male guardian to look after children's money and education. And boys needed a man's guidance. The Butler girls, Caroline and Eliza, were older and spent most of their time with their mother until they married. But the younger two, Edward George Washington and Anthony Wayne Butler, boys of four and one, frequently visited. Like Andrew Jackson Donelson, Edward Butler lived at the Hermitage and attended school there. All these children looked on the Jacksons as a second set of parents.

Older family members also needed to be looked after. When Andrew exposed the Glasgow land frauds, one of the men substantially involved was Rachel's brother Stockley, who lived in eastern Tennessee. At forty-five, he had married James Glasgow's daughter, Elizabeth Glasgow Martin, a widow with children. Unlike Sevier, both Glasgow and Donelson were disgraced and suffered considerable financial losses. Andrew had had no desire to damage Stockley, but it was impossible to shield him.

The Jacksons urged Stockley and Elizabeth to move to Nashville, where they would receive considerable help from relatives in recouping their losses; Andrew offered to build a log house for them on his property. Elizabeth, however, refused to move so far from home, and the couple separated briefly in 1803. Andrew took the lead in attempting to remedy their problems with both money and advice. He wrote to Elizabeth, reassuring her of the willingness of family and friends to welcome her, "seeing that you alone [are] the only earthly being under existing circumstances that would make [Stockley] happy or contented."[16] Deeply in debt, they reunited and finally moved to the Nashville area. After Stockley's death in 1805, Elizabeth married another Tennessean, and some of the children of her first union married into the Donelson family.

The enslaved population at the Hermitage was rather small for the first ten years that they lived there. The Jacksons were not grandees with hundreds of acres under cultivation, worked by large gangs of slave laborers. By 1806, they owned nine slaves in all. The adults and teenagers were old Hannah, the cook; her daughter Betty, who later became cook; Charles, the carriage driver; Aaron, the blacksmith; another Hannah, who later became housekeeper; Dick, a dining room servant; and Dunwoody, a horse trainer from Virginia. All worked in the fields as well. The children were old Hannah's son Squire and George, perhaps also her son, joined later by Betty's son Alfred.[17]

Jackson bought additional laborers during these years. The number of slaves at the Hermitage grew to twenty by 1820, then doubled again to forty by the end of the decade. As their numbers increased, more cabins were built, with duplexes or triplexes to house families. Jackson was never given to wanton cruelty, and he saw that all the blacks on the plantation were well-fed, clothed, and warmly housed. But he was not a man who brooked any signs of independence from his workforce. He never hesitated to order slaves beaten when they defied orders or didn't work to capacity. Rachel sometimes had trouble inducing the household staff to obey her. When that happened, she called on her husband or the overseer to step in.

Family and personal affairs, however, were not sufficient to absorb all of Andrew's abundant energy. The future of the West was his preoccupation. Although both Kentucky and Tennessee had become states, their needs and the political opinions of their citizens were sharply divergent from those of the Atlantic coast. With a burgeoning population and increasingly valuable economy, the leaders of Kentucky and Tennessee believed that the United States needed to address their needs and concerns.

White westerners were still deeply suspicious of the Indians remaining in proximity with them. Although the federal government asserted that Indian claims in Tennessee had been largely "extinguished" and that their remaining territory was to be respected by whites, settlers themselves were doubtful. They still had their eyes on the remaining Indian lands and expected further battles with the

Native Americans. Older members of the tribes might be willing to accept the status quo, but young men coming up were restive, willing to turn to violence to drive out the settlers and regain their ancestral lands.

Tennesseans' hostility toward Great Britain and Spain was also razor sharp. Britain wasn't yet convinced that the West might not revert to the Crown. From their western forts and trading posts, they encouraged Indian discontent. Spain was even worse in the minds of westerners. Following the Louisiana Purchase of 1803 and the American takeover of New Orleans and Natchez, the Spanish had retained Florida and a substantial swath of territory across the Gulf Coast, including parts of present-day Louisiana, Mississippi, and Alabama. They intended to hang on to what they had and, through trade and patronage of the Indians, to ensure the instability of the adjoining American territory.

Some white settlers still believed that independence might serve their interests better than statehood. The future of the entire area was still far from determined. Just then a new player arrived on the scene—Aaron Burr, one of the founding fathers of the nation and the former vice president. A man of multiple secrets and complicated plans, he was accused of trying to steal the presidency from Thomas Jefferson in 1800 while running as his vice president. Needless to say, he was not Jefferson's running mate in the reelection campaign of 1804, nor did he find himself welcome in many Republican political councils.

To make matters worse, in the summer of 1804 Burr had challenged Alexander Hamilton to a duel over political insults. Dueling was just being outlawed throughout the northern states. Still the sitting vice president, Burr had killed Hamilton and had been indicted for murder in both New Jersey, where the duel took place, and New York, where he lived, although he was not convicted in either state.

More or less a pariah in the East, his political career in shambles, Burr decided that his future lay in the West, whose future appeared as muddled and uncertain as his own. Dueling there was still acceptable, even required, behavior for a gentleman, despite its having been made illegal. It helped his reputation that Hamilton, the arch-Federalist, opposed most western interests while the Republican Burr had favored the statehood of both Kentucky and Tennessee. In fact, as a United States senator, he had done as much as anyone to ensure Tennessee's 1796 admission to the Union.

When he arrived in Nashville in May 1805, Burr was a welcome, even a celebrated visitor. It was quite a social coup that, during his five days in town, he stayed at the Hermitage, where he enjoyed the enveloping warmth of the Jacksons' hospitality as a stream of visitors came to pay court. Rachel was well known as a hostess of social gatherings, large and small, and was never at a loss to welcome and make her guests happy.

At the same time, Andrew organized banquets and entertainments in Nashville, where such events were part of the masculine purview. Most political business was conducted at hotels or taverns and required a strong constitution as toast followed drunken toast far into the night. Women were invited only for the occasional ball.

No one at that time or later knew the full scope of Burr's plans; and, in fact, he himself was trying to determine just what those plans might become. Basically, he planned a filibustering expedition into Spanish territory, perhaps even into Mexico. What might become of the "liberated" territory—annexation by the United States, an independent empire?—was never quite made clear. Jackson despised the Spanish "Dons," and believed that their departure from North

American soil was essential for peace. Throughout these years, the United States and Spain teetered on the brink of war. If war broke out, then Burr's private filibustering expedition would be not only desirable but perfectly legal.

At this point, Jackson's involvement with Burr wasn't very deep. Besides acting as his host, he had committed himself to building boats at his boatyard for Burr to go downriver to New Orleans and buying provisions for any proposed expedition. The men corresponded, and Burr stayed at the Hermitage again later in the summer, but the Jacksons had no concept of the notoriety that would follow their guest. After his departure, Jackson turned his attention to his favorite pastime—horseracing.

In early May 1805 Jackson had bought the stallion Truxton, one of the best-bred horses in America, for the princely sum of $1,500.[18] The whole purpose of such a horse was to win races (and large purses) and then be put at stud. The horse most likely to give Truxton a run for the money was another stallion, Joseph Erwin's Ploughboy.

A race was scheduled for November 1805 at Jackson's Clover Bottom racetrack. The stakes were set at $2,000; besides this bet between the principals, spectators were free to bet as much as they liked. If either owner withdrew before the race, he would pay a forfeit of $800. In the cash-starved West, the forfeit had to be paid with promissory notes from third parties. As it happened, the race was canceled because Ploughboy went lame. Erwin agreed to pay the forfeit, but he and Jackson disagreed about which notes had been pledged. Notes due on demand were practically as good as cash, but those with later dates might not be honored when they came due. They quickly agreed on a form of payment that was satisfactory to both, and that should have ended the matter. The race was rescheduled for April 1806; Truxton easily won both heats despite leg injuries and was retired to make substantial profits for Jackson as a stud horse.

Regrettably, however, that did not end the matter. According to one of Jackson's friends, Jackson had a run-in with Erwin's son-in-law, Charles Dickinson, at about the same time as the disagreement over the forfeiture payment in late 1805. Dickinson was in partnership with Erwin and was well known in the community as a wild young man given to drinking, boasting, and gambling. In the midst of an evening's revels at a local tavern, he apparently commented on Rachel Jackson in a lascivious way. Jackson soon confronted Dickinson, demanding an explanation. The young man said he didn't remember, having been drunk at the time, and had in any case meant nothing malicious. Drunkenness was considered a good excuse for bad behavior. Dickinson apologized for any impropriety, and Jackson accepted his apology, but he never really forgave and certainly never forgot.

Over the next months, Rachel's name never resurfaced, but friends of both men stirred the pot about the contested notes. Tittle-tattle, tale-bearing, and trouble-making interference kept the argument over the forfeiture payment alive long after Erwin and Jackson had settled the matter and run the scheduled race. Dickinson blamed Jackson for falsely impugning his and Erwin's honor; Jackson blamed Dickinson for using go-betweens and liars. This central storm spun off little twisters as two other duels took place between secondary characters.

As in the Sevier affair, insulting letters were exchanged between Jackson and Dickinson before the latter sailed off to New Orleans on business. In May 1806 Dickinson returned and renewed the quarrel. James Robertson, one of Nashville's founders, had all but prevailed on Jackson to let the matter go. Dueling was losing favor in the public mind, as well as in the law, and Jackson at thirty-nine was surely mature enough to overlook the boasting of the twenty-seven-year-old Dickinson.

That proved beyond Jackson's power, however, when Dickinson posted him a coward in the Nashville newspaper. Westerners paid to insert challenges and insults in local newspapers, a practice known as "posting" their enemies, to humiliate them publicly and force them into action. Their seconds set the now inevitable meeting for May 30 in nearby Kentucky. Well known as one of the best shots in the state, Dickinson roistered about the town, bragging that he would kill Jackson and even placing bets on his own marksmanship. Had it not been for Dickinson's insufferable attitude and his earlier insult to Rachel, Jackson might well have let the matter drop.

Early on that date, the rivals and their seconds met; Jackson had also brought along a doctor, and Dickinson, a party of the "gay blades of Nashville" in clear expectation of his own victory.[19] Because Dickinson was by far the better shot (Jackson was only mediocre), Jackson had decided to let his opponent fire first so that his own aim wouldn't be spoiled when he was hit by Dickinson's bullet. He was almost certain he would be hit and feared that he would flinch at the impact and fire wildly. If he survived the first shot, he should then be able to return fire. No one could doubt Jackson's nerve.

As agreed, a distance of twenty-four feet was paced off; the rivals faced each other with pistols at their sides. Thomas Overton,

Jackson's second, gave the order to fire. As expected, Dickinson got off a quick shot, aiming to kill, hitting Jackson inches from his heart, smashing ribs and part of his sternum. Jackson painfully raised his left arm, holding his wounded chest.

Dickinson, who had expected to kill his man with one shot, was staggered to see Jackson still standing. "Great God! Have I missed him?"[20] Overton ordered him to stand in his place. In terrible pain, Jackson raised his pistol and fired—to no effect. The hammer had stopped at half cock. Determined to hit his enemy, he then drew back the hammer, aimed, and deliberately fired. The bullet hit Dickinson in the abdomen, and he fell back into the arms of his friends. Within a short while, he bled to death.

Only as they walked away did Jackson's second realize that he was injured. One of his shoes was filled and overflowing with blood. He was very badly injured indeed. The bullet could not be removed because it was so close to his heart, and he spent more than a month convalescing at home. For the rest of his life, he suffered discomfort from this wound.

Under the vigilant eye of Rachel, Andrew recuperated physically, but his reputation suffered serious damage. It wasn't just that Dickinson was a much younger man with a young wife and new baby, but that Jackson had deliberately recocked his pistol while his opponent trembled in his place. That smacked not so much of a hotheaded quarrel as of a murder in cold blood. Of course, if Dickinson's quick shot had been a couple of inches to the side, the question would have been moot.

Dickinson's funeral was packed, and the next issue of the newspaper was bordered in mourning black at the behest of many local citizens. Jackson was furious and felt ill-used, but there was nothing to be done. This was his first real duel, and Dickinson was the first man he had killed, despite his ferocious reputation. The Dickinson affair would haunt him for the rest of his life.

And then Aaron Burr resurfaced in November 1805. President Jefferson and many others had become suspicious of his motives throughout the time Burr had been operating in the West. According to his own account, Jackson began to suspect that Burr might plan to detach the western states and form an independent empire in the fall of 1806 because of casual words let slip by one of Burr's lieutenants. Jackson sent swarms of warning letters out to cover himself with the president and other leaders. When Burr returned again to Nashville in November, Andrew was away. Rachel received him very coolly at the Hermitage and did not invite him to stay.

Jackson would have nothing to do with treason, and he wavered in his confidence in Burr's intentions. Only after Burr's arrest in Mississippi and return to Richmond to stand trial for treason on the orders of President Jefferson did Jackson finally make up his mind. Burr could not be guilty! He went to Richmond to testify on his behalf, but the defense attorneys turned down his offer. Burr was ultimately acquitted and spent several years in Europe.

Burr's reputation and his influence were completely destroyed, and Jackson's were severely damaged. Between the Dickinson duel and the Burr affair, Andrew's political future seemed to be as dead as Burr's. He devoted himself to business, drilled the militia, and spent time with Rachel. Reducing their expenditures and paying off their debts had restored their financial position. Although Andrew no longer considered running for office, his position as a wealthy and influential man grew. Anyone of importance visiting the area came to the Hermitage to pay their respects.

Despite the nieces, nephews, and wards who spent weeks and months at the Hermitage, Rachel still longed for a child of her own to rear. At forty-one, she must have given up hope of giving birth. On December 22, 1808, Elizabeth Rucker Donelson, the wife of Rachel's brother Severn, gave birth to twin boys, whom they named Andrew Jackson Donelson and Thomas Jefferson Donelson. By this time, among the children of Rachel's siblings and those of her nieces and nephews, there were almost as many namesake Andrews as there were little Rachels.

Within days, Elizabeth and Severn Donelson had agreed to allow Rachel and Andrew Jackson to adopt one of their twin boys. Andrew Jackson Donelson became Andrew Jackson Jr. and a permanent resident of the Hermitage. Both Rachel and Andrew doted on the new baby, who became the center of her life.

Adoption in the nineteenth century was considerably different from what it has become today. The adoption of strangers and secrecy about birth families were unknown concepts. Families frequently took in and reared orphans—relatives, godchildren, the children of friends or neighbors. Orphanages existed only in very large American cities; elsewhere the community took over. But these were not considered adoptions; more properly, they were fostering arrangements. The children in question never expected to become the heirs of the people who took them in.

True adoptions involved inheritance, as well as continuing a family name. Generally, childless wealthy couples adopted a child, usually a boy, from a relative with a large family and limited means. That boy, adopted as a baby or small child, assumed the surname of his new family and became the heir of his adoptive parents. There was no formal act of adoption; it was simply a matter agreed upon between family members, declared to the world by the adoptive parents, and accepted by the community.

Everyone knew about these adoptions, including the children and their siblings, and relations continued unbroken with their birth families. The motives of parents for allowing such adoptions were no doubt mixed—love and sympathy for childless relatives, desire to see a child rise in the world socially and financially, difficulty in caring for twins or very large families. Nevertheless, they stayed in close contact with their children, particularly in small communities such as Nashville. This was certainly the case with Andrew Jackson Jr., who remained stoutly attached to his twin Tom Donelson.

Now at last Rachel's dreams were coming true. She had a beloved husband, chastened somewhat against further adventures by his recent mishaps, a baby of her own, financial security, and peace.

CHAPTER 6

Great Convulsions

"And I beheld when [the Lamb] had opened the sixth seal, and, lo, there was a great earthquake; and the sun became black as sackcloth of hair, and the moon became as blood."[1] Thus one of the signs of the end of the world was portrayed as an earthquake in the apocalyptic Book of Revelation.

Throughout the Bible, beginning with Exodus, earthquakes wreaked destruction to punish sinners for their transgressions. In one vivid image, God's anger poured forth and "the ground clave asunder that was under them: And the earth opened her mouth, and swallowed them up, and their houses, and all the men...and all their goods."[2] Evangelical Protestants were well conditioned to see earthquakes as signs of divine displeasure. They also believed, however, that the Book of Revelation forecast the future so that a massive earthquake might be not just a punishment but a portent of the end of days.

Westerners understood earthquakes as natural phenomena but also feared them as biblical signs. No wonder they were terrified in the early morning of December 16, 1811, when a huge earthquake, estimated as greater than 8.0 on the Richter scale, violently shook an area of some 78,000–129,000 square kilometers, including the states of Tennessee, Kentucky, and Ohio, and the territories of Arkansas, Missouri, Illinois, and Indiana. It was followed a few hours later by an equally monstrous shock, interspersed with the constant rumble of smaller aftershocks.

These massive quakes were felt all the way to the East Coast, from Boston to South Carolina. In a great circle from the epicenter, chimneys were shattered and thrown down, the walls of brick and stone buildings were split, and log cabins were shaken to bits. The New Madrid fault (named for a small town in Missouri) extends from southern Illinois through Kentucky, Missouri, Arkansas, and Tennessee, crossing beneath the Mississippi River at some points. The earth rose and fell, deep cracks opened in the ground, tall jets of water and liquefied sand blew high into the air from gaping fissures, landslides swept away hills and river bluffs, and the ground at times appeared to roll like water. River islands, some inhabited, were sucked underwater, and a large lake was created on previously dry land in western Tennessee.

Eyewitness accounts detail the terror. Eliza Bryan of New Madrid wrote of being awakened by the violent shock, along with "a very awful noise" like thunder, "complete saturation of the atmosphere with sulphurous vapor, causing total darkness." Everyone was running around screaming, "not knowing where to go, or what to do," accompanied by the cries of all the birds and beasts, the cracking of trees falling, and the roaring of the Mississippi.[3]

Over in Kentucky, George Crist wrote that the shaking was so strong and prolonged that no one was able to hold onto anything because "the shaking would knock you loose like knocking hicror [hickory] nuts out of a tree." No one was killed in his immediate area, but many were knocked out, blood was everywhere, and all their animals ran away in terror. In a subsequent quake, his little daughter was killed when a falling log crushed her. He observed, "A lot of people thinks that the devil has come here."[4]

Many flatboats and keelboats making their way downstream on the Mississippi were capsized or thrown about and crushed like matchsticks. Giant trees and riverbanks fell into the water, blocking the passage of boats and changing landmarks. It appeared that the river ran backward for a time; although the upriver motion was actually caused by underwater dams and huge waves, the phenomenon was enough to terrify the experienced boatmen who lived through it.

Still, many boats survived by luck or great care, among them the first steamboat on the Mississippi. Called the *New Orleans,* it was on its way to that city in a demonstration of the viability of steam power on western rivers. Aboard were its owners, Nicholas and Lydia Latrobe Roosevelt, and their crew. As they made their way cautiously downriver, they saw Indians paddling canoes among the boles of trees in flooded lowlands. As they approached New Madrid, much of which had disappeared "as the earth opened in vast chasms and swallowed up houses and their inhabitants," refugees begged to be taken aboard. But their boat could not take on so many, and they turned "a deaf ear to the cries of the terrified inhabitants of the doomed town," as death and destruction mounted on the frontier.[5]

On January 23, 1812, another earthquake of comparable strength to the first two struck at New Madrid, followed by another monster at the same spot on February 7, which was as strong as or stronger than any of the previous quakes. This series of four earthquakes, known collectively as the New Madrid Earthquakes, are some of the largest ever to occur in the United States since European occupation, all measuring over 8.0 on the Richter scale. Interspersed with these shocks were about 200 moderate to large earthquakes, as well as 1,800 associated aftershocks and smaller quakes. Despite the severity of and the huge area affected by these earthquakes, the death toll was relatively small, probably only a few hundred in all, because of the scattered population on the frontier.[6]

The day after the last huge quake, on February 8, 1812, Jackson wrote to Rachel's sister Mary Caffrey, who lived in the Mississippi Territory, regretting that he was unable to send her the slave she had requested. "I am fearfull," he wrote, "it would (from the convulsed state of the Earth and water from the frequent shocks of Earthquake) be difficult to obtain passage for him down the river—few Boats will venture the passage of the Mississippi this spring—and from the last shocks here, being so violent it is to be feared that a vast many of the Boats that are on the river is lost."

He continued with the reassurance that Rachel and their friends were well, "but very much alarmed, with the frequent shocks of Earthquakes, some of which have been so severe as to throw down chimneys, and to crack brick walls—but I hope these alarms will subside, and the shocks cease here."[7]

Indeed, after the February earthquake, the worst of the convulsions were over although smaller aftershocks continued for another month of painful suspense. Much of downtown Nashville burned to the ground in 1812, the conflagration probably caused by candles, lanterns, and hearth fires thrown over by the earthquakes. These dramatic natural manifestations contributed to a convulsion of another sort—this one spiritual. In the aftermath of the New Madrid earthquakes, the number of conversions by evangelists in the West increased dramatically among town dwellers and the gentry. Up until 1811–1812, such people had resisted the religious revival that had been building since the beginning of the century. Among those who found God at this time was Rachel Jackson. Whether or not she was influenced by the earthquakes in her conversion, her religious faith would be her foundation and strength for the rest of her life.

Early frontier Tennessee was, for the most part, a rip-snorting, hard-drinking, hell-raising, brawling, gambling, fornicating, cursing abyss of sin and ignorance. There were hardly any ministers, meeting-houses, or schools, and most people didn't feel their lack. Certainly some families like the Donelsons, gentry and common folk alike, maintained standards of respectable behavior, homeschooling, and private religious meetings, but most observers found them excep-tional. A few missionaries came over the mountains in the 1770s and 1780s, but, as one observed, these settlers were so indifferent to religion that they would "eventually lose their souls." Another char-acterized Tennessee as "a sink of iniquity, a Black Pit of irreligion." By the time of statehood in 1796, with a population approaching 100,000, fewer than 5,000 Tennesseans were church members.[8]

In Virginia, the Donelsons had been members of the Church of England; Rachel's father, John Donelson, was a member of the vestry at Camden Parish in Pittsylvania County in 1773. But in the years during and following the American Revolution, the Church of England lost ground. Many of its staunchest members had been wealthy conservatives who opposed the rebellion and left or were driven out of the country. Even before the war, Quakers and Baptists had made numerous converts, especially among younger and poorer people, who had a taste for soul-stirring sermons filled with hellfire and damnation. For many, the Anglican Church was too restrained, too boring. Too much liturgy, not enough drama.

After the war, the Church of England was disestablished in the South; that is, it lost its state tax funding. Although it re-created itself as the Episcopal Church in the United States, it saw a great falling off of the faithful. As for following settlers to the frontier, Episcopalians had never been great evangelists, and they only became a presence in the West much later.

There were probably Presbyterians somewhere in the Donelson family tree, given their Scottish ancestry, and Rachel's husband retained his family's bias in favor of that denomination. Like most Ulster Scots, however inactive, Andrew Jackson had been a Presbyterian at birth. His mother, showing a remarkable lack of insight into her son's character, had intended him for the ministry. That career, with its emphasis on learning, rectitude, and sobriety, had not been for him, but he continued to consider himself a Presbyterian.

In the late eighteenth century, traveling preachers began to arrive in Tennessee and Kentucky—Baptists, Methodists, and Presbyterians. No other denomination had a significant early presence on the frontier. Preachers rode alone or in pairs, stopping wherever they found a group ready to listen, camping out or staying with local families, bringing refreshment of the spirit to their listeners. Very small congregations started to build log meetinghouses for the infrequent but welcome arrivals of ministers.

By the 1790s, what became known as the Second Great Awakening, referring back to the first revival of Christianity that had swept the British colonies in the 1730s and 1740s, had burst out in the eastern United States and spread to the frontier. The work of the early frontier missionaries came together in June 1800, when members of three Presbyterian congregations met at a church in Red River, Kentucky, for a four-day sacramental meeting. It had an unusually ecumenical spirit for American Protestantism with a Methodist exhorter joining two Presbyterian ministers. On the fourth day of services, a spark took fire in the congregation, and they began shouting, singing, sobbing, and trembling. With renewed fervor the ministers shouted and exhorted, working the crowd into a frenzy. Many fell to the floor, swooning with ecstasy.

The excitement swept the neighborhood, and a subsequent meeting at the Gasper River, Kentucky, church in July brought out a huge crowd. Again, "the divine flame spread through the whole multitude," as one of the preachers described it, and westerners starved for religion (and excitement) rushed forward to be converted.[9] Evangelists quickly spread the movement to southern Ohio and Tennessee. For the next ten years or so, massive revivals of as many as 5,000 people became the hallmark of Tennessee religion. Baptist ministers joined the movement early, and all three Protestant denominations saw a great upsurge in membership.

Throughout these years, revivals were primarily rural affairs, and the majority of the attendees were country folk, naïve and uneducated. Because they had to travel such distances to gather together, most families brought food and supplies for a stay of several days or even weeks. Camp meetings supplied them with entertainment, social life, education, and inspiration, breaking the monotony of lonely lives devoted to constant toil. Physical manifestations of the spirit became progressively wilder, with convulsive seizures, dancing, falling into trances, running, rolling, and even barking becoming commonplace.[10]

More socially conservative Tennesseans were also swept by the longing for spiritual uplift, but they disliked the excesses of the camp meetings and of their sometimes uneducated ministers. The

confirmed revivalists among Tennessee Presbyterians in fact broke
off and formed a separate presbytery over the issue of ministerial
training. In Nashville, however, a minister who was both well educated and dynamic appeared in 1811.

The Reverend Gideon Blackburn, an adherent of mainline
Presbyterianism, was a tireless preacher and teacher, the founder of
many churches and schools across Tennessee, Indiana, Kentucky, and
Ohio, and a former missionary to the Cherokees. In Nashville, he at
once began gathering a congregation and started raising money from
the community to build a church. This First Presbyterian Church
of Nashville became a major force in the community, eventually
numbering such leading families as the McNairys, the Overtons,
the Ewings, the Grundys, and the Jacksons among its flock.

Reverend Blackburn's sermons were particularly admired for
their sound theology, fervor, and great length; he often spoke without pause for three hours. Rachel Jackson was impressed by his mix-
ture of fervor and dignity. Under his influence, she was converted
and joined the church. Their relationship was very close, and she
referred to him as "My father in the Gospel."[11]

The Presbyterians believed in salvation through faith by God's
grace freely given, but they also believed that converts needed a further
period of sanctification, that is, education in and acceptance of church
tenets before they could be formally received. Anyone was welcome at
revivals or services, but actual membership was much more restrictive.
At first, the majority of the church members were women; although
their husbands attended church, they sometimes waited until later in
life to seek full membership. Andrew Jackson often went to church
with his wife, but he didn't join the Presbyterian Church until 1838
when he was a widower, had retired from the presidency, and was able
to bring himself (reluctantly) to forgive his enemies.

The Presbyterian Church and its beliefs became essential to Rachel's life and to her decisions. Once she had accepted them as her guide, she saw everything through the lens of those views. She had repented her sins and been forgiven; attending church, reading the Bible, and praying became fundamental to her life. She was never, however, a churchwoman who took part in organized activities; she didn't serve on committees or join the Sunday School movement. Her home and her husband were her focus.

Her letters to her husband showed her newfound fervor. As always, she hated for him to be absent from home. She wrote that her desire that he was healthy "was my nightly prayers to the Almighty God." As she described her worries, she declared that "my blessed redeemer Is making intersesion with the Father for us to meet again [and] restore you to my bosom."[12]

One major tenet of Presbyterianism that would have future consequences for the Jacksons was that church members could not be indifferent toward sin or evil. This belief was expressed in individual congregations through calling members to account when they strayed. At first, ministers and elders spoke privately to erring souls, but in later years, members would be publicly shamed for such lapses as alcoholism or failure to attend church. Early on, this belief was not particularly relevant to Rachel, but as Andrew became more powerful, it would come to the fore in her own views and in the views of others toward her with quite mixed results.

Despite their very real, very deep, and abiding love, the Jacksons' views of a happy life couldn't have been more at odds. There was a fundamental disharmony in their desire to be together. Andrew's ambitions and his future hopes were all about gaining power through military and political success. Her happiness depended on the status quo—living quietly on their land, loving family and friends, doing good. She never appreciated that, to accomplish his wishes, her husband had to be absent from home often and for long stretches. And, although he always vowed to do anything to make his wife happy, Jackson never actually altered his habits or his course in life. She wanted him at home with her; he wanted to roam afield and bring her to join him at the scenes of his victories.

These last years, so delightful to Rachel, had been a period of waiting for Andrew. He always knew that he was meant for glory and intended to seek it out. The year 1811 would be a year of convulsion for the nation and the beginning of Jackson's upward climb in national politics.

In the years between the Louisiana Purchase of 1803 and 1811, the drumbeat of the West was constant—War, War, War. Against the British, against the Spanish, against the Indians. Westerners like Jackson wanted to strike out left and right against those who seemed to frustrate and contain their ambitions. Only the effete, dishonorable politicians of the East, they felt, kept frontiersmen from asserting their manhood against this triumvirate of enemies.

Andrew Jackson had settled opinions on politics and foreign affairs, standard for his time and place, from which he never deviated in his long life. He believed that common men, that is, white men, were the backbone of the United States, and that they should have every opportunity to succeed, to vote, and to hold office. He believed that Tennessee and Kentucky, along with the remainder of the West, were a paradise for these plain, hardworking men. In political and economic opposition to their ascendancy stood the eastern establishment, men of power, status, and education who refused to accept westerners as equals.

Rather than achieving its full potential, in his view, the West was fettered by the land claims of Native Americans and the sporadic violence that broke out between them and the whites, as well as the pretensions of the two foreign powers. From Canada, Great Britain continued to intrigue with Indian leaders, such as Tecumseh, to supply arms and to encourage attacks against American settlers. Although losing its chokehold on the Mississippi River with the Louisiana Purchase and the cession of New Orleans, Spain continued to bedevil westerners from its remaining Florida colonies, which stretched all the way to present-day Louisiana. The Spanish also traded with and armed Indians, and thus provided a safe haven for raiding parties. Their Indian policy was meant to discourage westerners' ambitions toward Mexico and Spain's other Latin American colonies by keeping them busy at home.

Jackson had not experienced the overwhelming violence of the early years on the Tennessee frontier with its constant attacks and counterattacks by settlers and the Chickamaugas and the Chickasaws. But he had wholeheartedly absorbed the point of view of early Tennesseans that Native Americans were untrustworthy and committed to killing whites. Even though he had never joined militia raids or retaliatory attacks on Indian villages, his views were as fierce as though he had been a seasoned Indian killer.

For nearly twenty years, he had written about Indian duplicity. As early as 1793, he had warned that the Cherokees would use a proposed treaty to "open a more Easy Road to Murder with impunity" and indignantly denied the viability of any treaty with Indians. He believed that they were savages who "will neither ad[here to] Treaties, nor the law of Nations."[13] His views never varied in this regard, and they underlay his determination to remove all Indians far away from white settlement.

Jackson had hated Britain since the Revolution, when he had lost both his brothers and his mother and had been insulted and wounded as a teenage messenger. Nothing that had happened since had changed, nor ever could, his settled enmity toward the former mother country. Spain, however, was a more recent obsession, all the more suspicious for having become an ally of Great Britain. Both strategically and viscerally, the Spanish set his teeth on edge. Having another nation determined to block the economic and territorial growth of the West enraged him. He also shared the knee-jerk prejudice of American Protestants against the Spanish, who were non-English speaking and members of the Catholic Church, the painted harlot of the Protestant Reformation. He always referred to them as "the Dons," using the honorific to underline their foreignness.

James Madison had inherited an impossible situation from his predecessor and mentor, Thomas Jefferson, in 1809. Like Jefferson, Madison wanted at all costs to avoid a war against the British, the Spanish, the Indians, or all three at once, but neither his potential foes nor his own countrymen were making it easy for him. The president's party, the Republicans, won an overwhelming victory in the midterm congressional elections of 1810, but the new men were far from peace loving.

Especially from the South and the West came fiery congressmen, some young, some old, who were deeply offended by what they saw as years of affronts by the former mother country. They were determined to seek a treaty "with honor" from Great Britain or go to war. The War Hawks, as they became known, were led by Henry Clay of Kentucky, chosen speaker of the House on the first day of the new congressional session, November 4, 1811; John C. Calhoun of South Carolina; and Felix Grundy of Tennessee, among others. All three were under thirty-five, and all of them were eager to prove that the current generation of Americans were equal to those who had won the American Revolution.

The issue that most engaged the entire nation was the British refusal to respect American rights on the high seas. The British had been fighting a war to the death against their traditional enemies, the French, since about 1793. Napoleon had seized power in France in 1799 and pursued a vigorous policy of European conquest. The Treaty of Amiens, which had been signed by Britain and France in 1802, collapsed in 1803, and the ongoing wars, which finally ended with the defeat of Napoleon at Waterloo in 1815, eventually became known as the Napoleonic Wars. Until 1815, there was only a single year of peace on land or sea. Napoleon and his huge armies dominated on land, but British control of the sea allowed them to attack French colonies around the world and to interdict trade with France.

The British Orders in Council of 1807 declared their right to board and search all ships suspected of trading with the French, despite the protests of the United States and other neutrals. They also assumed the right to examine all seamen's papers, searching for deserters from the draconian British navy and dragging them away, despite their officers' protests, even if those deserters were American citizens. The financial losses and interruptions of trade were onerous, especially to the merchants and shipowners of the Northeast. But to all Americans, the continuing insults and loss of honor were the most infuriating aspect of this seemingly endless war between European nations, which had no relevance to their own aspirations.

Britain treated the United States as a third-rate power, logically enough in their thinking, since the United States didn't have much of a navy, or an army, for that matter. The British had all the arrogance of the world's greatest sea power, one determined to bring down its only rival for global supremacy. The cock-a-hoop pride and sensitivity of these former colonials were mere annoyances, almost impossible to take seriously for a nation with a world war to win. And there was the nub of the matter: The Americans' exaggerated sense of honor was lacerated by being considered beneath contempt by Great Britain.

For westerners, a related and even more crucial issue was British and Spanish encouragement of Indian attacks. They wanted war, the sooner the better, to make the West safe for white settlers and to teach these intrusive Europeans a lesson. A significant underlying motive for many Americans was also territorial ambition. In the fall of 1810, Madison had proclaimed that the Spanish territory of west Florida belonged to the United States as part of the Louisiana Purchase of 1803. West Florida was a long narrow strip of land along the Gulf Coast, including portions of today's Florida, Alabama, Mississippi, and Louisiana. If it did come to war, the conflict would afford Americans a convenient opportunity to annex both British Canada and Spanish East Florida, the present state of Florida, making the United States supreme in North America with no European rivals at hand.

Jackson had previously turned against Jefferson and now opposed Madison as a cowardly, mealy-mouthed appeaser. For years, he had been champing at the bit for some important military action. It was all very well to be addressed as "General," but it would be all the better to go into action and win a victory. Of the inevitability of his victory, he had no doubt.

As the new Congress began its deliberations, Speaker of the House Henry Clay appointed men who shared his views to head important committees, and the nation moved closer to war. But events in the West outpaced political maneuvers in the capital. A growing movement among the Shawnees for a confederated Native American resistance to white expansion and to white culture was led by two chiefs, Tecumseh, and his brother, Tenskwatawa, a religious leader called the Prophet. They lived in a town called Prophetstown at the confluence of the Tippecanoe and Wabash rivers and eventually planned to retake ancestral lands occupied by whites.

While Tecumseh was away seeking allies among southern tribes, William Henry Harrison, governor of the Indiana Territory, led a force of militiamen and regulars in a preemptive action. After an initial meeting between Harrison and the Prophet, the white troops camped near Prophetstown for the night. That night the Indians attacked. The fighting was furious and bloody with heavy casualties, but eventually the larger American force prevailed. The following day, they discovered that the Prophet and his people had decamped. They destroyed the town and then retreated from the area to a secure fort. At first, it was unclear to either the War Department or the general public that Tippecanoe was a victory for the United States.

After receiving news of the battle, Jackson wrote to Harrison, offering to march to his aid with 500 or 1,000 "brave Tennesseeans. The *blood* of *our murdered Countrymen must be revenged*—That banditti, ought to be swept from the face of the earth—I do hope that government will see that it is necessary to act efficiently, and that this hostile band, which must be excited to war, by the secret agents of great Britain, must be destroyed."[14]

Most Americans believed incorrectly, as Jackson did, that the British were behind the confederation movement. The action at

Tippecanoe did push Tecumseh into allying with the British; for the next two years, until his death in 1813, he and his followers fought against American incursions into Canada.

Although not serving in Congress, Jackson kept abreast of their actions through his fellow Nashville lawyer, Felix Grundy, a member of the committee on foreign relations. The decisions of this committee were essential to the war movement.

Less than a month after Congress convened, Grundy wrote to Jackson on November 28, 1811, that "The Ruebicon is pass'd." The committee was preparing the way for war with their recommendations to raise the number of soldiers in the regular army by 10,000, to accept 50,000 volunteers, and to arm merchant vessels. He believed that the committee would soon report in favor of "actual War." He reassured: "Rely on one thing; we have War or Honorable peace before we adjourn."[15]

And, indeed, before the adjournment of Congress in the summer of 1812, President Madison had delivered a war message detailing British wrongs. The measure was bitterly fought in both houses, the opposition coming primarily from the Northeast; only last-minute politicking in a deadlocked Senate cleared the passage of a declaration of war on June 17. The following day, the president signed the declaration. At the last minute, finally realizing that war forces in the United States were going to succeed, the British had negated the most obnoxious of their maritime orders in an effort at reconciliation—too little, too late. Conciliation should have come earlier.

War! For Andrew Jackson, there couldn't have been better news. No longer would the men of the nation stand by and allow themselves to be shamed by foreigners. For several months, though, the war was confined to the Atlantic seaboard and the Canadian border. Naval battles, British blockades, and raids were the order of the day. Americans tried at several points to "rescue" Canada, but the Canadians would have none of it, fighting beside the British to repel their would-be saviors. Despite a few victories, the American showing was very poor overall and contributed to the closeness of Madison's reelection in 1812. Only solid support from western and southern states pushed him back into office.

For months, Jackson had been driven mad with frustration. He was ready to lead his men into immediate action, but the War Department gave no sign of wanting him, perhaps because of lingering suspicion about his involvement with Aaron Burr's schemes. Finally, through the friendship of Governor Willie Blount, the half-brother and political successor of Jackson's late mentor, William Blount, he got his chance for action. An obvious target for attack was the port of New Orleans; by taking the city, the British could starve the West. In October 1812, Blount received orders to send 1,500 Tennessee volunteers to help defend New Orleans in case of attack. Despite an administration suggestion to the contrary, Blount appointed Jackson as commander. Now he was not just a militia commander, but a major general of United States troops.

Jackson's ringing call for volunteers was answered with enthusiasm by Tennesseans from all walks of life, finally numbering more than 2,000. Despite a bitter, snowy winter, his men and supplies were assembled by January 1813. During this trying and expensive time (he received no salary), the Jacksons lived apart, he in Nashville, she at the Hermitage. On January 8, Rachel sent her husband an affectionate letter and a memento of her love—a miniature of herself by an unknown artist. Miniatures were often used to remind people of their absent loved ones in the early nineteenth century. Women wore them as dress ornaments, but men's attire had become much plainer and more tailored, so they wore miniatures in vest pockets or under their shirts as pendants around their necks.[16]

Jackson chose the latter course: "I shall wear it near my boosom, but this was useless, for without your miniature, my recollection, never fails me of your likeness." By now in their mid-forties, the couple still wrote in a most romantic vein. Later in the same letter, Andrew added, "I thank you for your prayers—I thank you for your determined resolution, to bear our separation with fortitude, we part but for a few days, for a few fleeting weeks, when the protecting hand of providence if it is his will, will restore us to each others arms." He ended with, "It now one Oclock in the morning the candle nearly out, and I must go to bed, May the angelic hosts that rewards & protects virtue and innocence, and preserves the good, be with you untill I return."[17]

The infantry and riflemen were sent downriver by boat to Natchez, while Jackson led the cavalry and mounted infantry down the Natchez Trace. Rachel had sent her husband another gift as well, the fruit of her newfound religious convictions. She had prevailed on him to include three traveling ministers in his party and later expressed her delight that he was pleased with their company. But when Jackson's forces rendezvoused in Natchez, he found letters from the commander at New Orleans, U.S. General James Wilkinson, ordering him and his troops to remain where they were and not to proceed to the city; those letters were followed by others with the same message.[18]

It was clear that Wilkinson did not care to have Jackson in the same city with him, even under his command. The two men despised each other and had for the past decade. Jackson believed and had proclaimed publicly that Wilkinson had been the traitor in the Burr affair. Dishonorable, traitor, thief—Jackson had applied many epithets to the general, but he had swallowed his pride and agreed to serve under Wilkinson for the good of the country. How infuriating, then, to have his enemy administer the rejection.

While he waited in Natchez, expenses constantly mounting and supplies running out, Jackson attempted to untangle the mess, writing to Wilkinson and to the authorities in Washington. He also had to deal with his beloved's anguish at their separation. On his arrival in Natchez, he had found a letter from Rachel waiting. In it, she wrote, "Do not My beloved Husband let the love of Country fame and honour make you forgit you have me Without you I would think them all empty shadows." Later in the same letter, she added, "I wish I was with you, vain wish pray my Dear write to me often Its a cordial its balm to my mind [In my] lonesome hours I treasure Them up as [a] miser does his gold."[19]

Many men might have been annoyed at the excesses in her letters, but Andrew found them endearing and answered regularly, usually beginning "My Love" and regretting that "I have but little time to spend in the sweet converse of writing to my boosom friend."[20]

In mid-March, a thunderstruck Jackson received the news from the secretary of war that his services and those of his men were no longer needed. The combination of executive distrust, Wilkinson's resentment of him, and the lack of clear plans for conducting the war had led to this mortifying insult. He was to send any government supplies (including arms) on to Wilkinson, muster his unpaid men out, and leave them to make their way back as best they could through some 450 miles (estimated by Jackson as 800 miles) of wilderness road. Nor was any transport provided for the sick among them.

He fired off a letter to Felix Grundy at the height of his indignation, charging that the secretary had "lost all feelings of humanity & duty." He declared to his friend his intention to "march [his men] to Nashville or bury them with the honors of war." He also informed Rachel of the disgraceful situation, declaring that "it is therefore my duty to act as a father to the sick and to the well and stay with them untill I march them into Nashville."[21]

And so he did. Thus was the legend of the indomitable Andrew Jackson born. Struggling along with inadequate supplies, inadequate wagons, inadequate horses, and inadequate money, Jackson brought his men back home within the month. He had the charisma to inspire them and the toughness to force them along when they weren't inspired. The troops began to compare him to the toughest thing they knew—hickory wood. And so "Old Hickory" entered the mythology of the West.

The earthquakes that shook the physical world of Rachel and Andrew Jackson had presaged even deeper convulsions in their lives. Rachel had been shaken by the fervor of evangelical religion and would find faith her compass for the rest of her life. And Andrew had begun the path to military leadership he had always believed was his destiny. He would finally play a role on the national stage.

CHAPTER 7

The Nation's Hero

The War of 1812 widened the yawning gap between Rachel and Andrew Jackson's desires and ambitions for their life together. So far, her greatest discontent had been caused by his absences from home, and her greatest fears were for his safety and health because of his casual disregard for them. While waiting for a command in the new war, Jackson got embroiled in a serio-comic duel that almost led to his death.

On the march home from Natchez, conditions had been terrible, the men hungry, tired, on edge, and the officers stretched to their limits. On behalf of a friend irked by a number of trivial matters, Jesse Benton challenged Major William Carroll to a duel after they reached Nashville. Carroll was Jackson's protégé, as well as brigade inspector, a rank inevitably leading to friction with testy officers. Benton was the brother of Jackson's aide, Colonel Thomas Hart Benton, who was away in Washington on militia business.

Jackson at first persuaded Benton to withdraw, but the young man reissued the challenge when egged on by his friends. Perhaps annoyed at Benton's persistence, Jackson finally agreed to act as Carroll's second. As their commander and a man in late middle age, Jackson should have prevented or stayed out of the meeting between the young hotheads. Because Benton was a dead shot and Carroll "remarkably defective," however, they set the distance at ten paces to nullify Benton's advantage in marksmanship. On June 14, 1813, the men stood back-to-back, paced off the distance, and whirled to fire. Benton sank into a crouch to take his shot, hitting Carroll in the thumb. Because of Benton's squatting position, Carroll's shot raked his buttocks.[1]

In the raucous masculine society of western Tennessee, bawdy humor and ridicule went hand-in-hand. Jesse Benton became a laughingstock; the raillery escalated when he tried to argue that he had been taken advantage of. Beginning in Washington and continuing throughout the journey homeward, Thomas Benton bombarded Jackson with accusatory letters, blaming him for his brother's humiliation. Formerly one of the general's warmest supporters, Benton became a deadly enemy. Once he returned to Nashville, the question wasn't whether there would be violence between them but how soon. Hurt and furious at his aide's turnabout, Jackson threatened to horsewhip him the next time he caught sight of him.

On September 4 that year, Andrew Jackson could be found, as usual, at the Old Nashville Inn. Most Saturdays found him there, doing errands, going to the post office, and enjoying a convivial masculine evening with friends and relatives. The Benton brothers checked into the City Hotel, supposedly to avoid trouble. But when Jackson, John Coffee, and two of Rachel's nephews strolled past, they saw Thomas Benton watching them from the doorway. Jackson rushed forward, whip in hand, to carry out his threat. Benton backed up before the onrush while his brother Jesse fired and hit Jackson in the arm and shoulder. Everyone on both sides was armed, shooting wildly and roaring with rage, but no one else was hit. Daggers were drawn, and both Bentons were stabbed several times, but not seriously. Finally, bystanders broke up the affray.

Jackson was carried to his hotel, bleeding so heavily that he soaked a mattress through while waiting for a doctor to arrive. The bullet wound had severely damaged his shoulder and broken his arm; medical practice of the time called for amputation, as he well knew. Before passing out, he announced to the doctor that he would "keep my arm."[2] Fear of his wrath was so powerful that the doctor didn't dare bring out his wicked bone saw, merely cleaning up the mess and setting the compound fracture as well as he could, leaving another bullet in Jackson's body. Massive blood loss, shock, and trauma from the pain of the wound and the treatment had almost done Jackson in. Within a short while, his admirers made the Benton brothers' lives impossible in Nashville. They headed out permanently for Missouri.

The war came south with a vengeance in 1813, not with the British but with the Creeks. All summer long, both sides of the frontier had rumbled with talk of potential Indian attacks on white settlers. During the Battle of Tippecanoe in 1811, Tecumseh had been in Alabama and Georgia seeking Creek allies for his confederation. Most of the Creeks had rejected his advances, but one group known as the Red Sticks listened to him. In fact, a few of them went north and joined Tecumseh's men in battle against American attackers in

Canada. On their way home in late 1812, they killed two white families. When American authorities insisted that they be turned over for trial, Creek leaders instead executed the leaders of the guilty party.

The Red Sticks broke furiously with their kinsmen, whom they saw as subservient tools of whites, and civil war erupted among the Creeks. The Spanish authorities at Pensacola favored the Red Stick faction because they were the most likely to harass Americans and distract them from any incursion into Spanish territory. On July 27, 1813, Alabama troops ambushed these Indians, who were returning from Florida with packhorses loaded with Spanish weapons. The inconclusive encounter came to be called the Battle of Burnt Corn. Terrified settlers along the Alabama and Tombigbee rivers forted up in a series of log stockades.

One of these stockades, Fort Mims, was located about forty miles north of Mobile. Some 500 people took shelter there, including militiamen, local farmers, women, and children. On August 30, hundreds of Red Stick warriors stormed the fort in vengeance for the attack at Burnt Corn. Despite the general state of alarm and a specific report of armed warriors in the vicinity, the whites had put down their weapons to eat lunch and had left the large front gates ajar. The Creeks suffered heavy losses, fighting their way in through the gates and attacking armed men who had sheltered in the buildings of the inner stockade. When the Indians prevailed, they wiped out all the stockade's remaining inhabitants—men, women, and children. Buildings were set ablaze, burning alive those within.

In the massacre that followed, children were seized by their feet and their brains bashed out against the stockade walls; pregnant women were cut open and their unborn babies pulled out of the womb to die on the ground. Most of the victims were scalped, and the fort was looted. Slaves were spared to be driven back to the Creek nation by their new owners. Soldiers who came a couple of weeks later to bury the dead in mass graves found vultures and wild dogs fighting over the putrid bodies. Even the most battle-hardened were sickened by the scene. As reports of Fort Mims spread slowly through the nation, prints graphically depicting the massacre rolled off the press.

By mid-September, the news had reached Nashville. James Robertson, one of the founders of the town, wrote to Jackson in great distress since he assumed that the general would not be able to take command of Tennessee's troops. At the Hermitage, Rachel had nursed her husband devotedly, but his injuries were too serious for a quick recovery. Because of heavy fighting along the Canadian border, the federal government chose not to send regular army troops but ordered out the militias and volunteers along the southern frontier. On September 24, Jackson sent out a call to the Tennessee volunteers who had accompanied him to Natchez, writing that "we must hasten to the frontier, or we will find it drenched in the blood of our fellow-citizens." He ordered that 2,000 men were to meet him near the Alabama border at Fayetteville on October 4, well armed and ready for action. Warning that "Your frontier is threatened with invasion by the savage foe!," he expressed his confidence in their patriotism and bravery. With very considerable overstatement, one might even say falsehood since he could barely walk, he wrote, "The health of your General is restored—he will command in person."[3]

Rachel must have been beside herself when he rode away—still in awful pain, weak and pale, his arm in a sling—to meet his men at Fayetteville on October 7, 1813. As usual, she cared for the plantation, and now she had two ten-year-old boys living with her and Andrew Jr. full time while they went to school—Andrew Jackson

Donelson and Edward Butler. A young lady named Margaret Walkins, a friend's daughter, also lived at the Hermitage, helping her run the house, entertain visitors, and take care of correspondence. When Margaret married in 1814, Rachel gave her a heifer and a bedstead, a very expensive gift, typical of her generosity to her young protégés.

The Hermitage remained snug and welcoming, still with only three rooms in the main house but endlessly expandable in a day when people didn't expect a bed to themselves, much less an entire room. Little Andrew slept in the Jacksons' room, and Margaret may have slept in the other bedroom or on a trundle bed next to Rachel. The older boys could have been in the other bedroom or on pallets in the big downstairs room. Guests were usually put up in the upstairs bedroom or in a small cabin.

With Jackson's friend John Coffee commanding the cavalry, the troops cut a road through the mountains into Alabama, established a base at Fort Strother, encouraged Creek and Cherokee allies to hold firm, and sent cavalry and mounted riflemen to destroy the hostile village of Tallushatchee. Most of the Indian men there were slaughtered; the surviving women and children were taken prisoner.

On the battleground littered with the dead and dying, the American interpreter found a dead Creek woman still clutching her baby, a little boy less than a year old. The women prisoners refused to take the child, suggesting that he be killed since all his family were dead. Instead, the interpreter brought the boy, called Lyncoya, to the general for a decision. Hell-bent on wiping out Indian foes, Jackson had bragged by letter to Governor Blount about the Tallushatchee killing ground and his retaliation for the destruction of Fort Mims. And yet, something about the orphaned little boy touched his warrior's heart, and he decided to send Lyncoya to the Hermitage to be reared.

He first wrote to Rachel about this decision on November 4, a mere mention appended to his account of death and devastation. The child would be "for Andrew," he said, perhaps intending the boy to be a servant and lodge in one of the slave cabins. But he continued puzzling over the boy's fate, writing a month later that "charity and christianity says he ought to be taken care of and I send [him] to my little Andrew, and I hope [we] will adopt him as one of our family."[4]

Despite all the intense exertion of a difficult military campaign, Jackson continued to think about Lyncoya. At the end of December, he requested that Rachel "Keep Lyncoya in the house—he is a Savage [but one] that fortune has thrown in my h[ands] . . . I therefore want him well taken care of, he may have been given to me for some Valuable purpose—in fact when I reflect that he as to his relations is so much like myself I feel an unusual sympathy for him—tell my dear little Andrew to treat him well."[5] For Rachel, another boy more or less about the house was never a problem, but until the following spring Lyncoya was cared for by a family in Huntsville. Jackson had placed the little boy there and paid for his care until he could take his new foster son to the Hermitage at the end of the campaign.

A partial victory at Talladega, Alabama, in November heartened the troops, but hunger (they often had only parched corn to eat), cold, lack of promised reinforcements, and expiration of enlistments caused dissension and then mutiny. Practically everyone except Jackson wanted to go home and return the following spring.

Suffering from severe dysentery, Jackson barely ate anymore but insisted on staying in the field. He, Coffee, and a few others faced down attempted desertions, but eventually they were forced to let most of the men return home. Their situation was desperate.

During the long, frustrating autumn and winter, Andrew wrote frequently to Rachel. He blamed the officers more than the men, vowing that "hereafter when Some cry out Boisterously at home that he is a patriot he will be met in the teeth with their shameful abandonment of the camp in the face of the enemy."[6]

Since the troops were merely holding on, not actively fighting, Rachel saw no reason why she shouldn't be reunited with her husband. Andrew would have loved to have her comforting presence, but the situation was too grim. "I would to god, I had a place I could bring you to, I would certainly send for you and my little Andrew...My heart is with you, my duty compels me to remain in the field." A friend was waiting to take the letter to Nashville, so he had to close even though he had "many things to say to you—It may not be long before I can either send for you or see you at home But you know my motto, I know you approve of it—that is death before dishonor."[7]

Marooned at home, Rachel did her duty as best she could. As always, she was responsible for the home front, looking to the harvest, coping with impertinent and incompetent overseers, keeping an eye on their businesses, and welcoming her widowed eldest sister Mary Caffery to the Hermitage. The endemic fevers and stomach problems of the frontier afflicted them all. She and little Andrew were frequently unwell, as were the plantation slaves, and she had to bring in a doctor to tend to all of them. Making sure that all of their own cotton, as well as that of their customers, was ginned and baled was her responsibility, as was seeing to the grinding of wheat into flour and its safe storage in barrels sealed against bugs and mice. In the virtually cashless world of Tennessee, she had to confront a defaulting debtor, either retaining his cotton at their gin or taking him to court. As she could, she also sent supplies to the camp, which her husband was very pleased to acknowledge since "for a few days we have had ample supplies of bread & meat."[8]

With the beginning of 1814 and the arrival of a few hundred new recruits, Jackson was able to carry out a couple of skirmishes against the Red Sticks that were inconclusive but encouraging. Then Rachel sent him word that enemies in Nashville were defaming him and Coffee. Most of the "vile miscreants" were officers who had refused to remain in the field and had led their men back home. Particularly galling was the charge that Jackson was drinking heavily. Although he frequently drank a lot with friends on social occasions, he was incensed by the charge that he was intoxicated while at war. He indignantly replied, "as to the vile slanderous vipers, I despise them as the crawling worm that rolls through the slime untouched, unnoticed by any—you may assure yourself and my friends, that intoxication is not a crime in me nor have I been intoxicated since I left you and this thousands can prove."[9]

Rachel was furious with "those wretches" who tried to cover their own flaws by injuring her husband and Coffee. In her opinion, they made the brave soldiers look all the better and "Disgraced themselves Etarnaly [eternally]." "Let me assure you," she added, "[that] no man is or Can be more praised and applauded then you are." Even William Henry Harrison, who had retaken Detroit, couldn't compete. People said that General Harrison "was makeing his appearance in the [presidential] Drawing room and ball rooms [while] Gnl Jackson was making Conquests through . . . Every disadvantage possable."[10]

Both Jacksons were aware of the importance of publicity about his exploits. Despite her reluctance to see her husband go to war, Rachel admired his spirit and his success. On her own initiative, she sent some of his letters to influential friends. Andrew also sent congratulatory letters from the secretary of war and his commanding officer for her to read, have copies made, and pass on. Success was good in itself, but it was even better that everyone know about it for the sake of his reputation and for future opportunities.

Military victory was bought at a price. In January 1814, Rachel's nephew and Andrew's aide, Alexander Donelson, was killed in battle. She was distraught at his loss and even more so at the fear of never seeing her husband again. "My Dear pray Let me Conjur you by Every Tie of Love of friend ship to Let me see you before you go againe...I never wanted to see you so mutch in my life...let me know and I will fly on the wings of the pureest affection I must see you." She added that "*you* have been gone a Long time six monthes in all that time what has been your trials daingers and Diffyculties hardeships oh Lorde of Heaven how Can I beare it."[11]

Andrew replied in his usual loving, soothing vein. "I am grieved to think the pain my absence occasions," he wrote, but asked her to realize that he "cannot retire when I please, without disgrace." Also he reflected, "I am protected by that same overruling providence when in the heart of the creek nation, as I am at home."[12]

With the cooperation of Governor Blount, who sent fresh militiamen in the spring, and of U.S. General Thomas Pinckney, who made army troops available, Jackson at last had sufficient troops to penetrate to Horseshoe Bend in Alabama, the heart of Red Stick country. Leaving a contingent at Fort Strother, Jackson and some 4,000 men, including Indian allies, marched south to his enemies' heavily fortified town on the Tallapoosa River, which was defended by about 1,000 warriors. On March 27, the Americans attacked and won a major victory after a bloody battle lasting all day. In the following days, Jackson's troops mopped up the survivors, breaking the power of the Red Sticks forever. A few hundred escaped to Florida, where they planned to regroup with the aid of the Spanish and the British. The general went on to the Creek holy ground at the confluence of the Tallapoosa and Coosa rivers, where he built a stockade he called Fort Jackson.

After mustering out his troops at Fayetteville, Jackson rode on to Nashville, arriving in mid-May. He had written ahead to Rachel to meet him there on May 13. She brought Andrew Jr. with her; Jackson had in his train Lyncoya, by now a sturdy toddler who had been cared for by an Alabama woman until Jackson could bring him to the Hermitage. Rachel had written to her husband in April that deep snow had made all the plants look mournful, but when spring returned and "the sun shone on them theay all wer vivifyed. so will you have that Effect on my spirits when I see you returning to me againe nothing will animate or inliven me until then." And no doubt her prophecy came true when they were reunited after eight months' separation.[13]

Andrew Jackson was feted in Nashville as a conquering hero the day after his arrival. The Dickinson duel, the Benton affair—all were forgotten. During his brief return home, he received the welcome offer of a brigadier generalship in the U.S. Army, promoted to a major generalship after William Henry Harrison resigned his commission. Besides a respectable salary and even more respectable allowances for expenses, there was the prestige of the thing. He now commanded the Seventh Military District, comprising Louisiana, Tennessee, the Mississippi Territory, and the Creek nation. No more begging unsympathetic commanders for troops.[14]

Two months later, in July, Jackson was back at Fort Jackson, negotiating a treaty not just with the fallen Red Sticks but with his Creek
allies as well. To their astonishment, he demanded a huge cession of
land—23 million acres, half their nation, which opened a route from
Georgia to Mobile for white settlers—to compensate the United States
for the expenses of the war. After futile arguments about loyalty, justice, and their rights, the Creek chiefs eventually gave in and signed
on August 9. The Creeks, like other Indians in the future, found that
the man they called Sharp Knife negotiated with two interlocking
objectives in mind—acquiring Indian lands for the United States and
breaking the power of independent Indian nations.

After sending the Treaty of Fort Jackson to Washington, Jackson
had planned to return to Nashville, but "fortune that fickle dame,
mars all my wishes." He had received reports of British activities in
Pensacola and along the Gulf Coast and was duty bound to go south
to see what they were up to. As he put it, "I owe to Britain a debt of
retaliatory, Vengeance—should our forces meet I trust I shall pay
the debt."[15]

British strategy for ending this annoying little sideshow with
their former colonists had changed drastically with their defeat of
Napoleon. Driven back to Paris by the allied armies of his enemies,
the emperor abdicated the throne of France on April 11, 1814, and
was sent into exile on the island of Elba. Now the British were free to
unleash major army and naval forces against the United States and
finish things off.

The month of August 1814 was pivotal for the War of 1812. That
month, banks suspended specie payments, and the American

government's public credit collapsed. Even while opening peace talks with the United States in Ghent, the British campaigned aggressively in America, blockading ports, occupying Pensacola, and taking the capital. Their strategy was to negotiate peace from strength, planning to end the war with expanded territory in North America.

Of all the affronts to American pride, the British capture of Washington, D.C., was the worst. Landing on the Maryland coast, British army units plowed through the capital's confused and disorganized defenders, including President Madison, who fled before them. Dolley Madison became one of the heroes of the war when she gathered important government documents and a large portrait of George Washington before leaving the presidential mansion for the countryside. In the largely deserted city, the British carried out their orders to fire everything in sight. The Capitol building, the presidential mansion (where soldiers first enjoyed dinner and wine), government buildings, ships in ports, ammunition magazines, rope walks, warehouses, and anything else that caught their fancy was set afire. Besides the leaping flames, the shocks of exploding gunpowder and weapons could be heard for miles around. Strategically, the city was of little importance, but its destruction dealt a huge psychological blow to Americans.

Jackson, by ensconcing his troops in Mobile in the meantime, foiled the British plan for a grand advance through Mobile Bay into the heart of the country. By moving rapidly north and west from Mobile, the British planned to create havoc in American territory and cut off the port of New Orleans in the process. Vice Admiral Sir Alexander Cochrane, commander-in-chief of the North American Station, headed the expedition. At the invitation of the Spaniards, British troops had landed in Pensacola and were in communication with neighboring Indians who were hostile to the Americans.

On September 15, as the first step in the planned invasion of Mobile, British ships attacked Fort Bowyer on Mobile Bay, which Jackson had refortified. Through a series of misadventures, two of the British ships came under the guns of the fort while two others were unable to approach. Under the command of Major William Lawrence, the fort's defenders bombarded the enemy vessels until one blew up with a roar that Jackson could hear at his headquarters. With this defeat, Cochrane abandoned the original plan and sailed away. Although warned by Washington that a large British expedition was heading for New Orleans, Jackson still determined to attack Pensacola, one of his longtime aims. Jackson wrote to Monroe that sheer self-preservation made the move necessary to put down all foreign interference with southern Indians. With 4,000 men, he marched to Pensacola, arriving on November 6, 1814.

Although the Spanish were allies of the British in the Napoleonic Wars, they were officially neutral in the War of 1812. Nonetheless, the British made use of Pensacola and its fortifications as they saw fit, including supplying Indian allies during the war and maintaining a force at Fort Barrancas. When Jackson demanded that the Spanish governor of Florida, Mateo González Manrique, expel the British, he knew quite well that the governor lacked any such power. On November 7, Jackson's American troops approached the town unexpectedly from the east, preventing any bombardment from British ships, which were arrayed against a western attack. When Pensacola was securely occupied by Americans, the British blew up Fort Barrancas and sailed away with several hundred Indian allies. Having made his point, Jackson returned Pensacola to its governor, convinced that he had broken a Spanish/British/Indian conspiracy against the frontier. He wrote to James Monroe: "I am pleased to learn that my visit to Pensacola has had a good effect. The advices from that place...contain the most friendly expressions relative to the American character and forces."[16]

That Spain was a neutral in the war and that he had no orders to attack Pensacola was of little moment to Jackson. He believed the attack was necessary, he was satisfied with the results, and he was finally ready to march off to New Orleans to face the combined army/navy force that was on its way. He arrived in the city that would make him a national hero on December 1, 1814.

Throughout his absence from Nashville, he had been preoccupied with getting Rachel and their son to New Orleans, apparently not apprehending any danger to them in a city about to be attacked by crack British regulars. In August he had sent her a promissory note for collection; she was to use the money for a good pair of horses. He requested that she go into Nashville and make arrangements herself to repair their old carriage or exchange it for a new one.

Showing consciousness of their new social status, he added that "you must recollect that you are now a Major Generals lady...as such you must appear, elegant and plain, not extravagant, but in such stile as strangers expect to see you." He also suggested that she start assembling supplies, a continuing preoccupation, since buying food in New Orleans would be an unnecessary expense for people with their own farm produce. By November the carriage was repaired, and he reminded her how much bacon, flour, and vegetables would add to their good living and economy.[17]

Each letter brought fresh reminders—most unusual in their correspondence. Andrew was apparently feeling nervous about the impression they would make among sophisticated people in the big city. He discussed what servants to bring, not forgetting a nurse for little Andrew, and the necessities for housekeeping, such as two beds and bedsteads, tables with a dozen Windsor chairs, and her knife box. Dishes and plates could be bought in New Orleans. And again he obsessed about food. He wanted one hundred bushels each of threshed oats and ears of corn. "Some good corned Beeff will be an excellent thing." If the pork hadn't been slaughtered yet, she should do it at once and get hams and roasts smoked. He last wrote to Rachel on November 21, expecting that she would soon be on her way downriver to New Orleans.[18]

Perhaps his very poor health was behind all this concentration on food. Although he could now put his arm into a jacket sleeve and had discarded the sling, it had been a painful process. While he was at Mobile, stray pieces of broken bone worked their way to the surface of his skin; he sent them to Rachel, presumably as souvenirs.[19] Dysentery, though, had been his most debilitating enemy ever since October. While on the march to New Orleans, he didn't eat for eight days. As treatment for this distressing condition, he took doses of jalap and calomel, both harsh and effective purgatives. By the time he reached New Orleans, the always skinny Jackson must have been skeletal from the combination of his ailment and ill-advised medications. It wasn't until February 1815 that he was finally free of dysentery.

In New Orleans, Jackson's major strategic concern was the myriad of routes by which the British could attack the city and the impossibility of blocking them all with the troops under his command. The British had a different problem—which of the many approaches to take. The Mississippi River, lakes, bayous, man-made canals—every route had its advantages and disadvantages.

From the fleet's anchorage at the Mississippi Territory's barrier islands, Admiral Cochrane assessed the situation. Shortage of shallow-draft vessels caused him to reconsider his first plan of attacking from Lake Pontchartrain through Bayou Saint John into the back of the city. He did send a naval force on December 14 into Lake Borgne, which lay between Lake Pontchartrain and the Mississippi Sound, to attack the fleet of American gunboats there. The greatly outnumbered Americans fought a losing battle but gave Jackson extra time to call in reinforcements for his troops.

Jackson's army included the men he had brought with him and the white militia and volunteers of Louisiana, as well as troops from Mississippi. Against the wishes of many Louisianians, Jackson accepted the services of two battalions of free men of color, some of whom had served as militiamen under the Spanish, others emigrants from Saint Domingue and its revolution. All were seasoned fighters, whom Jackson welcomed with full pay; his only racially based stipulation was that they be commanded by white officers.

Another decision that met with mixed reactions was his acceptance of the offer of Jean Lafitte and his band of smugglers from Barataria Bay to help defend New Orleans. Lafitte and his brother Pierre owned ships and dealt extensively in slaves and other contraband goods, but their men included the only trained artillerists in the area. Governor William C. C. Claiborne, Jackson's former friend, was furious, but Jackson wasn't turning down any useful volunteers. Meanwhile, now that he knew for sure that the British meant to attack New Orleans, Jackson urged the swift arrival of John Coffee, the militias of Tennessee and Kentucky, and William Carroll and his troops.

In New Orleans, with the success of the British at Lake Borgne, panic overcame the city. Among its polyglot population, there were many spies, as well as some inhabitants who wouldn't be averse to British occupation. The Louisiana legislature was obstructive, disputing command with the imperious general. So on December 16, Jackson declared martial law in New Orleans. Now securely in charge, he gave orders for all bayous and canals leading to the city to be blocked and a watch kept on them. He also set guards out the Chef Menteur Road toward Lake Borgne, the route he considered most likely for an approaching army.

On December 23, still unsure when or by what route the enemy would attack, Jackson was worrying about Rachel. He complained to Robert Hays, "I have not recd a letter or paper from Tennessee since the last of Octobr." He thought that his wife would have been on her way by this time, and, in contrast to his usual habit of frequent letters, he hadn't written to her. If she was still at home, he asked Hays to "say to her the reason I have not wrote her."[20]

That very afternoon, he learned all he needed to know about the British plans. The day before, barges loaded with troops had left Lake Borgne and entered Bayou Bienvenue. They were the cream of the British army, seasoned veterans of the long war against Napoleon in the Iberian Peninsula. Unseen, they had continued into Bayou Mazant until they could embark on solid ground and march over to the plantation of Jacques Philippe Villeré, the future governor of Louisiana. None of the approaches to these bayous had been blocked.

The planter's son, Gabriel Villeré, was captured by the British as they took the plantation and formed up along the Mississippi River. Desperately, young Villeré leaped from a window and escaped into a cypress swamp, eluding pursuing soldiers. He and two other Creoles finally made their way to Jackson's Royal Street headquarters on the afternoon of December 23. They warned the general that the British had reached the river ten miles south of the city and had a clear road to New Orleans.

When Jackson heard the startling news, he burst out, "I will smash them, so help me God!"[21] Quickly summoning his troops, he made his dispositions to guard the city and the Chef Menteur Road in case of a feint. At the head of his army, he rode south to attack the British in a flat area known as the plains of Chalmette. For several hours, the armies fought in the dark, ending in a deadlock. Earlier disagreements between the British commanders had caused them to miss their chance for a surprise attack and the almost certain fall of the city. Instead, they secured their position and considered their options. Now there would be no immediate attack on the city, but neither were the Americans strong enough to pursue the British or to destroy their advance guard.

The Americans withdrew to the Rodriguez Canal, and both sides spent the next few days fortifying their positions, assembling reinforcements, and setting up their artillery emplacements. On Christmas Day the Duke of Wellington's brother-in-law General Sir Edward Pakenham arrived to take command of the assault. Although neither army knew it yet, nor would they for weeks, the Treaty of Ghent had been signed on December 24, providing for peace between Great Britain and the United States and a territorial return to the prewar status quo.

What with the uncertainty about the action downriver and with problems at the Hermitage, Hays and other friends had advised Rachel to put off her departure. She needed more money from the sale of produce for the trip, but work at the plantation was going slowly. Although crops had been harvested in the fall, cotton needed to be ginned and baled, wheat milled into flour, corn dried or ground, whiskey distilled, and fruits and vegetables dried. The overseer, John Fields, had trouble controlling defiant slaves. Hays thought that Fields's hard drinking was the root of the problem.

Jackson continued to inquire anxiously about her whereabouts in the midst of his frantic defensive efforts.

The Americans threw back another assault on New Year's Day 1815, and the British fell back. On Sunday, January 8, the British made their final assault. Although the British forces numbered more than 8,000 to Jackson's fewer than half that number, the assault was a massacre. The Americans stayed ensconced behind a breastwork that stretched from the Mississippi River into cypress swamps. Their artillery was magnificent in force, speed of firing, and accuracy; frontier sharpshooters helped carry the day. British soldiers ran straight into a wall of fire. The few who managed to climb the American ramparts were shot and shoved back. West Indian troops in the swamps were shot or mired down. Pakenham was cut down by grapeshot, and other senior officers died or were so badly wounded they couldn't assume command. Without commanders, British troops faltered, hesitated, and ran away in a confused retreat. Jackson refused to allow his men to pursue the enemy, knowing they didn't have the discipline to prevail in the open field if they ran into trained reinforcements.[22]

The main battle took only half an hour; an assault on the west bank of the river, two hours. Well before noon, the Battle of New Orleans was over. The men cheered General Jackson excitedly and then turned to survey the field of Chalmette. It was "covered with dead and wounded laying in heaps, the field was completely red." Small skirmishes continued over the next days, bringing new casualties, and many of the wounded died. Battlefield numbers are never completely accurate, but these are astonishing nonetheless. The final numbers for the Americans were 13 killed and another 58 wounded or missing. British losses were 291 killed, and 1,746 wounded, taken prisoner, or missing. The disparity between the numbers, especially with the Americans victorious, confounded everyone.[23]

Although he had triumphed at the Chalmette battlefield, Jackson continued to fear a new British attack by land or sea. During this time, there was merely a cease-fire in effect as the combatants buried the dead, tended the wounded, and exchanged prisoners. Jackson finally pulled his men back from the Rodriguez Canal to New Orleans, and there was a tremendous celebration in the city with a solemn *Te Deum* in honor of the city's deliverance. Grateful as they were, restless Louisianians saw no reason why they should remain on military duty, and they began to find the general overbearing. And still Andrew wondered, "Where is Mrs. Jackson?"[24]

By early January 1815, Rachel was in Nashville along with the young wives of two of her husband's trusted officers—her niece Rachel Hays Butler, wife of Colonel Robert Butler, and Harriet Winter Overton, wife of Major Walter Hampden Overton. All those desirable supplies had been accumulated, including some of her best butter (butter and eggs being the purview of women). Within two weeks, Nashville learned of the great victory, and Rachel's party set out downriver in a well-equipped barge on January 25. Dr. William Edward Butler, brother of Colonel Butler and a longtime friend, went along as the ladies' escort.[25]

Happily learning that Rachel was on her way, Jackson contended with the city's citizens who wanted to return to local rule immediately and to treat with the British privately for the return of escaped slaves. No one yet knew that the war was actually over. The general vowed to continue martial law until he was informed that a treaty was in effect, and he forbade any unofficial communication with the enemy. By February 4, the exchange of prisoners was still going forward with the British at Ship Island. The British forces were in a parlous state, running short of provisions, quarreling among themselves, eaten up by mosquitoes. The request of a wounded general for the return of his captured sword delighted Jackson, who crowed, "when a British Genl makes the request of an american Genl, to restore his *sword won in battle*—prospects of peace is opening to our View—and British pride much humbled."[26]

Jackson was right to remain on his guard. Disappointed of his expected prey, Admiral Cochrane had sailed away with most of the British fleet, laying siege to Fort Bowyer in Alabama and capturing it on February 11. The admiral planned to resurrect his original plan of taking Mobile as the base for a further southern invasion.

At the beginning of 1815, Washington was a blackened ruin, its citizens despondent at their defeat. Almost everyone, including the nation's leaders, had fled before the British and feared their reappearance. It was well known that a British fleet with a huge invasion army was landing somewhere in the South, and Washingtonians glumly assumed there would be another American defeat.

Two and a half years earlier, when war was declared, Americans believed that they would expand their nation both to the north and to the south, celebrate their independence in the eyes of the world, and teach the arrogant British a lesson. With a few shining exceptions, the United States had been the one taught a very painful lesson indeed.

In those days of snail-like communication, when express riders were at the mercy of bad weather and other vicissitudes, it was February 4 before reports of the Battle of New Orleans reached the nation's capital. What a carnival of liberty! The citizens gathered in the streets, cheering and singing, and illuminations lit up the night skies. Boston, Philadelphia, New York—the nation's great cities soon shared in the delight. And the name on everyone's lips was Andrew

Jackson. He had become the nation's Hero with a capital "H." The arrival of the news that the Treaty of Ghent had been signed was anticlimactic when it arrived a little over a week later.

On February 19, Rachel and her party arrived at the New Orleans levee to her husband's delight and to her shock at his wasted appearance. Besides the constant dysentery, Jackson had not taken one day off duty since his arrival in the city on December 1. Rachel understood well the cause of his illness. She wrote to Robert Hays, "of all men on Erth he does the most business from day light to ten at night [and] devotes little time to pleasure."[27]

Coming from the rude frontier town of Nashville, Rachel was wide-eyed at the elegance of New Orleans. She and the general attended a celebration of Washington's birth night. It was beyond "the power of my pen" to describe "the splendor the brillient assembleage the magnificenc of the supper and orniments of the room." Such mottoes as "Jackson and Victory" and "Vive Jackson" decorated the room. "I have seen more alredy then in all my life past," she added; "it is the finest country for the Eye of a strainger."[28]

Supper was served on the ground floor of the French Exchange building, which was decorated with flowers, colored lamps, and transparencies with inscriptions hung between the arcades. At the ball on the second floor, the Jacksons led out the first dance. Dancing had always been Rachel's delight, but her sun-browned, wrinkled face and virtually waistless figure did not make a happy impression on New Orleanians. "To see these two figures, the general, a long, haggard man, with limbs like a skeleton, and Madame la Generale, a short, fat dumpling, bobbing opposite each other like half-drunken Indians, to the wild melody of *Possum up de Gum Tree* [perhaps their own musical choice], and endeavoring to make a spring into the air, was very remarkable," wrote Vincent Nolte, a wealthy European businessman.[29]

Living in a comfortable house near Jackson's headquarters, they dined with other American officers. Rachel was beginning to tire "of the dissipation of this place so much amusement balls concerits Plays theaters &c &c but we don't attend the half of them." Under her ministrations, "the General looks better in health then when I came here."[30]

Already rumors had swept the city that a peace treaty had been signed, and the clamor rose for a return to civilian rule. News of the treaty finally arrived from the postmaster general on March 6, but it still had not been ratified by the Senate, a necessity for it to have legal standing. The following week official news of the ratification arrived, and on March 13, Jackson ended martial law.

The legislature, many citizens, and Judge Dominick Hall were still angry at what they saw as Jackson's unconstitutional behavior. While the city was under martial law, Jackson had jailed a legislator for sedition; Judge Hall had granted a writ of habeas corpus, which Jackson refused to honor. Now that Hall was back on the bench, he haled Jackson into court to answer a charge of contempt of court. The general finally appeared on March 27, but he had to leave to attend to Rachel, who had become ill. The judge fined him $1,000 on March 31. Although grateful New Orleanians raised that amount to pay the fine, Jackson insisted on paying it himself, publishing his replies to the charges in several papers and forwarding a copy to Washington.

The next week was a blur of congratulatory dinners and celebrations. The exhausted Jackson party left New Orleans, feted every step of the way, and arrived home on May 15 to a welcoming procession and a wild celebration in Nashville. Cynics then and later dismissed the Battle of New Orleans as insignificant because the Treaty of Ghent had already been signed. But they overlooked the amazing jolt to the American psyche and the probability that the British would not have returned either New Orleans or Mobile to the United States but would have given them to Spain. Large portions of the American Southeast might have been lost, not to speak of the damage to America's international reputation without the victory. Andrew Jackson was deservedly hailed as the Hero of the nation.

CHAPTER 8

Life in the Public Eye

The victory at the Battle of New Orleans changed everything in the Jacksons' lives. Andrew had become a national celebrity who could never return to his former regional identity. Newspapers reported on his movements, describing every detail of banquets and celebrations. A quiet home life and personal privacy were out of the question. His—and Rachel's—every move, present and past, would now be open to observation and intrusive comment.

Like any successful general, then or since, Andrew Jackson had to be considered a viable contender for the presidency. Politicians holding national office or eyeing the possibility of a campaign saw him as a potential rival. Ambitious cabinet members like William Harris Crawford and James Monroe started keeping a close eye on his every move, but no one yet had the nerve for an open attack. His prominence and public acclaim were enormous compared to the reputations of the men in government, none of whom had made a mark during the War of 1812 and its many failures. Then, too, his famous temper and irascibility, although much exaggerated, made most men pause before insulting him. He was not one to endure attacks on his reputation without a furious all-out response.

Jackson's command in the American army, undergoing reorganization in the wake of the war, would clearly be an important one. The same day their party arrived in Nashville, May 15, 1815, he received the news of his appointment as major general, Division of the South. Jacob Jennings Brown was major general in command of the Division of the North. On June 12, Jackson made a public announcement of his assumption of command. Treading carefully with the Hero, the War Department allowed him to designate the Hermitage as command headquarters. Working hard on his proposals for military reorganization, Jackson needed his staff at hand. Several lively aides lived at the house over the years, making work more efficient and enhancing the Jacksons' social life. Rachel loved the company of these young men and tended to them as surrogate sons. In turn, they worshipped their commander and adored his wife.

The Jacksons spent the summer and fall of 1815 in recuperation and improving their plantation. Both of them had been quite ill at the end of their stay in New Orleans. The capriciousness of New Orleans weather, freezing in February, then abruptly turning warm and muggy in March, was especially hard on those prone to bronchial disorders like the Jacksons. Andrew had been pushing himself relentlessly for nearly two years without a pause. He had two bullets lodged in his body, the latest (from Jesse Benton's gun) resting alongside a lung, causing horrible inflammations, and a very painful shoulder and arm. He had suffered months of dysentery and semi-starvation, while dosing himself with toxic levels of mercury. Rest and peace were what they both needed.

Jackson's patience—not that he had a lot to spare—was seriously frayed by inquiries from Washington about his incursion into Spanish Pensacola, his declaration of martial law in New Orleans, and his treatment of civilians there. Neither President Madison nor his acting secretary of war, Alexander Dallas, had the least desire for a confrontation with Jackson, but questions were being asked in Congress and in the press. Dallas wrote letters on April 12 and again on July 1 that were remarkable for their inoffensive and apologetic tone, requesting information from the general on his "conduct and the motives for [his] conduct."[1]

Jackson shot back a stiff reply, every line bristling with indignation and affront. Failing to take into account the constant turnover in the wartime cabinet, he made it clear that the second letter's two-month delay was suspicious. Pleading ill health and many engagements, he declined to discuss the matter by letter or with a subordinate. Instead, he would lay his proceedings in New Orleans before the president "& the world" when he arrived in Washington.[2]

Finally, in early October 1815, somewhat late in the season for comfortable travel, Andrew and Rachel, little Andrew and his nurse, Rachel's nephew Lemuel Donelson, Jackson's aide John Reid, and house servants set off by carriage and horseback for the capital. In their absence, Robert Butler looked after the Hermitage and their business affairs as well as the other boys. The journey through eastern Tennessee soon turned into a triumphal progress. The nation's first national military hero since George Washington, Jackson and his party were stopped all along the route by admirers who insisted on celebrating his feats. Rachel was always proud when her husband was properly appreciated.

Writing to Butler on October 18, Jackson described how they had been "met by a number of the most respectable citizens [of Knoxville,] conducted to the city, and pressed to stay and Dine with them today." He had felt compelled to agree, even though he was distressed by the delay and somewhat embarrassed: "you know how loathsome this parade is to my feelings."[3]

The Jacksons didn't arrive in Washington until November 16. Neither of them had ever seen the nation's young capital, where John Adams had first moved into the unfinished presidential mansion fifteen years earlier. Then a largely unsettled wasteland with large stands of trees cut through by streams and marshes, its roads were dusty (or muddy) lanes dotted with tree stumps and bushes, and government buildings and houses clustered in little islands at great distances from one another. By 1814, the American capital had grown closer to its founders' dreams with more than 25,000 permanent residents, besides the seasonal arrivals of the congressmen who filled all the city's boardinghouses to bursting. But in September of that year, the British conflagration had destroyed most of Washington and led some residents to despair of the city's ever coming back.[4]

By late 1815, however, the capital had begun rebuilding, and most of its people had returned. Still, the Jacksons stared out at blackened ruins as their coach pressed forward through a cold winter's rain. It would be another two years before the presidential mansion would again be habitable and before Congress could meet in the Capitol. The Madisons lived and entertained in one of the Seven Buildings, private row houses on Pennsylvania Avenue, while Congress met in a new brick building built for them the previous spring.

For all the destruction, the sheer size of the place must have taken Rachel by surprise. Earlier in the year, she had been amazed in

New Orleans by its more than 10,000 people. Now she was in a city more than twice that size. For all her life, Nashville had been her measure for urban life, and it had barely grown beyond a population of 1,000 by 1815.

Washington housed many people of wealth and elite social background. Protocol relating to the presidency was already a thorny subject, exacerbated by the widowed Thomas Jefferson's flouting of the very concept of protocol as unworthy of a free people. Dolley Madison loved a good party and used presidential balls, receptions, teas, and dinners as a way to bring political enemies together. She had also restored the custom of making calls on newcomers—a change very popular with the ladies of the city. The question of who called first was a matter of burning importance to many socialites, and the president's wife made it easy for them. Considering the many entertainments at which the Jacksons were the honored guests, Dolley and the cabinet wives must have called on Rachel at her lodgings.

Protocol for ladies and gentlemen was considerably different, reflecting elite gender expectations. While ladies waited to be called upon, gentlemen immediately called on their superiors, as well as their wives. The secretary of war and the president were also Jackson's military commanders. The day after they arrived, John Reid accompanied Jackson on official calls and wrote home facetiously about the formality and stateliness of their reception. They visited President and Mrs. Madison, Secretary of State and Mrs. James Monroe, as well as the secretary of the treasury and the secretary of war and their wives, and in Reid's seriocomic style, were *"not a bit afraid."* Reid mocked the rigmarole of separate visits to the women's upstairs parlors. He reported that "A few very 'civil things' are said by her & the General; & then we again retire with our *double bows.*"[5]

Their visit to the formally attired Madison with his "black, silk stocking, and powdered [hair]," Reid continued, was particularly uncomfortable, the conversation stilted, perhaps because the president was trying to figure out how to deal with the headstrong general. He observed of the president: "The truth is he was perplexed by the appearance of Genl. Jackson, who whenever the conversation 'flagged' was looking, with a melancholy air [ou]t at the window, on the ruins of our publick buildings."[6]

Within a few days, Jackson met with Secretary Alexander Dallas and accepted his assurance that both Madison and Dallas were satisfied on every point with his behavior at New Orleans. The essential business of the trip—his vindication—thus accomplished, they went on to social enjoyments. The weather continued nasty and bitingly cold while they attended dinners and soirees. Payne Todd, the beloved wastrel son of Dolley Madison, accompanied Jackson on a call. A visit to Mount Vernon was a highlight; the owner, Associate Justice Bushrod Washington, was away, so they were hosted by Washington's far more entertaining stepgrandson, George Washington Parke Custis of Arlington. The leaders of capital society made their visit a triumph.

Rachel, young Andrew, and Lemuel all took sick with heavy colds, but were recovered by early December just as Jackson was starting to feel very unwell. He held out long enough to attend a grand celebration ball in his honor, given by the Madisons at their temporary residence. Four days later, he was confined to bed with a massive infection in his left arm. His life was despaired of, and the president brought in a famous Philadelphia doctor. He gradually recovered, but his illness delayed their departure.[7]

They finally left on December 24, 1815, once again pushing through heavy snow in Virginia. Writing to Robert Butler in a dry tone, Jackson declined giving "a detailed account of the passing scenes at washington—suffice it for the present to observe, that I had the pleasure of seeing all the great men at the city, was friendly greeted by all—and was obliged to flee the profered hospitality of the surrounding cities to restore my health & preserve life."[8]

After their return to Nashville on February 1, 1816, Jackson set to work in earnest as commander of the army's Division of the South. The visit to the capital and the flattering attention of the country's leaders gave him a renewed sense of his own power to bring about change in the South and safeguard the nation. Besides putting army reorganization into effect, he saw his priorities as securing Mobile and the Gulf Coast from either Spanish or British attempts at recapture, neutralizing southern Indian tribes and negotiating land cessions with them, preventing Spain from supporting the Indians, and eventually forcing the Spanish out of North America. His aims were all concerned with the expansion of the United States, its military defensibility, and the security of its citizens. He was by no means alone in his expansionist dreams; most westerners and a majority of the rest of the nation shared them. But he had the power to accomplish them.

Jackson's view of the ideal United States was geopolitical. He saw it stretching from the Atlantic Ocean to the Mississippi River and from the Great Lakes to the Gulf of Mexico, in other words, the present-day map of the eastern United States. Once that was achieved, expansion to the far West would naturally follow. But in 1816 the reality was a patchwork of competing national claims—several nations of Indians, as well as Spanish colonies, with the British ready to support any or all of them. Such overlapping claims were, in Jackson's opinion, always a potential source of war. He saw

the future strength of the United States lying in a consolidated territory under American law.

Jackson didn't hate individual Indians per se, but he hated the fact
that Indian nations were interspersed throughout American territory
and that the Spanish maintained colonies on the nation's southern
and western boundaries. He regarded these various claims as dangerous to American sovereignty and open to British manipulation.
Anything that weakened this imperial foe was desirable. The previous year, he had crowed over Napoleon's March 1, 1815, escape from
exile in Elba and his welcome by the French army, writing about
"the *wonderfull revolution* in France" and the proof that "Napoleon
reigns in the affections of the soldiers." He hoped that, under those
circumstances, Britain would agree to an advantageous trade treaty
with the United States.[9] Napoleon's subsequent defeat at Waterloo
and exile to St. Helena quashed those hopes, and he continued to
regard Britain as a dangerous adversary.

For the next five years, Jackson spent months in pursuit of his
vision of the ideal United States. Rachel once again took on the task
of running the Hermitage and other businesses although she now
had additional help from her husband's military aides. One of her
deepest concerns was that Andrew Jr. was growing up without sufficient attention from his father. She was the sort of adoring mother
that the nineteenth century sentimentalized. Jackson loved their
boy dearly, especially because he made Rachel happier and more
contented.

When the baby was adopted in 1809, Jackson had been largely
at home, but little Andrew had hardly turned four when his papa
set off on his first expedition downriver. During the War of 1812
Jackson was seldom at the Hermitage. When the family was reunited
in February 1815, their son was seven and starting to study his letters

and figures. Jackson continued to be an often distant figure throughout his childhood although Rachel tried to alleviate the effects of his absence through talking constantly about him, even giving the child one of his father's letters to sleep with.[10]

In most ways, the Jacksons were more like grandparents than parents, spoiling and coddling the little boy. Discipline never played a large role in their relationship with him, and the results showed in later life. During these years, the loving son helped soothe his mother's sadness, wiping away her tears. His "sweet papa" appreciated the boy's efforts. He wrote, "The sensibility of our beloved son, has charmed me, I have no doubt, from the sweetness of his disposition, from his good sense as evidenced, for his age, that he will take care of us both in our declining years—from our fondness towards him, his return of affection to us, I have every hope if he should be spared to manhood, that he will with a carefull education reallise all our wishes."[11]

During one of his many delays in returning home, Jackson wrote, "Tell Andrew I fear he will think I am runaway from him—but kiss him for me and say to him truly, that in all my life I never wanted more to see you & him than I do at present."[12] Both the Jacksons made a clear distinction between their adopted son and their other wards. But despite his loneliness for wife and child, Andrew saw no alternative when he needed to be elsewhere to make his vision for the United States a reality.

The Treaty of Fort Jackson, which had been imposed by Jackson on August 9, 1814, continued to be a matter of violent dissension. Many Creeks and Choctaws still resisted its draconian terms, which divested them of 23 million acres, while white settlers were moving into their lands and refusing to budge. Jackson, needless to say, backed the settlers. President Madison was perplexed about how to handle the situation since the only way to remove the whites was with regular army troops—a public relations nightmare in itself and useless since they would return as soon as the troops left.

Politics, of course, were involved. The smooth functioning of the Republican Party called for Madison to be succeeded by his secretary of state, James Monroe, in the system devised by Thomas Jefferson. Nomination by their congressional caucus would guarantee his election in 1816, but in the meantime it was necessary to ward off the efforts of such challengers as William Harris Crawford. Jackson's name was also beginning to be noised about as a presidential candidate. Crossing the Hero might push him into the race.

To avoid a confrontation and fix Jackson's attention elsewhere, Madison named him to the commission to deal with Indian claims, in effect making possible a vast spoliation of their lands. The president and others in the government were in favor of westward expansion but were not quite sure how to accomplish it. By putting Jackson in charge, Madison handed over the Indians' fate to a man determined to acquire their lands for the nation. By this stroke, he also ensured Monroe's election in 1816.

Jackson never doubted his stars and was ready to push toward his goals at the slightest opportunity. In February 1816, he toured the nation's Gulf Coast defenses, returning home through New Orleans. When William Harris Crawford overreached himself by attempting a more favorable accommodation with the Creeks, Jackson stepped in. Over the next years, Jackson negotiated cessions of millions of acres from the Creeks, the Cherokees, the Chickasaws, and the Choctaws in the South.

At the same time, peace was concluded with scarcely any difficulty on the northern border of the United States. American leaders had finally accepted the notion that Canadians didn't care to be incorporated into the United States. In 1817 the United States and Great Britain signed the Rush-Bagot Agreement, which demilitarized the Great Lakes, and in 1818 the Anglo-American Convention, which established a permanent boundary with the British colony of Canada.

The southern border with the Spanish colony of Florida was quite a different matter. Florida was still an object of western lust, believed to be easy pickings for a determined force. One of the pretexts for still another incursion into Florida was Spain's sheltering of dissident Creeks and other hostile Indians from the United States. They had joined native Seminoles who frequently raided across the border into Georgia. Land speculators and settlers in the newly organized territory of Alabama cried out for protection.

With great brutality, an American force attacked a Seminole village on land claimed by the United States in late 1817. In revenge, the Seminoles attacked a convoy of American boats on the Apalachicola River and slaughtered all the party. That was the beginning of the First Seminole War. General Edmund P. Gaines was authorized to pursue the Seminoles into Florida if necessary. But on December 26, his commanding officer, Andrew Jackson, was ordered by Secretary of State John C. Calhoun to take command of the troops and end the Seminole hostilities.

Few could doubt the results of giving Old Hickory his head in an incursion into Spanish territory. He recruited volunteers in Nashville and marched south on January 22, 1818. A letter from

President Monroe, written in veiled terms, certainly appeared to encourage an attack on Florida. Jackson's letter, which crossed that of the president in the mails, asked him for direct orders, but that letter remained unread for a year and was not answered. Jackson, however, never doubted that the president approved of his invasion. By April 1, Jackson's troops had attacked and destroyed a major Seminole town; a week later they seized the Spanish fort of St. Marks, where they found two Red Stick leaders and two British merchants accused of encouraging attacks on American soil. The Indians were hanged immediately; the British were brought before a military tribunal and found guilty as charged. One was hanged and the other shot by a firing squad. By the end of May, Jackson's forces had occupied Pensacola, the Spanish capital of East Florida. On June 26, Jackson was back in Tennessee, where he discharged the volunteers, arriving two days later in Nashville for the customary celebrations.

For American expansionists, Jackson's six months away from home had been a tidy little operation, dealing smartly with both hostile Indians and Spaniards. Unfortunately, there had been no declaration of war. Not only had Jackson attacked a nation with which the United States was at peace, but he had executed two foreign nationals. In Washington, all was in an uproar during the summer of 1818. The Spanish minister, Luís de Onís, indignantly demanded the return of the captured Florida forts in July. The cabinet met daily to discuss what to do about Jackson and how to respond to Onís. Calhoun and Crawford wanted to censure Jackson and return Florida. John Quincy Adams, the secretary of state, defended Jackson and planned to acquire Florida. Monroe wriggled, somehow wanting to please everyone, provide no international provocation, and still get hold of Florida.

Letters flew back and forth between Washington and Nashville, and Jackson's aides collected depositions about the necessity for taking Pensacola. Monroe's suggestion that Jackson might have transcended his authority was rebuffed with indignation. When Congress convened that fall, the general's enemies began brandishing their finely honed knives. Even though negotiations for the purchase of Florida were under way (which was only possible because of Jackson's conquest), Congress began an investigation of his actions.

There were many reasons to disapprove of Jackson's actions—principled, philosophical, and politically motivated—but in combination they could lead to the end of his career. As always, Jackson saw conspiracy in the attempt to bring him down, and there was much truth in his suspicion; he saw William Harris Crawford, secretary of the treasury, and Henry Clay, speaker of the House, as the leaders of his enemies, and there was much truth in that belief as well.

The debate about Jackson's censure began on January 20, 1819. Having ridden like the wind since the beginning of the year, Jackson arrived three days later, spending every day consulting with his supporters to counter the rhetoric of Clay and his allies. On February 8 he was exonerated, and on February 22 the Adams-Onís Treaty, by which the United States purchased Florida, was signed. The crisis had passed, and Jackson's reputation was intact and even enhanced.

After all their years in the small log Hermitage, Andrew decided it was time to upgrade his residence and began construction of a large new brick house despite the effects of the burgeoning Panic of 1819. As some western banks failed and the price of cotton plummeted, the Jacksons were more careful than ever of their finances.

Despite the belt-tightening, however, they could still afford to build the new house.

That spring, after Congress adjourned, Monroe made a southern and western tour, soothing Jackson's ruffled feathers by spending time as a guest at the Hermitage and inviting the general to accompany him to Kentucky. The president had no intention of losing such a valuable ally. In the two years during which the Spanish delayed ratification of the treaty (which the Americans had ratified at once) for their own advantage, Monroe always had in mind that Jackson should be the governor of Florida when it became American territory. During the interim, Monroe was reelected to the presidency in 1820.

The consultations and negotiations leading to Jackson's resignation from the army and his assumption of the governorship of Florida were byzantine. Congress's decision to cut the peacetime army drastically would mean the demotion or resignation of one of the two commanding major generals, leaving the other in sole command. General Jacob Brown was the senior officer in length of service, and he had strong government supporters, including William Harris Crawford. Jackson, the junior general, had very strong congressional support, along with the admiration of the nation. Getting Jackson to Florida and Brown in command without offending either officer or his supporters was one of James Monroe's political masterpieces.

The Senate re-ratified the Adams-Onís Treaty on February 19, 1821, and Monroe was inaugurated for his second term the following month. Having gone back and forth about accepting Monroe's offer of the governorship, Jackson at last agreed to serve despite Rachel's "repugnance" at the whole idea. Serving as governor, he felt, publicly vindicated all his actions in Florida. Although he would have to resign his army commission, the governorship carried the same salary—$5,000—and expenses.[13]

On April 14, Rachel and Andrew, along with Andrew Jr. (now thirteen), a Donelson niece and nephew, staff, and servants, left Nashville by steamboat for New Orleans. Andrew Jackson Hutchings, the orphaned son of Jack Hutchings, who had joined the household in 1817, was left at home in the care of another niece to attend school. A week later they docked in New Orleans, where all controversial memories were forgotten. They were feted at dinners and the theater, where the audience broke into cheers in French and English.

But Rachel was a far different woman from the country mouse who had been so dazzled six years before by the citizens' sophistication and glamour. In the ensuing years, she had developed a coherent worldview that saw her through any situation. With Andrew away from home for months on end, she had spent much of her free time in Bible study and in the company of ministers and the devout women of the First Presbyterian Church. Having seen the light herself, she could no longer be intimidated by people she considered ungodly—and Catholics were not among the godly as far as Evangelical Protestants were concerned.

A central tenet of religion for many American Protestants was sabbatarianism. To them, it meant not only keeping the Sabbath holy with church, prayer, and cessation of work, but also refraining from almost anything at all, including social gatherings, parties, theater, sports, hunting, or travel. By the 1820s they went even further: non-believers should be prevented from profaning the day and tempting believers. The Catholic conviction that innocent entertainments or travel was acceptable on Sunday was denied with scorn. Presbyterians like Rachel saw the Catholics of New Orleans and Pensacola as wicked idolaters. By allowing such people to continue in their sinful ways, the godly were neglecting their duty to carry out God's commands.

During her time in the city, she wrote a long letter to her friend Elizabeth Kingsley, one of Nashville's leading Presbyterians. Where before she saw elegance, she now saw "unspeakable...riches and splendor." New Orleans was the "Great Babylon," a metaphor from the Book of Revelation that appeared in the writings of other Protestant visitors about the city. She begged her friend to pray for her "in a heathen land, far from my people and church."[14]

In a time of tight budgets, governmental inertia, and very slow mails, Jackson found himself struggling for money to carry out his new duties. After he arrived near Mobile on May 1, aggravations multiplied for an impatient man. The president ignored his advice, announcing unwanted and unwise appointments. Even though the treaty had been signed two years previously, the Spaniards still dilly-dallied about sending the commander, Colonel José María Callava, final orders to turn Pensacola and Fort Barrancas over to Jackson. And Callava himself delayed at the behest of his government. There was a stormy quarrel over cannons at the fort, and the American party moved nearer Pensacola.

Although Jackson sent Rachel, their son, and much of their party into Pensacola to live in a rented house on June 28, he refused to enter the place until he could ride in with the American colors flying high. Finally on July 17, 1821, delays at an end, Jackson entered the city for the third time in his life, the object of his ambition since 1814, officially took over from the Spanish governor, and ran up the United States flag "high in the air, not less than one hundred feet."[15]

Meanwhile, Rachel oversaw the repairs and furnishing of their house on the little town's main street. With a population of some 700, including slaves, Pensacola made Nashville look like a metropolis. As she observed the ceremonies from her upper galleries, she felt for the citizens: "O how they burst into tears to see the last ray of hope departed." With the exodus of officials and soldiers, "How did the city sit solitary and mourn. Never did my heart feel more for any people."[16]

But feeling sympathy for their plight and allowing rampant Sabbath-breaking were different things. As she recounted to her friend Elizabeth Kingsley, "I was not an idle spectator." After observing three riotous Sundays, she sent an American major to lay down the new rules to the populace, with her husband's blessing. The following Sunday, "Great order was observed; the doors kept shut; the gambling houses demolished; fiddling and dancing not heard any more on the Lord's day; cursing not to be heard.... What, what has been done in one week!" Her husband's imposition of these ordinances and fines against Sabbath-breakers certainly helped make it so.[17]

Now that she was assisting people who were "living far from God," she was happy and busy. She was also able to appreciate the town with its white sand, abundant fruit trees, beautiful flowers growing wild, views of the water, and fine sea breezes. "There is something in it so exhilarating, so pure, so wholesome, it enlivens the whole system." Already the Americans who would quadruple the size of Pensacola in a year were pouring in. Rachel's main complaints were heat, rain, mud, and lack of Christian society. As usual, she admired her husband, who "has indeed performed a great work in his day," using a common biblical phrase for godly actions. To her mind, the governmental changes he was achieving in Florida would make it more like Tennessee, "a land of gospel light and liberty." As had often been the case, though, his nonstop schedule contributed to his ill health.[18]

Jackson had always intended his governorship in Florida to be a short one—to establish American law in the new territory, set up and staff an effective government, arrange for a system of ascertaining landownership and registering new grants, and then go home. Overall, he did well in his objectives, also bringing two of Florida's future leaders, Richard Keith Call and James Gadsden, to the territory. But his noisy and out-of-control responses to the slightest provocation terrified Floridians and provided scores of critical column inches in Washington's *National Intelligencer,* part of Crawford's campaign apparatus, and other newspapers. Jailing the former Spanish governor and ordering Spanish officers out of the country seemed to his critics undiplomatic behavior, but there was a matter of justice behind his actions. Given the still overwhelming American public support for Jackson, no official inquiry was held about his governorship.

Instead, Jackson completed what he saw as his fundamental work and announced to the president that he was leaving for home, giving Rachel's ill health as his excuse. Actually, Andrew was the one who was sick from a lifetime's accumulation of wounds, illnesses, and carelessness of his own well-being, as well as being sick of the minutiae of office. On October 8, 1821, Rachel and Andrew Jackson left Pensacola for Nashville in a carriage drawn by four showy gray horses. On November 13, Andrew sent his official resignation to the president.

Andrew Jackson had long talked about retirement and its pleasures. Now fifty-four, an advanced age at the time, he had driven himself mercilessly for years. He was in pain most of the time and tired of the constant quarrels of public life. Rachel was the same age, also in poor health, and definitely ready for her husband to remain at home. He had achieved a great deal, and she had supported him through his career. Their finances still suffered from the effects of the Panic of 1819, and their affairs needed attention. Then there were the three boys—Andrew Jr., Andrew Jackson Hutchings, and Lyncoya, stair steps from thirteen down to nine—all of whom needed care and guidance. It was time for the Jackson family to enjoy the new Hermitage "under their vine and their fig tree," in the biblical image for peace and retirement.[19]

CHAPTER 9

Out of the West

Home at last in 1821, the Jacksons could enjoy their fine new house, completed after two years of construction. After having lived so long in their conglomeration of log buildings, they now enjoyed a house of some elegance, described by Andrew as a gift to Rachel but also a symbol of his arrival as a national personage—famous, but not wealthy. Their home was large and respectable enough, but far from being a mansion. The site, chosen by Rachel, was over the top of a rise near the site of the old blockhouse. Reflecting her modest character, it did not stand atop the hill, dominating the landscape when visitors arrived.

The new Hermitage was a large two-story Federal-style building, red brick with a wide central hall graced by a simple dogleg staircase. There were four rooms on each floor, the upper floor housing bedrooms for their boys and guests; the lower, two parlors, a dining room, and the Jacksons' bedroom. During the sweltering summertime, the doors and windows in the house were kept open, and the central hall, with both front and back doors, made a breezy sitting area.

The furniture in the house was the comfortable sort carried by middling companies in eastern cities. The one note of true elegance was imported French wallpaper in the entry hall, chosen by Rachel. Printed by hand from woodblocks at the Dufour firm in Paris, these papers were very expensive and highly prized, more art prints than conventional wallpaper. It took more than 2,000 woodblocks and 85 separate colors to create the Hermitage paper. Its colors are strong and glowing, predominantly greens and blues, giving the impression when standing in the hall of being inside a painting.

The theme of Rachel's paper was Telemachus on Calypso's Isle, one of the adventures of a young man in search of his father, Odysseus, who had been absent for twenty years. Popularized as an anti-authoritarian novel, *The Adventures of Telemachus,* by the French writer François Fénelon, the story originated in the *Odyssey.* The happy ending in which father and son reunite, return to Ithaca, defeat the rival claimants for the throne and the hand of Telemachus's mother, Penelope, and reunite the family was just the sort of story to appeal to the Jacksons, with their sense of family and their belief in lasting love.

Rachel's taste is also shown in the new formal garden, designed and planted by William Frost, an itinerant English gardener. The garden was her special joy, protected from livestock by a wooden fence. She ordered geraniums, daisies, wallflowers, and polyanthus from a nursery in Cincinnati for the garden. It also included old roses, peonies, iris, and crape myrtle. She loved making little posies from her garden for departing female guests, sending them on their way with a keepsake from the Hermitage.[1]

Many of the Jacksons' wards had grown up by now, and several of them attended the United States Military Academy at West Point, the source of an excellent free education, with their appointments secured by their Uncle Andrew. Their favorite ward and nephew, Andrew Jackson Donelson, who had lived at the Hermitage for most of his life, graduated second in his class from the Academy. He served for two years as Jackson's aide-de-camp during the Seminole War in 1817–1818 before resigning his commission. When they returned home from Florida, this Andrew studied law at Transylvania University in Kentucky, but he frequently returned home during the holidays.

Permanently in residence were the "two little Andrews," their adopted son, Andrew Jr., and Andrew Jackson Hutchings, as well as the Creek orphan Lyncoya. At first apparently intended as a sort of body servant for Andrew Jr., Lyncoya had become part of the family, though not quite on a social level with the other boys.

To its citizens, Nashville seemed quite sophisticated when a Frenchman opened a dancing academy where the Andrews learned everything from cotillions to hornpipes. All the boys attended school locally, but neither Hutchings nor Lyncoya cared for the discipline of the classroom. Lyncoya always remained a child of the forest who would have preferred living with his own people.

Rachel couldn't have been happier to be back at home with her family and friends. As she had written from Pensacola to her brother, she believed fervently "that Tennessee is the best Country [in the United States]."[2] Nashville was growing into a fine town with a population of nearly 3,500. A stone bridge from the public square across the Cumberland River was nearly complete, and steamboats chugging both up- and downriver docked regularly at the port to take on cotton and other crops and deliver manufactured goods. With

the growth of the town, the area's natural springs were not sufficient to provide pure water for everyone, so a municipal water system
was in the works. Many streets were paved, and oil lamps had been
installed along them. One drawback to the increased population for
Evangelical Christians was the corresponding growth of gambling
dens and tippling-houses, which the religious found to be public
nuisances as they sold liquor on Sunday.[3]

No doubt Rachel was dismayed by the Sabbath-breaking taverns,
but her husband's health was her main concern. He had come peril-
ously near a complete breakdown on their return from Florida, and
she believed he needed rest and relaxation to recover. Twenty years
earlier, Andrew had written to her "how precious health is, and how
carefull we ought to be, to acquire it," advising her to let business stop
rather than succumb to fatigue or ill health.[4] Unfortunately, he had
never taken his own advice, and it had been years since he enjoyed a
pain-free day. Every letter he wrote mentioned his poor health, including debilitating chest pains, lung congestion, a persistent cough, rheu-
matism, hemorrhages, abscesses, fatigue, and other ills.

Jackson had truly meant to pass his retirement quietly at the
Hermitage, tending to his own affairs, entertaining guests, and
sitting quietly by the fireplace with his beloved wife, chatting and
smoking their pipes, their favorite evening pastime. Rachel, like
many western women, regularly smoked a pipe. Taking snuff had
been common among eastern women, including Dolley Madison,
in an earlier period, but now using any form of tobacco was considered a repulsive and unladylike habit. As with most things, though,
Rachel continued to follow her own convictions, savoring her pipe
and unconcerned by the new straitlaced social mores.

John Sevier (Courtesy of the Tennessee State Library and Archives)

Charles Hammond (Cincinnati Museum Center—Cincinnati Historical Society Library)

Peggy Eaton (The Hermitage: Home of President Andrew Jackson, Nashville, Tennessee)

John Henry Eaton (State Archives of Florida)

Andrew Jackson Donelson (The
Hermitage: Home of President Andrew
Jackson, Nashville, Tennessee)

Emily Tennessee Donelson (The
Hermitage: Home of President Andrew
Jackson, Nashville, Tennessee)

Andrew Jackson Jr.
(The Hermitage:
Home of President
Andrew Jackson,
Nashville, Tennessee)

Old Hannah, the
Jacksons' housekeeper
(The Hermitage: Home
of President Andrew
Jackson, Nashville,
Tennessee)

Main room of a typical two-story log
house (Courtesy of the Iennessee State
Library and Archives)

The first Hermitage, a three-room log
house where the Jacksons lived from
1804 until 1821 (The Hermitage:
Home of President Andrew Jackson,
Nashville, Tennessee)

Frontier log cabin
(Library of Congress)

Hermitage kitchen
and slave quarters
(The Hermitage:
Home of President
Andrew Jackson,
Nashville, Tennessee)

French wallpaper
at the present
Hermitage,
selected by
Rachel Jackson
(The Hermitage:
Home of
President
Andrew Jackson,
Nashville,
Tennessee)

The massacre at Fort Mimms (author's collection)

The Battle of New Orleans (Library of Congress)

"The President's Levee," the crowd celebrating Jackson's 1829 inauguration (Library of Congress)

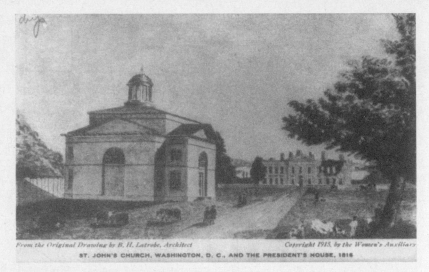

The presidential mansion, 1816, two years after the British burned Washington (Library of Congress)

The tombs of Rachel and Andrew Jackson (The Hermitage: Home of President Andrew Jackson, Nashville, Tennessee)

As Jackson wrote to Andrew Donelson, "my sole ambition is to pass to my grave in retirement."[5] His competitive disposition, however, made that fate all but impossible, especially once he became convinced that President Monroe, whom he had previously admired, was dishonest and hypocritical. Corruption was rampant in the national government, he believed, and newspaper investigations bore out his opinion as they uncovered evidence of dishonesty at all levels.

At the same time that he was becoming convinced that the government must be returned to its early republican purity, admirers began sounding him out about running for president. His combination of military fame, personal honesty, and egalitarian beliefs would make him a formidable contender. In the elections of both 1816 and 1820, he had been mentioned as a possible candidate, but he had made it clear that he wasn't interested because he was pursuing his military career and supporting Monroe.

But in 1824 the long Republican—and Virginian—ascendancy had fallen apart. Monroe had followed Madison, who had followed Jefferson, each serving as secretary of state in the previous administration and being selected as the party's presidential candidate by a congressional caucus. Given the Republican lock on Congress, winning in the caucus was tantamount to winning the election.

Now there were rumblings and grumblings of discontent. The latest would-be nominees, Republicans to a man, didn't want to wait patiently in line for their turns in power. John Quincy Adams was Monroe's secretary of state, but he had several drawbacks as a candidate. Brilliant, able, and likeable in private company, he had no social charm and offended many people with his icy demeanor. Too, he was a New Englander, son of the Federalist John Adams, and suspected by many Republicans of holding aristocratic principles. Wildly impatient to push Adams aside and scoop up the nomination for himself was William Harris Crawford of Georgia, longtime secretary of the treasury. Henry Clay of Kentucky, speaker of the House, had high ambitions, and Congressman John C. Calhoun of South Carolina, just turned forty and considered too young for such an important post, thought he had a chance.

Both within and outside the party, many observers believed the caucus system was another form of corruption, anointing a guaranteed successor and giving the voters no real opportunity to choose a candidate. The views of the candidates tended to vary depending on how likely they were to be chosen by the caucus; Crawford defended the caucus system because he seemed to have a lock on the congressional vote. Jackson was militantly opposed to the caucus because it ignored the will of most citizens and gave too much power to eastern states.

The dark horse that all the politicians dreaded and tried to keep out of the race was Jackson. With his broken health and official retirement at the end of 1821, it seemed that they would get their wish. And yet, no one quite knew what he would do. A Tennessee friend, Samuel Overton, had written to Jackson in August 1821, while he was serving as governor of Florida, that if he were willing, he would be the favorite for the Pennsylvania party nomination. These party votes, held in many states, were not binding, but they did inform congressmen of the electorate's preferred nominees. In Pennsylvania, party leaders had been considering the matter, and they were satisfied "that you [Jackson] have more popularity, and greater claims to the office [of president], than any other individual who can be presented to the people of the United States."[6]

A man as opinionated and emotional as Jackson brought all his passions to bear on politics. He wrote several letters to friends about his judgment of the potential candidates. In December he wrote that he planned to support Adams unless Calhoun should come forward. As secretary of state, Adams had supported Jackson's incursions into Florida and had negotiated the Adams-Onís Treaty acquiring the Spanish colony. Jackson declared his high opinion of Adams's "Talents, virtue, and integrity." Crawford, on the other hand, who had worked behind the scenes to censure his actions, he abhorred, declaring "I would support the Devil first."[7]

In January 1822 the *Nashville Gazette* floated the idea that Jackson could be a winning candidate. Still not taking the possibility very seriously, Jackson was nonetheless flattered and began to think that perhaps it wasn't completely far-fetched if the nation needed his services again as it had in 1814.[8] As they sensed that Jackson was wavering in his refusal, his supporters took heart and pressed on.

By that summer, Tennessee state legislators decided to push through a recommendation of Andrew Jackson as their nominee for president. Being told by his friends of their plan, Jackson did not attend the meeting in Murfreesborough, the capital, to avoid any appearance of seeking office. On July 27, the Tennessee House nominated him and was followed by the Senate on August 3, 1822. Their resolution declared that they considered him "as a person the most worthy, & suitable to be the next President of our union." His protégé Sam Houston immediately sat down to write him the news. Houston was elated by this success because "The Canker worms have been (already too long) gnawing at the very core & vitals of our Government & corruption stalks abroad."[9]

Three days later, by August 6, Jackson had decided to run for the presidency. Clearly he had discussed the matter with Rachel, and just as clearly she was opposed. Such a decision ran counter to all her wishes for a long and peaceful retirement. As she later wrote to a sister-in-law, "I saw from the first it was wrong for him to fatigue Himself with Such an important office. Even if he obtains it, in the End it will profit Him nothing. Mr. Monroe is going out poor & much Dissattisfyed."[10]

Nonetheless, her husband was determined both because he was ambitious and because of his beliefs about republican government. The public ideal for all presidential candidates was George Washington, who had refused to seek the office but accepted a unanimous vote from the electors. As the first president, however, Washington had stood alone in the admiration of the country. Since then, while pretending to be above sordid politics, candidates privately connived and schemed, snarling like dogs fighting over a bone.

Jackson genuinely believed that he had never been an applicant for any office, conveniently forgetting his politicking for command of the Tennessee state militia. To Andrew Donelson, he declared that he would follow "the same independent, republican course" in this election as he had in the past. If the people freely chose him, then he, like "every individual composing the republic, when they people require his services, is bound to render it." In other words, if the people needed him, he would accept their call.[11]

Over the next year, his correspondence snowballed as he and his supporters analyzed the moves of his opponents. His stance of inaction was not quite perfect since he frequently gave advice and suggestions to his adherents. The Republicans of Pennsylvania were among his strongest supporters, but they couldn't mount a winning campaign unless they were assured that he would accept the presidency. In February 1823 Jackson made a pledge to party leaders that he would serve if elected. He was now completely committed.

At the same time, having ignored his wife's wishes by getting involved in politics, Andrew donated some of the Hermitage land in 1823 to build a neighborhood church. He and his neighbor Edward Ward, a Presbyterian elder, put up most of the money for the neat little brick building, which was completed in January 1824. Rachel had longed for a church close at hand because weather or illness sometimes interfered with their drive into town to attend First Presbyterian, and he wanted to please her. Although not yet a formal church member, Jackson was a thoroughgoing believer. During the construction project, Ward confided to Jackson that Nashville clergymen supported the general because they believed "he will come out more decidedly in favour of religion than any other of the candidates."[12]

The political landscape changed dramatically in the fall of 1823. William H. Crawford, the undoubted frontrunner, suffered a debilitating stroke in September and was unable to attend cabinet meetings for several months. Even though his supporters continued working for his election, voters at large had little faith in his ability to perform as president. At about the same time, two of Jackson's closest advisers, Senator John Henry Eaton and William B. Lewis, warned him of their concerns about Tennessee's other senator, John Williams, who had often criticized Jackson. They feared that opposition from his home state could be very damaging to a successful campaign. After canvassing for a candidate strong enough to unseat the popular Williams, they urged Jackson to allow them to put up his name. Convinced by their arguments, he agreed and was elected to the Senate in October 1823.

The sudden election upset all the Jacksons' calculations. Andrew would need to leave for Washington within the month and travel fast to take his seat in the Senate. There was no hope of making arrangements in that time for the care of the Hermitage and the boys and thus no hope that Rachel could go along. Just days before he left on November 11, he wrote John Overton that "Mrs. J. is more disconsolate than I ever knew her before, & I u. ssure you I leave home with more reluctance than I ever did in my life. It was so unlooked for, unwished for, & so inconsistant with my feelings."[13]

One bit of good news was that Andrew Donelson had returned to live at the Hermitage and so was available to help run the place and keep his aunt company. Several nieces and young friends of the family came for long visits, as did any minister visiting the neighborhood. The three boys were usually a pleasure, and Jackson frequently admonished them to obey Rachel and not to cause her worry. But nothing could take the place of her husband. None of her letters from this period are extant, but judging from his replies, she was miserable at this sudden turn of events. On November 28, from Staunton, Virginia, he wrote about the gratifying welcome he had received all along the road: "were you only with me I could be satisfied—But should providence once more permit us to meet, I am solemnly resolved, with the permission of heaven, never to seperate, or be seperated from you in this world."[14]

Arriving in Washington on December 3, Jackson soon joined John Eaton and Richard Call as boarders at the house of Rhoda and William O'Neale and their daughters, whom he regarded as a worthy family. He was very comfortably situated with his intimates and the O'Neales, spending pleasant evenings while their married daughter, Margaret Timberlake, played and sang. The family's

Methodism was quite compatible with his Presbyterianism. He went to church every Sunday, as did Mrs. O'Neale.

Soon after his arrival, Eleanor Parke Custis Lewis, known as Nelly, Martha Washington's granddaughter and the Washingtons' adopted daughter, presented him with a china plate that had been used by the Washingtons at birthday feasts. Jackson's former ward Edward George Washington Butler was a friend of the Lewis family and was soon to become a suitor and then the husband of Nelly Lewis's daughter, Frances Parke Lewis. But apart from the family connection to Jackson, all the Custis family abhorred Jefferson and other Republican Party leaders. During George Washington's presidency, Jefferson and Madison had attacked Washington anonymously in partisan newspapers as a way of damaging his secretary of the treasury and their political opponent, Alexander Hamilton. The Custises had never forgiven these attacks. For the first time since 1800, they saw a candidate they could respect.[15]

In January, Nelly Lewis's brother, George Washington Parke Custis, like his sister adopted by the Washingtons, stage-managed an even grander gift to Jackson. Presenting the military hero with a pocket spyglass used by Washington during the Revolution, he had also encouraged the gift of Washington's pistols. Owned by another branch of the family, these pistols had been a gift from the marquis de Lafayette. Trying to avoid seeming vain, Jackson was swept away by the honor of receiving these gifts belonging to *"the mighty chieftain, the father of his country, the immortal Washington."*[16]

Many friends had inquired after Rachel and sent their greetings. He wrote to his wife weekly, but he missed her terribly: "This seperation has been more severe to me than any other...we must travel together, & live together whilst permitted to remain Tennants [tenants] here below." Before leaving the city, he planned to book her rooms for the following autumn.[17]

Jackson joked about the response of Washingtonians to him. His only visit to the capital had been eight years before, and at that time he had remained only six weeks. "I am told the opinion of those whose minds were prepared to see me with a Tomahawk in one hand, & a scalping knife in the other has greatly changed—and I am getting on very smoothly." Many easterners did indeed suppose the Tennessean to be a savage, thinking him "unfit for civil life; and many here, strangers to me, had expected, I understand, to see a most uncivilised, unchristian man when they beheld me."[18]

Far more disturbing were the rumors about the Jacksons' marriage that started to surface in late December 1823 in Pennsylvania, then in Ohio and the District of Columbia. Like most rumors, they were lurid and exaggerated. Evoking Andrew's reputation for violence, gossips claimed that he had driven Rachel's husband away and then lived with her for several years before she was divorced. Still imagining the general to be an outside choice, his political enemies didn't yet bother to go into print with these charges.[19]

Whispers were moving through Washington society, and people were trying to find out the truth. In February 1824, Nelly Lewis wrote to a friend in Philadelphia about the Jacksons' marriage. At her request, a family connection, Congressman George Tucker, had looked into the matter. "I am happy to assure you my dear Friend that Gen'l Jackson is not the wretch he is represented." Tucker had conversed with several persons "of great respectability & well acquainted with every circumstance, within the last week." Her account of the true version of the Jacksons' story was wildly inaccurate, casting Rachel as a child bride and Andrew as a longtime family friend. Nonetheless, it satisfied her of the respectability of the couple.

Nelly added "that the circumstances of this case gained Jackson the esteem & approbation of the whole neighborhood in which they occur'd." James Gadsden had assured her that Mrs. Jackson was an excellent woman. She concluded that "these are most honorable & very correct evidences. I shall like him [Jackson] or Mr. Calhoun. I think them the most honest & pure patriots."[20]

When the Pennsylvania party convention chose Jackson as their candidate in a landslide on March 4, toppling Calhoun and Crawford, he became a major candidate. His rivals immediately started looking for dirt. The following week, Eaton wrote to John Overton in Nashville looking for a possible defense for the circumstances of the Jacksons' marriage. As he put it, until now his opponents "have not dreaded him; but now seemingly a most prominent rival, they are bringing all their batteries to bear against him." Jackson was disgusted by personal attacks, urging his friends to support him on his "own merits and not by destroying the charector of others."[21]

Since Eaton knew about these early stirrings of scandal, Jackson surely knew as well. None of his letters to Rachel back home breathe a word about the danger to their reputations. Perhaps he told her when he arrived at the Hermitage. Or perhaps he kept silent to avoid worrying her. At this time Jackson did not believe that his rivals would stoop to smearing a man's wife.

Newspapers supporting the other candidates had so far contented themselves with noting Jackson's lack of executive experience in civil government and his impatience with rules. Now that he was a real threat, they began to explore the themes that would be the basis of savage campaign attacks. Lack of civil experience was expanded to include suspicions about his role as a "military chieftain," that is, a military leader who might overturn the law, even the Constitution. The specter of dictatorship by a victorious general, à la Napoleon, loomed large in their columns. His ungovernable temper and violent actions were explored at length, including the duel with Charles Dickinson, the executions of mutinous militiamen, the declaration of martial law in New Orleans, the jailing of a judge there, the execution of two British subjects in Florida, and the imprisonment of the former Spanish governor.[22]

Despite this barrage, Eaton remained very positive about the chances of Jackson's election. Along with general news about health, society, and church attendance, Eaton wrote to Rachel that his (Eaton's) head was full of "politics bills laws and such like trash" that wouldn't entertain her. However, since "there is a very strong probability that ere long you may be required to come into our political Corps and join with us in the great affairs of the nation," perhaps he should begin to tell her "all about the little workings, management & intrigue" in Congress.[23]

Jackson was well aware that his enemies were trying to goad him into a public outburst that would prove their point about his unsuitability for the presidency. In contrast to his previous stint in the Senate, this time he attended sessions regularly and gave his attention to business, comporting himself with great dignity. Not once did he lose his temper, no matter the provocation. He also made "peace all around" with men whom he had been at odds with for years. Jackson wrote: "This has destroyed the stronghold of my enemies who denounced me as a man of revengefull Temper and of great rashness."[24]

In one of the friendly letters John Eaton wrote to Rachel, he remarked on the great pleasure it would give her to know that her husband had settled all his old quarrels. Jackson returned from an evening engagement to add a postscript: "It is a pleasing subject to me that I am now at peace with all the world."[25]

The most important of these reconciliations was that with his former aide and friend Thomas Hart Benton, now an important and influential senator from Missouri. From nearby seats in the Senate chamber, at social events, and at the president's mansion, the two made cautious approaches to mending their quarrel. Finally, with a firm handshake, they agreed to let the past go and resume their old friendship. Benton became one of Jackson's most reliable political supporters.

His brother Jesse, of course, was another matter. His foolish duel and humiliation had been the source of the original quarrel. Jesse continued to blackguard Jackson, even publishing an anti-Jackson/Adams, pro-Crawford pamphlet. His target wrote laughingly about the efforts of the "Redoubtable *hero, of Squating memory.*"[26] No wonder Jesse hated Jackson until his death. Enmity is far more bearable than contempt. But Thomas Benton remained Jackson's enduring ally.

Although he was forced by his political ambitions to take some part in the hectic social life of the capital, its stylized minuet was not at all to Jackson's western taste. As a rising political force, he received hundreds of visits from his friends, his enemies, his admirers, his detractors, the curious, the ambitious, and practically everyone else in Washington.

An elaborate protocol governed the whole business of calling, including who visited first. If the person wasn't at home, the visitor left a calling card, preferably engraved. He or she might also write a short message, such as "General Jackson for Mr. and Mrs. Adams." And then, every call from an equal required a return call. As Andrew complained to Rachel, "there is nothing done here but Vissitting & *carding each other.* you know how much I was disgusted with those scenes when you & I were here, it has increased instead of diminishing."[27]

He refused most invitations to evening parties except those given by the wives of such friendly cabinet members as Adams and Calhoun. On January 8, 1824, John Quincy and Louisa Adams gave a ball in his honor on the anniversary of his victory at the Battle of New Orleans. With Rachel at the Hermitage, Andrew restricted his own entertaining to men. On March 15, he had a large dinner party on his fifty-seventh birthday. Presided over by John Eaton and Richard Call, the guest list of Washington leaders included friends like Edward Livingston of New Orleans, Adams, and Calhoun. Even Henry Clay, whose scorn for Jackson was reciprocated with interest, was there.[28]

Loneliness continued to be a theme of Andrew's letters. Although he was very busy, he wrote that "the attentions I have recd. loose all their relish I assure you, whilst you are absent." He continued to fret over her misery as well. Although she had promised to bear up in his absence, she was finding it all but impossible. He reminded her that her health depended on "keeping your mind calm & at ease."[29] Neither was made any happier by his continued stay in Washington. Important matters were before the Senate, including a tariff bill and recompense to Rachel's father's estate for surveys made long ago. Jackson voted for a strong tariff, unpopular in the South and West, and payment to the Donelson heirs, both of which passed before he set off for home, traveling as fast as possible.

When Andrew finally arrived at the Hermitage on June 4, Rachel was "rejoised to see him in his own house after an absence of nearly seven monthes." To a cousin, she lamented, "Oh the time was long." This was their longest separation since the War of 1812, and it had been hard on both of them. During his absence, the little neighbor-hood church, now called the Hermitage Church, had been dedicated and held occasional services when traveling preachers were available. But, to Rachel's deep regret, they still lacked a full-time minister.[30]

Rachel's faith was the bedrock of her life. Joining with a congregation in prayer, being touched by emotional sermons, discussing the Gospel with other believers—these things kept her going. Camp meetings were still a feature of evangelical life in Tennessee, and she had begun attending each summer for the refreshment of her spirit and the camaraderie of the faithful.

The summer passed quickly as Andrew corresponded regularly with friends and admirers. His campaign gained momentum across the nation. From being an outside hope, he had become the favorite in the race. The mundane affairs of farm and business also had to be taken care of, and there were many visits from family and friends who had missed Jackson during his long absence.

A very happy family event was scheduled for September 16. Their ward Andrew Jackson Donelson was to marry his lovely seventeen-year-old first cousin, Emily Tennessee Donelson. That very day, unfortunately, another of their first cousins, Rachel Donelson Donelson, died. She was the elder sister of Andrew Jackson Jr., and her husband was Emily's elder brother. In the heavily intertwined Donelson family, any death reverberated beyond simple sorrow. Since the minister was already there, their elders decided they should go ahead with the ceremony, but it was mournful indeed.[31]

Despite all her resistance and uneasiness about Andrew's course, Rachel had no doubt that he was the best man for the job. Attacks on him infuriated her, and she believed that all their friends should support him or be considered traitors. James Jackson (no relation), a longtime friend who had done business with Andrew for years, disagreed with his pro-tariff vote and said so in a newspaper. Rachel was appalled, declaring that "he is gilty of black ingratitude to one of the best friends he ever had."[32]

She dreaded the winter in Washington, during which the next president would be elected: "At my time of life it is disagreeable." But she had determined to accompany her husband. The choice was simple: "I must go with him or be as unhappy as I was last winter and how could I bare it."[33]

Unlike Andrew's trip the year before, the Jacksons traveled in some style with their party, which included the newlywed Donelsons and several servants. Andrew Donelson had become his uncle's secretary, and Emily would be company for her aunt. The two little Andrews had been left behind to attend school. The group steamed up the Ohio River to Wheeling, Virginia, where they disembarked and boarded their private coach drawn by a team of gray horses. Their trip was stylish but exhausting. After twenty-eight days of continuous travel, they arrived in Washington on December 7 at 11 AM.

They stayed at the fashionable Gadsby's Hotel, at the northeast corner of I and 21st streets facing Pennsylvania Avenue. Besides the Donelsons, John Eaton and Richard Call and his new wife also stayed there, making life at the hotel congenial to them all. What a change Rachel encountered in the nine years since she had last seen the capital. All the public buildings had been rebuilt since the British conflagration. The president's mansion, beginning to be called the White House because of the whitewash coating its stone walls, was more impressive than ever since the addition of the South Portico with its stately columns. There were still acres of vacant land, unpaved streets, and mosquito-ridden marshes along the river's edge. But to the Jacksons and the Donelsons from little Nashville, it was quite an impressive city.

Two weeks after their arrival, Rachel wrote to Elizabeth Kingsley declaring it the first day she could call her own since her arrival "in this great city." She was happy to report that there were many churches and able ministers, and that she had enjoyed the services at the Second Presbyterian Church, whose minister was "a plain, good preacher."[34]

The expense and social whirl in the city upset her, especially "the extravagance...in dressing and running to parties." At the Hermitage she was accustomed to a peaceful existence. Now she felt beset: "Oh, my dear friend, how shall I get through this bustle. There are not less than fifty to one hundred persons calling in a day." She enlarged on the theme of the demands on the time of Mrs. General Jackson. "The play-actors sent me a letter, requesting my countenance to them. No. A ticket to balls and parties. No, not one....Indeed, Mr. Jackson encourages me in my course. He recommends it to me to be steadfast."[35]

Andrew reiterated her theme in a letter to John Coffee about the constant bustle "during the Holidays, although Mrs. J. & myself goes to no parties." They avoided the grand crushes, but they did dine out and go to tea on occasion. The young Donelsons thoroughly enjoyed themselves at parties, dances, and the theater while "Mrs. J. & myself [were] at home smoking our pipe." Like many westerners, Rachel and Andrew enjoyed smoking clay or corncob pipes, sometimes each with their own pipe, sometimes passing a common pipe back and forth. Money was a constant worry, what with the expenses at Gadsby's and the high prices of everything in Washington.[36]

An unexpected blessing for Jackson's candidacy was the arrival in America of General Lafayette, a hero of the Revolution and the sole surviving general from that era. Invited by President Monroe to visit the United States as the guest of the nation, he arrived in the port of New York in August 1824. His visit of more than a year became a celebration of liberty with every wide spot in the road eager to welcome the visiting hero. The amazing hoopla reflected the deep desire of Americans to hark back to an earlier, simpler era when, they imagined, the nation was free of corruption and vicious political infighting.

Andrew Jackson was thrilled by Lafayette's visit. Like himself, Lafayette was a military leader who had taken whatever action the situation required. In early September, he had written the hero, welcoming him to America. Lafayette had soon responded, stating his determination to meet Jackson before leaving the United States.

In December, they first met on the entry to the stairs at Gadsby's Hotel, where Lafayette was also staying. Jackson had set off to pay the first visit to Lafayette, while Lafayette was on the same errand to him. They immediately struck up a friendship, based on "the emotion of revolutionary feeling," when they had their accidental encounter and afterward spent many hours in one another's company. Considering the adulation that Lafayette received throughout the United States, it seemed hypocritical for his opponents to criticize Jackson for being a military hero.

Rachel was impressed by Lafayette as well: "I am delighted with him. All the attentions, all the parties he goes to, never appear to have any effect on him." He had "the happy talent" of recalling anyone he had ever met. She was especially impressed by his ability to go to every party every night and remain healthy.[37]

◦∞◦

Jackson had duly taken his seat in the Senate in December 1824. Election returns began trickling in, and it soon became clear that he had received a plurality of the popular votes, but not a winning majority. The votes of the Electoral College were made public long before they were officially counted by Congress in February 1825. In December, everyone knew that Andrew Jackson had received 99 votes, John Quincy Adams, 84, the debilitated William H. Crawford, 41, and Henry Clay, 37—as with the popular vote, a plurality for Jackson, but not a majority. To Jackson's delight, Clay was out of the race. Only the top three candidates would be considered by Congress, as specified by the Twelfth Amendment.

But Jackson had another worry, though not yet a pressing one. One of his supporters, Charles Pendleton Tutt, a Virginia planter, had written to warn him that his political opponents intended to publicize Rachel's divorce. On January 9, Jackson replied that he was well aware that his enemies had no honor, "but that they would attempt to disturb the repose of an innocent female in her declining years is a species of wickedness that I did not suppose would be attempted."[38]

Nonetheless, he wrote that he had no fear of any investigation. "I as well know how to defend my & her charecter as I have the rights of my country." He still didn't believe that any sustained attack would be made against his wife. He thought of these threats as a mere ploy against him: "I am aware of the plan of my enemies, to endeavour to exite & provoke me."[39]

Behind the scenes, Henry Clay had no intention of allowing his western enemy to scoop up the prize that he had lost. As speaker of the House he had tremendous influence. Crawford might have been his choice, but poor health made him an untenable option. Instead, through friends, he began to make overtures to Adams. All his adult life, Clay had lusted after the presidency, and, based on the evidence of the last twenty-four years, he believed that being secretary of state was the natural path to it. Clever as he was, he had not yet realized that the election of 1824 had altered presidential politics forever.

Of the other candidates, Adams most respected and liked Andrew Jackson. He thought he would be a fine vice president. Implicit in all his thinking was that he (Adams) was the man for the job. He had spent long years in distinguished government service; he had been a brilliant secretary of state. He was the best educated and most grandly visionary of the candidates. By his own calculations, he *should* be president.

Adams had always disliked and distrusted Henry Clay, frequently making disparaging remarks about the speaker in his diary. After Jackson's birthday party, he fumed that Clay "is so ardent, dogmatical, and overbearing that it is extremely difficult to preserve the temper of friendly society with him." Clay was also well known as a gambler who loved the high-stakes risk of cards. Regarding Clay's presidential hopes, Adams wrote: "He plays brag [a bluffing card game], as he has done all his life."[40]

But Adams also knew his only hope of becoming president was through Clay's maneuvers in the House. Beginning in mid-December 1824, Clay's men began dropping by Adams's office, letting him know that Clay was disposed to favor him for president even though they denied having any direct authority for their remarks. They wanted to know Adams's disposition toward Clay. Diplomatically, he said that he "harbored no hostility against him."[41] Negotiations continued as Adams agreed that, as a representative of the West, Clay deserved an important position in the new administration.

Finally, on January 9, 1825, Clay made an appointment to visit Adams for a long talk about their political differences. As a result, Clay decided to support Adams even though the Kentucky legislature sent instructions that the state's vote should go to Andrew

Jackson. Clay declared that "he should consider the elevation of the Hero as the greatest calamity which could befall the country."[42]

Everyone knew something was going on, and Jackson was becoming more anxious and fearful about the election with each passing day. On January 23 he wrote scathingly about Washington politicians to John Coffee, declaring that there is "nothing of pure principles of friendship in these crowds" and that "hypocrisy and hollow heartedness predominates in this great city."[43] The following day, Henry Clay announced his support for John Quincy Adams.

Not knowing how far Clay would go to keep Jackson out of office, many people still believed that the Hero would prevail. On January 26, Nelly Lewis wrote, "The City is full of strangers & very gay. It appears *most probable* that Old Hickory will gain the day, but it is not certain. *Madme. H.* is an excellent plain *motherly* woman, but by no means elegant. I intend to teach her the *graces,* what think you of it. Will it entitle me to rank with *Hercules of old.*"[44] The Jacksons would certainly have been flabbergasted if she had made such an attempt.

Meanwhile, Rachel didn't allow remarks about her elegance or lack thereof worry her. Enjoying her Presbyterian church, she and a religious friend went to church services twice on Sundays and to prayer meetings twice on Thursdays. The rest of the week she spent, as Andrew did, "in receiving and paying vissits & so much for our time."[45]

On February 9, John Quincy Adams was elected president on the first ballot. In an unresolved election such as this, each state's congressional delegation has one vote. There were then twenty-four states in the Union. Clay's persuasive powers were amazing. Adams received thirteen votes, including that of Kentucky, where he had not received a single vote in the Electoral College. Jackson received seven votes and Crawford four. John C. Calhoun became vice president. When the count was finished, John Randolph of Virginia supposedly remarked, "it was impossible to win the game, gentlemen, the cards were stacked." Although he had been suspicious, the actual event made Jackson wild. He wrote to John Overton that "the voice of the people of the west have been disregarded, and demagogues barter them as sheep in the shambles."[46]

That evening at the presidential mansion was Mrs. Monroe's drawing room, as these events were known. Despite a heavy snowstorm, the reception was a crush with everyone excited about the electoral results and their implications—and excited about seeing Adams and Jackson meet. As a matter of public appearances, they both had to be there. Louisa Adams was with her husband, but Rachel Jackson was at the hotel, having been sick for several days. Early in the evening, there were so many people that it was impossible to move.

Nelly Lewis was there with a party that included Lafayette and his son. She wrote that "[we] had the pleasure to see our candidate greater in defeat, even, than when his prospects were most flattering. . . . When Jackson congratulated Adams, the latter blushed to the *top of* his *head*, as well he might." Adams saw it otherwise: "General Jackson was there, and we shook hands. He was altogether placid and courteous."[47] He would soon get over this false impression.

Friends of William Crawford returned to his house after the drawing room to report on the momentous encounter. Crawford thought that Jackson's handshake was the right thing to do, "but the congratulatory speech might have been omitted. I like honesty in all things." Everyone united in despising Clay, "walking about with exultation and a smiling face." Several people pointed to Adams, whispering, "there is our *'Clay President.'*"[48]

Demonstrating his lack of any political instinct, Adams almost immediately asked Clay to serve as his secretary of state. With Clay's acceptance on February 14, Jackson and many others were convinced that this was the suspected "corrupt bargain" in action, Clay's payoff for securing the presidency for Adams. As Jackson raved, "so you see the *Judas* of the West has closed the contract and will receive the thirty pieces of silver."[49] He had always respected and admired Adams, but now he hated him with all the considerable venom he was capable of.

The Jacksons still remained in Washington because Andrew wanted to oppose Clay's appointment to the cabinet. Without his permission, on February 25 the *Nashville Gazette* announced that Andrew Jackson would run for president again in 1828. Certainly he would run, but he didn't want to appear to seek the office. He wasn't the only one who thought the election had been stolen. People throughout the West were indignant.

On March 3 Congress adjourned, and the following day John Quincy Adams and John C. Calhoun (following two sleepless nights) were sworn in. Adams read his speech. After the inauguration, a crowd came to the Adams house to congratulate him; then he went to the presidential mansion, where he was again congratulated. That night he attended the inaugural ball at Carusi's spacious assembly rooms at the corner of 11th and C streets.[50] Of course, the Jacksons attended none of these events.

The Senate was called back into session, presided over by the new vice president. Adams sent them his list of nominees for the cabinet, most of them holdovers from the Monroe administration.

On March 7, all of them were approved unanimously, except for Henry Clay. The vote was 27 in favor, 14 opposed, 7 absent. Jackson and Eaton were among the nays. Adams continued to be blind to any impropriety in his appointment of Clay. Instead, he saw the opposition votes as all politically motivated, noting, "This was the first act of the opposition from the stump which is to be carried on against the Administration under the banners of General Jackson."[51] Like Jackson, Adams had turned against his former friend and returned his hatred.

Three days later, the Jacksons and the Donelsons left Washington, stopping in Baltimore and then Elkton for a series of entertainments in Andrew's honor. Their steamboat was detained again at Cincinnati for a further tribute. Finally on April 13 they reached the Hermitage. Jackson spent the entire spring in meetings and correspondence with supporters, planning their strategy for the next election while Rachel immersed herself in what she considered real life—family, friends, and church.

General Lafayette, making a lightning tour of the southern and western states, arrived in Nashville on May 4. His goal was to visit every one of the twenty-four states, and he did it despite age and infirmity. Everyone wanted to meet the hero of the Revolution, and his two-day stay in Nashville was another tribute to Jackson's importance.

Lafayette was met at the dock by a welcoming committee headed by Jackson. As usual at every stop he made, there was a parade through the streets, followed by public speeches. Immense crowds—cheering and shouting loud huzzahs—thronged every public appearance. Following a public banquet and a Masonic reception, Lafayette spent the night in town. The next day, again under Jackson's chaperonage, he reviewed the militia, visited the Nashville Academy and Cumberland College, and then went to lunch at the elegant new Hermitage, where he was received warmly by Rachel. There Jackson presented him with Washington's pistols, which he had just received in the capital. After an evening ball in Nashville, the indefatigable Lafayette boarded his steamboat and set off the next morning, heading for the Ohio River.[52]

This was the sort of public event at which the charismatic Jackson shone. He was genuinely fond and admiring of Lafayette, but he also knew the boost this visit gave to his campaign. Newspapers covered every day of Lafayette's tour, reporting everything that happened, everyone who was present, and every word spoken, down to the last after-dinner toast. These stories put Jackson in the spotlight all over the nation, one hero welcoming another.

A somewhat hesitant candidate in 1824, Andrew Jackson was now a steely-eyed, clenched-jaw avenger, determined to win in 1828. As he saw it, he and his constituents had been wronged, their victory stolen by crooked politicians. Immediately on his return home, he leapt into action. This campaign, beginning four years before the election, would change the political culture of the nation.

CHAPTER 10

Triumph and Heartbreak

Corruption—Andrew Jackson saw it festering at the very heart of the Republic. His perception that the Monroe administration was riddled with fraud had caused him to run for the presidency in 1823–1824. And the following year Monroe's secretary of state and the speaker of the House of Representatives had stolen the election from him and the American people. Governmental honesty, a return to republican principles, and the right of the people (read: white men) to elect their leaders were basic tenets of the Jacksonian campaign.

Certainly there had been a pattern of dishonesty in the Monroe administration, particularly in the Treasury Department. But just as disturbing to Jackson's mind was Monroe's vision of the end of hostile political parties. For twenty-four years the Republicans of Thomas Jefferson, James Madison, and James Monroe had effortlessly dominated politics. The old-time Federalists, the party of Alexander Hamilton and John Adams, were a pitiful minority with strength only in New England. Monroe dreamed that this rump group would join the majority. Chosen by a congressional caucus, Republican president would follow Republican president calmly and peacefully, representing the nation as a whole.

To Jackson and his followers, this system smacked of aristocracy, a throwback to British tyranny. In the election of 1824, they had broken the caucus system for good. Never again would a presidential candidate be chosen by so few. Over the next years, Jackson's adherents, joined by the supporters of William Crawford and John C. Calhoun, would become the Democratic Republicans and then the Democrats, with their doctrine of limited federal power and popular suffrage.

The branch of the party led by John Quincy Adams and Henry Clay became known as the National Republicans and then the Whigs. They had a more expansive vision of federal power and countrywide development, including a national bank, extensive road building and other public works, and even a national university. Inevitably, the bitterness and partisan strife of the election of 1824 and the decision for Adams orchestrated by Clay led to the formation of the two great parties of the mid-nineteenth century. Both still claimed to be republicans, with both a lowercase and a capital "R." George Washington and other founding fathers had assumed that the best men of the Republic would govern together without partisanship because they believed political parties were the creation of monarchy and aristocracy. But by this time it was clear that this ideal could not survive. The two-party system became permanently embedded in American politics, no longer labeled an aberration but lauded as essential to good government and democracy.

Rachel supported her husband's aspirations, understanding his fury at having had victory snatched away. Her role was to sympathize, to listen, to bring him peace at home. Absorbed by her three teenaged boys, all the Donelsons, and a stream of political visitors, she was always busy. Her friend Katherine Duane Morgan, the daughter and wife of pro-Jackson newspaper editors, wrote with the latest news from Washington, obviously including an account of Louisa Adams as presidential hostess. Rachel replied that she preferred her country life to the "duties which would have fallen to me had the Presidential election terminated differently." She added that "referred to my own wishes that question would no longer disturb Mr. Adams, so far as the General is concerned. To me the *Presidential charms* by the side of a *happy retirement from Public life* are as the tale of the candle and substantial fire, the first of which it is said is soon blown out by the wind but the latter is only increased by it."[1]

Even as she wrote, she knew perfectly well that her own wishes would never prevail. Andrew was obsessed with his campaign, corresponding, meeting, organizing, maneuvering, analyzing, planning, manipulating, managing. Breaking out in anger at the opposition with Rachel and his friends, he kept a tight rein on his temper in public. Refusing invitations that might look like out-and-out office seeking, he accepted many others to public events such as Independence Day celebrations and banquets throughout Tennessee and Alabama—the line between political and civic events fuzzy at best. Adams, who could barely bring himself to be civil in public, fumed and muttered, turning down quite legitimate opportunities to appear at public occasions in his role as president. As he wrote, "This mode of electioneering suited neither my taste nor my principles."[2]

On October 6–7, 1825, the Tennessee General Assembly nominated Andrew Jackson for the presidency. A week later, he appeared before the Assembly to submit his resignation from the U.S. Senate. Like so much else that involved Jackson, this formal nomination of a presidential candidate in opposition to the incumbent was a first in American history. While Adams refused to make most ceremonial appearances as president, Jackson had the advantage of his military reputation in staging public events. As a former militia general, he had the thoroughgoing support of militias throughout the United States, who turned out to parade in his honor wherever he appeared. But the real godsend for his campaign was the victory at the Battle of New Orleans. As the War of 1812 was considered by many Americans to be the second war for independence from Great Britain, the anniversary of the January 8, 1815, battle was celebrated nationally, second in importance only to the Fourth of July.

The Jacksonians' strategy was twofold: to lionize their Hero with his fitness to lead a free people and to assail the "corrupt bargain" that had elevated Adams to the presidency. Ignoring the will of the people, they asserted, made Adams unworthy of respect and unfit to lead. Jackson himself believed incorrectly that Clay had offered to swing the election either to him or to Adams in return for a promise to make him secretary of state and thus a natural successor to the presidency. He was wrong about that. Clay would never have supported a man he despised as much as he did Jackson.

At the time of the supposed approach, Clay had already decided to support Adams. Clay and Adams also disliked each other, but not with the degree of hostility that existed between Clay and Jackson. Beginning in December 1824, when it was clear that Clay could not be elected, his followers approached Adams with the word that Clay might support him. Eventually the two principals met for long discussions. It is doubtful that Adams would have responded favorably to an outright suggestion of tit-for-tat, the so-called "corrupt bargain."

But even in his diary he wrote that he would be willing to appoint a western leader if his support came from the West. An understanding can be reached without blatant promises. Both Adams and Clay were tempted by the presidency and so blighted their future hopes. Like his father, Adams would be a one-term president. Henry Clay would never grasp his dreamed-of prize.

The election of 1824 was the first in which most adult white males could vote for president of the United States and the first with meaningful electoral returns. By the election of 1828, the idea of the people's power to choose their leader had taken hold. That was the beginning of political parties based on support from the mass of voters rather than elections controlled by elite political leaders.[3] There were hundreds of thousands of potential voters in 1828. The question was how to reach them.

The answer was a war of words—spates, torrents, floods, tidal waves of words. As in so many other ways, the Democratic Republicans or Jacksonians held the advantage over the National Republicans. John Quincy Adams was very much an eighteenth-century man of the Enlightenment, rational, intellectual, and reserved. Andrew Jackson was all nineteenth-century Romantic, spontaneous, intuitive, and emotional. Even their home cities underlined the dichotomy in their philosophies—refined, formal Boston versus exuberant, earthy Nashville.

Although maintaining a dignified stance in public, Jackson was able to admit to himself and his associates that he wanted the presidency desperately and was willing to fight for it. Adams believed that he deserved the presidency, but knew he had achieved this desire "not...in a manner satisfactory to pride or to just desire; not by the unequivocal suffrages of a majority of the people."[4] Never one to court the public, he was overwhelmed by the violent opposition to his election. Henry Clay, a brilliant orator, natural politician, and gut fighter, led the administration's reelection campaign.

Jackson's campaign was distinguished by its organization. Most major cities had their Jackson committees that coordinated campaign activities. The capital's committee was crucial. John C. Calhoun, Martin Van Buren (won over from Crawford), John Henry Eaton, and Thomas Hart Benton met when in Washington and otherwise corresponded regularly. Committee organizations in some states went all the way down to the town and school district level. Voter registration soared all over the United States, and most states held nominating conventions in 1828.[5]

Adams generally relied on members of his cabinet to travel and speak on his behalf. The Jackson committees appealed to the general public through rousing campaign meetings featuring stump orators, music, liquor, and barbecue. Much like camp meetings, but for men only, they provided an opportunity for people to come together in a good cause. Reaching out to the general public took good planning and money. Broadsides to attract an audience, slogans, emblems, jokes (at their opponents' expense, of course), musicians—all the right elements had to be brought together to ensure a big, rowdy crowd. Nicknames too helped make the candidates seem more accessible to their support-ers. Jackson's "Old Hickory" was made to order for politics with its res-onance of strength, leadership, and heroism. Henry Clay was "Harry of the West," which also played well with most audiences. John Quincy Adams simply wasn't the sort of man to accept a nickname.

The Jackson men had a lot of fun with the hickory theme, planting hickory trees, giving out hickory brooms, carrying hickory canes, wearing hickory leaves in their hatbands. Their campaign song was "The Hunters of Kentucky," the lyrics written by Samuel Woodward in the 1820s in tribute to Jackson's victory at the Battle of New Orleans. His verses were set to the familiar music of "Poor Miss Baily," also known as "Allie Croaker." That was often the way with new lyrics. Setting them to well-known tunes helped ensure their wide circulation. Think of "America," also called "My Country 'Tis of Thee," being sung to the tune of "God Save the King [or Queen]." Or the carol "What Child Is This?" set to the traditional "Greensleeves."

Americans loved to sing together and joined in whenever a familiar tune was struck up. Anytime "The Hunters of Kentucky" was played, Jacksonians rose to their feet and bellowed out the lyrics, whether it was tactful or not. Shortly after Adams's inauguration, he and his wife went to the theater, where the orchestra in the pit started playing the new favorite. Most of the audience stood, laughing and joining in the song to the president's severe mortification.

This campaign anthem had several verses celebrating Jackson and his Kentucky allies, including:

> But Jackson he was wide awake, and wasn't scared at trifles,
> For well he knew what aim we take with our Kentucky rifles;
> So he led us down to Cypress swamp, the ground was low and mucky,
> There stood John Bull in martial pomp, and here was old Kentucky.
> Oh, Kentucky! the hunters of Kentucky.
>
> They found at last 'twas vain to fight, where lead was all their booty,
> And so they wisely took to flight, and left us all our beauty,
> And now if danger e'er annoys, remember what our trade is,
> Just send for us Kentucky boys, and we'll protect your ladies.
> Oh, Kentucky! the hunters of Kentucky.

For the contemplative and intellectual Adams, everything about this campaign was a nightmare, an affront to his taste and habits. He would have preferred a debate on ideas and policies, not a personality contest in which he was doomed to failure. From his election in 1825 until his defeat in 1828, he seldom enjoyed a serene moment. He did, however, have a campaign song. It's hard to imagine who chose such a terrible song, impossible to play anywhere but New England and certainly not a sing-along. Called "Little Know Ye Who's Comin'," it's almost apocalyptic in tone, as these verses show:

> Slavery's comin', knavery's comin',
> Wonder's comin', plunder's comin',
> Jobbin's comin', robbin's comin'
> If John Quincy not be comin'!
>
> Tears are comin', fears are comin',
> Plague and pestilence is comin',
> Hatin's comin', Satan's comin',
> If John Quincy not be comin'!

Campaign oratory was stirring, but it was the printed word that dominated the election. Cheap postage and increased literacy made newspapers the vehicle of choice for reaching the masses of Americans. Stories from one paper were picked up by others and thus circulated rapidly. Since 1824, the number of newspapers in the United States had tripled, and the excitement of the election caused new ones to pop up like toadstools. Everybody wanted to have his say in this election.

Newspaper editors evolved from the old working-class printer/ editors into major opinion makers and political heavyweights. Jackson welcomed editors into his councils. No one thought that newspapers should be impartial or evenhanded. They set out to be politically partisan and grew more vehement as the campaign progressed. Controversy sold newspapers and subscriptions. Many editors believed that two contending parties were necessary to expose inequities and corruption and to right wrongs at the polls. There were men of passion on both sides who fought savagely for their beliefs, hunting out and magnifying the misdeeds of the other man, explaining away the slips of their own. Like today's tabloid editors, they weren't above making up scandalous or preposterous charges to spice up a story.[6]

In the capital, Adams was supported by the *Washington Intelligencer,* a major source of political news for provincial papers. To establish a Jackson presence, John Eaton bought the *Washington City Gazette* in February 1826 and renamed it the *United States Telegraph.* Its prospectus avowed a determined opposition to the Adams administration. Under the editorship/ownership of Duff Green, who came to Washington from Missouri, the *Telegraph* kept that promise. Jackson's supporters also subsidized, promoted, and wrote for dozens of papers throughout the country.[7]

Newspaper stories, especially the several-part series so popular in this campaign, were republished as pamphlets for wider distribution. The Adams men published pamphlets on Jackson's alleged unfitness for office, citing his violence, ignorance, dueling, mishandling of military accounts, treasonous support of Aaron Burr, slave trading, poor judgment, instability, and illegal acts in Florida. Enemies rifled the records of the War Department and Jackson's Nashville bank box, for ammunition. His bank box, the forerunner of today's safety deposit box, should have been secure, but one of the bankers had allowed the search.

One member of the Adams cabinet asserted that James Monroe, then secretary of war, should be credited rather than Jackson with the victory at New Orleans. A group of friends in Nashville headed by John Overton, labeled by the administration the "white-wash committee," was kept busy writing rebuttals. The group was formally organized as the Nashville Jackson Committee in 1827. This pamphlet war was conducted with some particularly choice invective. For instance, in *Truth Is No Slander,* Samuel Clement of Nashville declared that worshipping an ignorant, violent liar like Jackson was like "the dung plastered on as a crown for the Hottentots."[8]

Graphics too became important. Glaring black headlines, tricky type designs, and ornamental dingbats screamed for the reader's attention. Editorial cartoons, the more vicious the better, became a minor art form. Since most people were unlikely to set eyes on a presidential candidate, the public was hungry for images of famous men. At least three engraved editions of prints based on portraits of Jackson were printed during the campaign. Engravings were inexpensive and popular home decorations.

The rallies, the newspapers, the pamphlets—everything in the new mode of campaigning cost money, lots of money. The outlay on the election of 1828 soared beyond anything seen before in American politics. Overall, the Democratic Republicans spent about a million dollars, an immense sum at that time, to elect Andrew Jackson president; the National Republicans spent considerably less on John Quincy Adams's losing campaign. Large sums were donated by wealthy supporters, state committees raised money locally for their own efforts, tickets were sold to public dinners and banquets, dues were levied on party members in some places, and admission fees were charged for some meetings. Martin Van Buren was a genius at tapping manufacturers and major businessmen in the big cities of the Northeast for sizeable donations.

Government printing contracts for newspapers and the congressional franking privilege were major factors in this election. Congressmen could send mail free, and both sides did so with a vengeance. Not only did they send out newspapers and pamphlets, but they franked, that is, signed, wrappers and gave them to partisans to insert mountains of political material to forward at no cost.[9]

As the midterm congressional elections approached in 1826, the administration's supporters were becoming desperate. No matter what charges they flung at Jackson, he was still a hero to the American people, and the ranks of his supporters kept growing. Adams was incapable of drawing the ardent devotion that Jackson inspired and would have scorned to try. The president was supported by those who agreed with his ideas and policies, but few people felt a personal attachment to the man. In a mass popular election, charisma always trumps aloofness.

Finally, Charles Hammond, an Adams supporter and a former Federalist who abhorred everything about Jackson, took drastic action to try to ruin the candidate's reputation for good. An attorney who had recently become editor of the *Cincinnati Gazette,* in 1825 Hammond began investigating the titillating rumors about the Jacksons' marriage. Harrodsburg, Kentucky, the seat of Mercer County and the place where Rachel lived during her unhappy first marriage, was only 125 miles from Cincinnati. Using an Englishman named Edward Day as his agent, Hammond discovered many of the facts about that marriage. Day traveled throughout the area, picking up gossip and acquiring a copy of the court records of Lewis Robards's divorce, including the uncontested grounds that Rachel was guilty of adultery. Not aware of the Jacksons' marriage in 1794, Hammond believed that they were not legally married.

In October 1826 at a reading room in Steubenville, Ohio, Hammond first spoke publicly about the divorce. In the *Gazette* of November 14, he declared that he had spoken "quite freely and plainly of both Gen. Jackson, and the woman who he and others call *'Mrs. Jackson.'* . . . It is said . . . that I *traduced* the General and *abused* the woman. I spoke truths of both." All his charges were true "but little known." He argued that the public had a right to know these facts to understand Jackson's true character and that he would make them all known in time.[10] In the charged political atmosphere of that year, Hammond's hostility toward Jackson is fully understandable, but his scorn for Rachel is less clear. No respectable man would refer to a lady of her standing as "the woman," an appellation connoting low social and moral standing. The mere suggestion that she had committed adultery apparently disgusted him.

Jackson wrote to his former ward, Edward G. W. Butler, aide-de-camp to General Edmund P. Gaines, requesting copies of the offensive papers. Butler was stationed in Cincinnati, the headquarters of the western division of the U.S. Army. In his reply, Butler referred to the "rude and indelicate" remarks about Rachel. Somehow, Hammond had been deterred from publishing more information for the moment. Allegations about Jackson's marriage had a double advantage for his enemies. The stories were damaging in themselves, but they also might provoke the general into violent action that would be even more damaging. Like all of Jackson's friends, Butler knew this and begged him to ignore anything flowing from "the *Sources* or *Tributaries* of corruption." As he pointed out, "The character of my Dear Mrs. Jackson has ever been above the suspicion of friends and honest men."[11]

An anonymous letter in November from "An Enquirer acquainted Jackson with the role of Edward Day in Kentucky. The letter charged that Henry Clay had delivered the documents to Charles Hammond and was behind the whole affair. Always ready to believe the worst of Clay, Jackson directed Eaton to confront the man and demand an explanation. After three unsuccessful attempts to meet with the secretary of state, Eaton finally saw him on December 21. Clay declared all the accusations "unfounded & untrue" and denied having any role in the attack; at his request, Hammond subsequently wrote to Eaton affirming this. Eaton believed Clay, but Jackson never did.[12]

Although Adams and Clay denied any knowledge of Hammond's intentions, there are indications that their denials may have been disingenuous. They both had a tendency to stick to the strict letter of the truth, while ignoring its wider implications, as in denying any "corrupt bargain" without explaining why two longtime political enemies had become allies. Clay and Hammond were certainly in regular communication throughout this time. In April 1825, Adams recorded in his diary that he and Clay met and that Clay left with him a letter from C. Hammond at Cincinnati, "containing some information." Whether that information concerned the Jacksons' marriage is unknown. But certainly either of them could have called Hammond to heel after his initial publication in November 1826. Without ordering these personal attacks, both men enjoyed their benefits.[13]

As the results of the congressional elections and senatorial appointments of 1826 (Eaton was reappointed senator from Tennessee) began to trickle in, it became clear that the Twentieth Congress, to be seated in December 1827, would have a solid Jacksonian majority. Adams was traumatized that a decided majority of both houses would act in opposition to the administration—"a state of things which has never before occurred under the Government of the United States."[14]

Clay was shocked, but game. If Adams lost the election of 1828, his own plans for a smooth succession to the presidency were doomed. He redoubled his efforts in 1827 and 1828 to defeat Jackson. The rest of their party followed suit, and the attacks on Jackson in administration newspapers were unceasing.

Meanwhile, the Nashville committee, under the chairmanship of John Overton, was hard at work on their rebuttal of Hammond's charges. Throughout his life, perhaps because of his early career as an attorney and judge, Jackson gathered depositions to support his case in any dispute. Writing to his friend and neighbor William B. Lewis, a member of his Nashville circle, Jackson enclosed a deposition from an elderly neighbor lady and suggested others who could attest to Rachel's good behavior at the time of her first marriage. Then he broke out with the pain he felt for his wife: "the Rascallity of the attempt to blacken the character of an ancient & virtuous female who has thro life maintained a good reputation & has associated with the best circles of society in which she has been placed, and this for the basest purpose . . . raises in my mind such feelings of indignation that I can scarcely control—but a day of retribution . . . must arrive."[15]

As Jackson's friends assembled their evidence, hostile versions of the divorce and remarriage began to appear, first in a pamphlet published by Thomas D. Arnold of Knoxville in February, picked up in March 1827 by the Richmond *Whig,* followed ten days later by the Washington *National Journal,* and soon reverberating through administration newspapers nationwide. Arnold's attack was vicious, charging that one of Jackson's friends boasted that he "had driven Roberts [Robards] off like a dog, and had taken his wife."[16]

Seeing that he was being scooped, on March 23 Charles Hammond jumped into print in the *Gazette* on the subject of the marriage. He wrote that Jackson had prevailed upon the wife of Lewis Robards "to desert her husband, and live with himself, in the character of a wife." He printed portions of the court records and continued his attacks throughout the remainder of 1827.[17]

Without waiting for the publication of the committee's report, Jacksonian newspapers countered these attacks as best they could with preliminary information and affidavits. The opposition upped the stakes with racial innuendoes, a tactic that always played well in racist America. In a parody illustration, a Kentucky newspaper likened Rachel to "a dirty black wench!"[18]

Finally, on June 5, 1827, the Nashville Jackson Committee published its rebuttal of charges relating to the Jacksons' marriage, along with supporting affidavits. The information was published within the month in the *United States Telegraph* of Washington and throughout the nation in other Jacksonian newspapers. Later it appeared in pamphlet form as *A Letter from the Jackson Committee of Nashville . . . upon the Subject of Gen. Jackson's Marriage* (Nashville, 1827).

The basic narrative of the Nashville Committee's defense was the truth. Backed up with depositions from respectable elderly ladies, a member of the Robards family, and several contemporary witnesses, they wrote about Rachel as "a respectable and virtuous female" tormented by the jealousy of an "irrational and cruel" husband. Fudging the dates a bit, they wrote of a chaperoned flight to Natchez, the news of the supposed divorce (the Virginia legislative act), the Jacksons' marriage in Natchez, return to Nashville, shock when they realized the divorce wasn't final, and remarriage.[19]

The one vital piece of missing information is a description of the wedding in Natchez. Who married them, when, and exactly where? A sympathetic Catholic priest in his vestry? A traveling Protestant clergyman? A friendly justice of the peace at Springfield Plantation? All have been asserted, but no evidence has ever been discovered by the most diligent researchers. In a sense, it doesn't matter. None of these projected scenarios would have been legal because Rachel was still married to another man.

But this wedding was key to the Jacksons' assertion of innocence and good faith. To admit that they had eloped to rescue Rachel from an intolerable situation would have been social and political death in 1820s America. If they had named the place and the person who married them, the opposition hounds would have gone baying off to Natchez. What isn't stated can't be disproved.

On June 1, Lyncoya, the Jacksons' Creek foster son, died of tuberculosis while still in his teens. Rachel had loved this boy and mourned him deeply. Her health was always affected by her emotions. Lyncoya's loss combined with the unremitting personal attacks left her exhausted and sick at heart. On her physician's orders, the Jacksons planned to recuperate at a nearby health resort but were forced to postpone the trip when lightning strikes killed two of their carriage horses. Andrew was beside himself with worry, writing: "When the midnight assassin strikes you to the heart, murders your family, & robs your dwelling, the heart sickens at the relation of the deed: but this scene loses all its horrors when compared with the recent slander of a virtuous female propagated by the minions of power for political effect. It is a case unheard of before in civilized life."[20]

On June 10, it was Rachel's turn to receive an anonymous letter, this one from "A female friend." Sympathizing with her about "the brutish attack upon your reputation," the writer identified the instigators as Henry Clay and John McLane of Delaware. Accurate or not, the letter's statement that McLane "is constantly detailing his stories of your illiterate chat as he calls your remarks" must have been a blow to her pride.[21]

Duff Green, the editor of the *Telegraph,* was blithely unaware of the cumulative toll these months were having on Rachel. Writing to her husband, he sent his congratulations to Mrs. Jackson on "the satisfactory and conclusive vindication of her innocence" presented by the Nashville Committee. He continued, "Let her rejoice—her vindication is Complete—the voice of slander is hushed."[22]

A ferocious antagonist himself, Green had seen the need of "bringing home the matter to Mr. Adams' own family," hinting at the frequency of pregnant brides in the Adams family. He laughed at the consternation of the administration, reporting that "I was denounced in the most bitter terms for assailing *female* character by those very men who had rolled the slanders on Mrs. J. under their tongues as the sweetest morsel." He didn't follow through on his threats to write more about the Adams ladies but did criticize the administration press for its efforts to present Louisa Catherine Adams as a republican and "to demonstrate how much better qualified she was to discharge the duties of the drawing room, than the unassuming plain, old housewife of the Tennessee Farmer."[23] Jackson refused to countenance such attacks and demanded that they stop.

In July, Rachel wrote about her severe trials to Elizabeth Watson, the friend with whom she attended church in Washington: "the Enemyes of the Genls hav Dipt their arrow in wormwood & gall & sped them at me." She lamented, "to think that thirty years had past in happy social friendship with society, knowing or thinking no ill to no one." She went on, "let not your Heart be troubled—I am on the rock of ages."[24]

Andrew was also suffering from cumulative emotional exhaustion. Despite his ill health, they were "surrounded with Crowd from one weeks End to an other as one Carriage full goes another Comes, well I am fond of Society." Rachel wondered about their many friends: "will theay Bear the test—in times of trial."[25] She and Andrew did manage to leave for Tennessee's Robertson and Tyree Springs in late July and stay through part of August before returning home. That fall's political season was wildly active because everybody had their eyes set on the presidential election of 1828.

On December 3, the Twentieth Congress convened, with both houses dominated by pro-Jackson men. Printing contracts were one of the major sources of underwriting for partisan newspapers, and Green's *Telegraph* was chosen as the printer for the Senate the following day. The hostile speaker of the House was quickly replaced with Philip Barbour of Virginia, a politician whose views were more in keeping with Jacksonian ideas.

Back at the Hermitage, the Jacksons were packing up for a momentous trip downriver. In March, the Louisiana legislature had invited the Hero to attend a grand celebration of the Battle of New Orleans. After being reassured that this was a civic, not a political, event, he determined to go. The Louisianians did it up right, even sending a steamboat upriver to fetch the Jackson party. On December 27, Rachel and Andrew, a large group of family members, friends, veterans of the War of 1812, and political supporters boarded the *Pocahontas* and set off for New Orleans.

Their stop at Natchez on January 4 was a dress rehearsal for their reception in New Orleans, with cheering crowds, a parade, artillery salutes, dinner, and a ball. On January 8, their boat was greeted by the roar of cannons and a flotilla of steamboats (twenty-four in honor of the states of the Union) that the flag-bedecked *Pocahontas* led into port. Receptions by uniformed veterans, respect shown to Rachel by the great ladies of the city, speeches, banquets, adoring crowds—their four days in New Orleans were a constant festival. And every day's events were covered by newspapers in every state.

In Washington, the president wrote angrily of Jackson's New Orleans triumph. He had exhibited himself "in pompous pageantry." Jackson's speeches—no doubt ghostwritten, harrumphed Adams—were in a style of "tawdry elegance."[26] The general's celebrity and the overwhelming public response to his appearances were impossible to counteract, no matter how many charges were flung at him. The majority of voters simply didn't care if he had a hot temper, wrote poorly, or had eloped with a married woman.

But the inimitable Charles Hammond had not given up his crusade against the Jacksons. In January 1828 he began publication of *Truth's Advocate and Monthly Anti-Jackson Expositor*, its mission inherent in its title. The first article in the first issue was called "View of Gen. Jackson's Domestic Relations, in Reference to His Fitness for the Presidency." Hammond rejected, he wrote, the Jacksonian assertion that investigating a man's marriage and his wife's reputation was "a violation of all the charities and all the decencies of life," as well as the "shivering moderation" of some members of his own party. Because the president must bring his wife to the capital, it was important to examine her worthiness for the position—"his wife...must share the distinction of the station he occupies." It was his duty to examine Mrs. Jackson's fitness for the place; if she was unfit, then her husband's judgment and fitness to be president must be rejected.

Rather than see "a degraded female placed at the head of the female society of the nation," he urged voting against her husband. Having uncovered the fact of her divorce for adultery, he asked, "ought a convicted adulteress, and her paramour husband to be placed in the highest offices of this free and Christian land." His answer was a resounding no.

For sixteen pages, Hammond laid out the justifications of the Nashville Jackson Committee and rebutted each one scornfully. He was particularly offended by the idea that thirty-seven years of blameless life could wipe out her sin, comparing her unworthiness to that of a notorious murderess. Satisfied that he had disposed of Rachel's reputation, he went after Jackson. As the cause of her fall "from the virtue of chastity," Jackson should have lived with her in "unobtrusive retirement." Any sense of propriety should have made him do nothing "to bring his wife before the public," where her shame would be uncovered. With obviously false sympathy for Rachel, Hammond accused Jackson of exposing her "to the ribald taunts and dark surmises of the profligate or to the cold civility, or just remark of the wise and good."

He trotted out the maxim about Caesar adapted for this case. "The wife of a distinguished public man, should not only be pure but unsuspected." He ended his long tirade by appending copies of the Virginia bill that granted Lewis Robards the right to seek a divorce and of the Mercer County divorce records. He published the article as a stand-alone pamphlet in March.[27]

The damage to Rachel's reputation was devastating. Accusations of sexual impurity against a woman in nineteenth-century America stuck forever, whether they were true or false. A respectable woman, according to society's expectations, would never allow herself to be put in a position where she could be accused. Hammond had made sure to smear her as thoroughly as possible.

Such a humiliating attack on his beloved—and Jackson could do nothing to avenge her. The Nashville Committee printed extra copies of their vindication and sent them far and wide, but Hammond's pamphlet had all the spice of sex and scandal. It was read all over the nation. Jackson believed that nearly 15,000 copies of the vile piece had been franked by various congressmen.[28]

Barely held in check by his friends throughout the summer, Jackson threatened to make a public response to all the charges swirling about him. Racial taunting had again appeared with the story that his mother was a British camp follower, that is, a prostitute, and his father a mulatto slave. Jackson wrote to his confidant John Coffee, "How hard it is to keep the cowhide [whip] from some of these villains—I have made many sacrafices for the good of my country—but the present, being placed in a situation that I cannot act, and punish those slanderers, not only of me, but Mrs. J. is a sacrafice too great to be well endure[d]."[29]

Throughout the emotionally charged summer and fall of 1828, the Jacksons tried to maintain some semblance of normal life at the Hermitage. The stream of visitors never slowed down, and Rachel tended to their comfort. There were Donelson family births and deaths, and the ever troublesome Andrew Jackson Hutchings was expelled from college. In October, Andrew Jr. graduated from the University of Nashville, where his father was a trustee.

Earlier visitors to the Hermitage left few reminiscences, but in the 1820s many of them wrote in their journals, to friends, or to the newspapers about their stays at the now-famous Hermitage. Anyone traveling in the neighborhood felt the need to call on the great man. One of the touchstones of every visit was the way in which they were embraced as part of the family even if they had never met before. Coming upon Jackson sitting on the front porch reading and smoking his pipe or Rachel going about her chores in a blue-checked apron with her large ring of housekeeping keys at her waist made them all feel like intimates.

The Jacksons kept open doors, welcoming all comers. Even in the old Hermitage, a long table was kept set for whatever guests might drop in to dinner. In the new house, they seldom sat down with fewer than twenty guests at table—with the number rising to thirty or more at busy times.

The rigid economy practiced by Rachel at the Hermitage allowed them to treat everyone with generous hospitality. She and Andrew sat at the head and the foot of the table, delighting in their guests' company. They both enjoyed young people and frequently drew them near. Most of the food served came from their plantation. Dinner would typically include several kinds of meat and vegetables, followed by a pudding course. Although Jackson had been known as quite a drinker in his earlier years, by this time he had become abstemious from principle and because of his poor health, so guests were not offered wine or other alcohol.

Jackson frequently told stories of the past after dinner, served at 3:00 PM, showing off his presentation swords and medals. Rachel would sit knitting socks from their own wool. He also walked guests around the place or rode with them over the fields. He and Rachel rode to services at the nearby Hermitage Church, and everyone was encouraged to join them there.

Eliza Gould of Alabama was charmed by a day spent with Rachel in Andrew's absence. Her hostess read aloud to her from the love letters "the General" wrote to her during the Creek War. The "childish heart" of young William Galt of Virginia, traveling with his father for his health, was won by Rachel's pleasant attentions to him.[30]

Almost everyone described Rachel's looks, and few of them were flattering. Now in her fifties, Rachel had become quite fat. Being so short made the weight all the more noticeable. From days spent in the sun on plantation business, she was tanned, an unappreciated look in the days when magnolia-like skin was the mark of beauty. But one sympathetic writer discovered lingering traces of her former beauty. Another claimed that "her eye still burns with a luster that first extorted allegiance from the intrepid Jackson."[31]

About her character, everyone agreed. Benevolent, friendly, hospitable, gracious, pious, and spirited were adjectives that loomed large. Young people found her company very congenial because she encouraged rather than repressed their amusements. She was talkative and entertaining with company. Although one visitor found her "excessively fond of laughing," most people found that an attractive trait. Her grammar might not be perfect, but she was a lady in her manners. To sum up the impression she made, a guest wrote: "She may not make so splendid a court lady as Mrs. Adams, but I venture to say, quite as candid and as useful to her country & the poor."[32]

Despite the best efforts of Henry Clay and the administration party, by the fall of 1828 it was obvious that Jackson would prevail. Fearing social slights for Rachel in the capital, Andrew had at first thought that she might stay at home until after the inauguration to give the gossip a chance to die away. By early December, however, they decided that another separation would be too painful. Even though full election results were not in, the Jacksons made their plans without doubting that he would be the next president. Rachel wrote a friendly letter to Louise Moreau Davezac Livingston. Edward Livingston had recently visited the Hermitage, where he passed on his wife's offer "to assist in the selection of such articles of dress as might be considered necessary for the [best?] circles of the city," as she had in 1815 in New Orleans.[33]

Louise was socially prominent, elegant, and much admired, and her taste was to be depended on. But she was also a good friend who had stood by them when the Jacksons were surrounded, as Rachel put it, "by the dark mists of slander & detraction." Rachel enclosed a tape marked with the measures for her waist and skirt—by now quite large. She asked to have two dresses made, leaving the color and style "to your better taste & judgment." Rachel was also adding to her wardrobe in Nashville.[34]

Soon after her letter to Louise Livingston, Rachel replied to an acquaintance's letter, mentioning the near certainty of Jackson's election. She repeated, as she did in most letters, that she would prefer to remain at home rather than in Washington "were it not for the many base attempts that have been made to defame the characters of my husband and myself, and the ungrateful exertions that were used to prevent his election." They both saw his election as a vindication. Under the circumstances, "it is my duty to follow without a murmur, & to rejoice at not being separated from him who is dearer to me than all other earthly considerations."[35]

In December, electoral returns continued to trickle in. The final count was 647,286 popular votes for Andrew Jackson versus 508,064 for John Quincy Adams. The Electoral College showed a sharper skew of 178 versus 83. Hezekiah Niles, editor of *Niles' Weekly Register,* called this election "the most anxious and ardent, as well as the most rude and ruthless political contest that ever took place in the United States."[36]

Not aware that Rachel had already decided to accompany Andrew to Washington for the inauguration, John Eaton wrote about the regrets of her many friends that "it can be even considered doubtful what your determination may be." Despite the delicacy of the topic, he mentioned the assaults made on her. Since they were politically motivated and now fading from memory, she shouldn't feel "a moments pain."[37]

He wanted her in the city for the sake of appearances, but also reassured her that she wouldn't be embarrassed. Ladies from far across the Union will show "their feelings & high regard." If she stayed at home, "Your persecutors then may chuckle, & say that they have driven you from the field of your husbands honors." He begged her to arrive by March 1, "ready & rested for the 4th."[38]

Eaton was wrong about society's forgetfulness about her elopement and divorce. She might well have suffered the "cold civility" that Charles Hammond had predicted. In a letter to her sister, Margaret Smith discussed John Eaton's attachment to Margaret O'Neale Timberlake, a boardinghouse owner's daughter whose moral and social standing were suspect. Smith reported that Jackson's "enemies laugh and divert themselves with the idea of what a suitable lady in waiting Mrs. Eaton will make to Mrs. Jackson and repeat the old adage, 'birds of a feather will flock together.'"[39]

Congratulations poured in from old friends and supporters as news of Jackson's triumph spread. On December 18 he was finishing a letter of acknowledgment. Dramatically, he added a postscript: "Whilst writing, Mrs. J. from good health, has been taken suddenly ill, with excruciating pain in the left shoulder, arm, & breast. What may be the result of this violent attack god only knows, I hope for her recovery, & in haste close this letter."[40]

Rachel had been busy about kitchen chores with Hannah, the housekeeper. Hannah was a slave woman whom the Jacksons had owned since they moved to the Hermitage. For the past several years, she had run the household, directing the work of all the rest of the house staff. Rachel depended entirely on her and considered her a friend.

Rachel's pain was so terrible that she had fallen into a chair with an agonized shriek, clutching at her heart. For years, she had endured the discomforts of congestive heart failure, but this was a full-fledged heart attack.[41]

Two doctors were summoned to the Hermitage from Nashville and applied all the useless and painful treatments available to nineteenth-century medicine. She was bled every day and dosed with mercury and castor oil while her heartbeat continued to be very irregular. Grim-faced, Jackson lived by her bedside, *willing* her to recover. A grand ball in honor of his victory, scheduled for December 23 in Nashville, was cancelled.[42]

On December 22, Jackson wrote Richard Keith Call with an account of Rachel's attack, "such the contraction of the heart, that suffocation was apprehended." Although she seemed to be getting worse, he hoped that she would regain "her usual health in due time to set out for washington." As president-elect, Jackson needed to be in the capital by March 4 for the inauguration. He couldn't decide what to do. Rachel was clearly too ill to travel by coach, so he considered taking her by steamboat up the Ohio. Going to Washington alone was unthinkable: "I cannot leave her, believing as I do, that my separating from her would destroy her, & the persecution she has suffered, has endeared her more if possible than ever to me."[43]

Painfully stiff, on the night of December 22 he finally heeded Rachel's wishes, going into an adjoining room to rest. Hannah helped her to a chair while the maids straightened the crumpled sheets of the sickbed. Only minutes later, Rachel cried out loudly and fell forward into the housekeeper's arms. A death rattle deep in her throat signaled the end. Andrew burst into the room, clasped his wife in his arms, and lifted her to the bed, insisting that she wasn't dead, that the doctors must revive her.

At his command to bleed her, one of them cut her arm—no blood flowed. When her heart stopped beating, the blood had stopped circulating. Jackson was committed to the therapeutic value of bleeding. He ordered, "Try the temple, Doctor."[44] The doctor suffered for him, knowing there was no hope. Only two tiny drops from the cut at the side of her head stained her cap.

Still Jackson refused to believe that she was dead, staying by her side throughout the night, praying that she might awaken. Only when her body grew cold and stiff did he accept the truth. At dawn, friends found him at her bedside, grieving, head in hands, all but speechless with despair. Throughout the day, as funeral arrangements were made, he tightly embraced his wife of thirty-seven years. He left her only briefly while some of her nieces prepared her for burial. They washed the body, arranged her hair and cap becomingly, and dressed her in the white gown that had been intended for the gaieties of Washington.

The day before Christmas, the afternoon bleak and dreary, an immense throng of family, friends, and admirers arrived for the funeral and burial in Rachel's beloved garden at the Hermitage. Businesses in Nashville were closed by order of the mayor, and all the church bells tolled throughout the hour of the service. Quiet and unpretentious, Rachel Jackson was treasured wherever she was known for her warmth, charity, and loving kindness. Jackson was still like a man in a trance, white-faced and staring. Finally, at the end of the eulogy, he broke into tears. Her burial site was protected by a wooden structure until a formal tomb could be designed and built.

He blamed the unremitting attacks on Rachel's character for the loss of "the partner of my life," declaring that "those vile wretches who have slandered her must look to God for mercy." He later expanded, "May God Almighty forgive her murderers as I know she forgave them. I never can."[45]

Andrew Jackson never truly recovered from what he called "a loss so great, so sudden and unexpected." He wore her miniature around his neck and thought of her every day. His political enemies were to feel the lash of his grief and vengefulness. Instead of the triumph he had expected in Washington with his wife at his side, all was ashes. Boarding a steamboat to begin the journey to his inauguration, dressed in mourning black, he said to the friends and well-wishers seeing him off, "My heart is nearly broke."[46]

EPILOGUE

The President Alone

After all the hoopla surrounding his inauguration, Andrew Jackson settled quietly into the presidential mansion in March 1829. His companions in its lofty halls, dwarfing the Hermitage and the plantation homes of his friends back in Tennessee, were his secretary and foster son, Andrew Jackson Donelson; Donelson's young wife, Emily; and the Donelsons' cousin Mary Eastin. He considered them his family, but it was Rachel who had been their aunt. It was his beloved wife who had provided the family that Andrew so desperately wanted and now depended on to support him in his grief. Their very presence emphasized what his wife had meant to him and the loss he had suffered. All of them were in heavy mourning for the woman who had seen to the happiness of those around her. They accepted few invitations and seldom entertained.

Washington society was sympathetic to the president's emotional plight to a point, but the mansion was, after all, the social center of the capital. Margaret Bayard Smith and her friends had expected the "triumphant party" to relieve the gloom cast over the city by John Quincy Adams's loss and the departure of such fixtures as the Crawfords and the Clays. But Jackson and his family remained largely in seclusion for the first several months of his administration, "not known, or seen, except at formal morning visits," to the chagrin of those who had expected more interaction.[1]

Andrew Jackson now had to imagine how he would live without the woman who had been the emotional center of his life for nearly forty years. Without the distraction of social events, the new president concentrated single-mindedly on the business of government. But even that focus only reminded him more vividly of Rachel. He was drawn—or rather, threw himself—into a social controversy that would bring the executive department to a near halt for the next two years, baffle and infuriate the president, and contribute to his social isolation.

Before the inauguration and with little consultation, Jackson had chosen his cabinet and announced its members in late February 1829. With the exception of Martin Van Buren as secretary of state, he chose second-rate politicians to fill the positions, which signaled his intention to dominate the decision-making process in his administration. In choosing the secretary of war, however, Jackson had determined to please himself by appointing a personal friend with whom he could freely discuss confidential matters. Thus he selected John Henry Eaton, whom he considered the best of friends and a man worthy of his "warmest gratitude so long as I live."[2] Tennessee senator, bosom friend, and unwavering supporter, Eaton was another of Jackson's surrogate sons.

Although not a man of the greatest talents, Eaton would have been an unexceptionable choice had it not been for his two-month-old marriage. When he had first come to the capital as a widowed senator ten years earlier, he had boarded with the O'Neale family, becoming friendly with their beautiful daughter Margaret and her husband John Timberlake, a naval purser. Eaton continued to live with the O'Neales whenever he was in Washington. Besides being their boarder, he had become an intimate friend of the entire family, helping both William O'Neale (Margaret's father and his landlord) and John Timberlake financially and professionally. At Eaton's suggestion, Jackson himself had boarded with the family while serving as senator from 1823 to 1824.

Although some Washingtonians considered Margaret Timberlake brassy and forward, Jackson liked her and her family very much indeed, and introduced them to his wife the following year. Rachel also found the family acceptable. Nonetheless, gossip surrounded Eaton's relationship with his landlords, portraying him as Margaret's lover. Margaret was beautiful, talented, well-educated, independent, and indiscreet—a woman who liked being the center of attention. When her husband committed suicide while at sea in April 1828, critics whispered that her infidelity with Eaton and others was the cause. Depressed and ill, Timberlake had been in financial hot water throughout his career. There were other possible, even probable, explanations for his act, but few in the capital considered them.

Eaton found himself in a quandary over his relationship with the newly widowed Margaret. Although stoutly denying that they had ever been lovers, he believed that her reputation had been damaged by all the talk. In his perplexity, he wrote to his mentor for advice in December 1828. Admitting his attachment to the lady, he asked if it would be proper to marry her. As always, Jackson was on the side of love. Besides, he truly liked and admired Margaret. He replied that Eaton should propose to the lady or move to another boardinghouse.

Eaton concurred and asked Margaret to marry him. Even though Timberlake had been dead only eight months, she not only accepted Eaton's proposal but pushed up the marriage date. And so they had married on New Year's Day, 1829, with mostly men in attendance. Almost all of the women of Eaton's acquaintance declined to attend. Jackson was still at the Hermitage, but his former ward Edward G. W. Butler was among those at the ceremony. Most of Washington sneered at Eaton's indiscretion in marrying a lady whose reputation was "totally destroyed," and one, moreover, who had never been part of "good society."[3] At this time and later, most of the matrons who considered Margaret beneath their notice swore that they despised her because they would not countenance vice. But somehow her father's profession as a tavern keeper always crept in. It is clear that her opponents were as exercised by her ungenteel background and her independence as they were by her possible sinfulness.

Jackson's enemies laughed and diverted themselves with the idea of what a suitable lady-in-waiting Margaret Eaton would make to Rachel Jackson. Not very creatively, they frequently quoted the adage "birds of a feather will flock together."[4] Their view was that the slandered Margaret was a fit companion for a woman with the soiled reputation of Rachel Jackson.

After the news of Rachel's death reached the capital, the snickers about her largely disappeared. In death, she became a guardian angel who would have softened her husband's temper, as indeed she frequently had. Yet, even her new deification was no proof against sneers at her frontier background. She was described as "a wife fondly and excessively loved!," implying that the depth of Andrew's love was somehow more than she deserved. "Strange that a single woman," mused Margaret Bayard Smith, "possessed of goodness tho' destitute of talents, could thus influence the destiny of nations."[5]

But Margaret Eaton remained an object of scorn. Some of Jackson's supporters begged him to drop Eaton from the cabinet because his new wife was socially unacceptable. Jackson was furious. To him, the parallel with the attacks on Rachel was clear. Another innocent woman, someone he knew and liked, was being maligned and slandered for political reasons.

Generally, in the past, members of the cabinet and their wives had socialized regularly as an extension of their official relationships. Soon, however, the situation in Jackson's cabinet was unbearable. Margaret Eaton called on Floride Calhoun, the wife of Vice President John C. Calhoun, as required by Washington etiquette. Floride received her politely enough, but refused to return the call as protocol dictated and soon returned to South Carolina to avoid the situation completely. All but one of the other cabinet wives followed her lead, and soon most of the women who made up the official society of the capital did as well. At public events, they conspicuously snubbed and humiliated Margaret. Instead of politics and reform, the government came to occupy itself with social events. Jackson could not believe that the wives of his cabinet members refused his command to treat his friend's wife courteously. Even more maddening was that little Emily Donelson had fallen under the influence of society leaders and also refused to become an intimate friend of Mrs. Eaton, whom she genuinely disliked.

The president devoted endless hours to investigating all the charges against Margaret and John Eaton, berating meddlesome ministers who were the sources of many rumors, soliciting depositions in Margaret's defense, and, all in all, behaving with considerably less than common sense. His judgment twisted by heartache for his lost wife, he was obsessed with the need to protect Margaret as he had been unable to protect Rachel. Andrew Donelson supported his wife's refusal to grow closer to a woman she considered immoral while their uncle had decreed her "as chaste as a virgin."[6] To maintain control of his own household, Jackson sent them packing back to Nashville to his own and their grief.

Throughout the affair, known as the "Eaton Malaria" by wags, Martin Van Buren, a widower, had devoted himself to Margaret's defense and thereby ingratiated himself with the president, while Calhoun steadily lost influence. Ultimately, in 1831 Van Buren suggested to Jackson that the stalemate could be broken by the resignation of the present cabinet and the formation of a new group of advisers. He and Eaton then resigned voluntarily, the rest following at the president's insistence. Margaret was sorely disappointed when her husband was appointed minister to Spain and they were forced to leave the capital and her social ambitions behind. It is the only time in American history that an entire cabinet has been dissolved.[7]

Besides all its wider political and social implications, the contretemps over Margaret Eaton illustrated several of Andrew Jackson's deep-seated characteristics—loyalty, stubbornness, rage at not being in command, high-handedness, sympathy for the afflicted, and tenderness toward women. Had Rachel lived to become first lady, the situation would have been different—perhaps far worse. Jackson's political enemies might have merged her and Margaret's reputations as adulterers. It staggers the imagination to picture a capital where the president's wife was ostracized.

But Jackson's support for John and Margaret Eaton also reflected his core belief that people who loved one another, as he and Rachel had, should be together despite the odds against them. In a choice between propriety and love, he was always on the side of romance. Years before, Rachel's brother Sam Donelson fell in love with Mary Smith, known as Polly, the only daughter of the wealthy Daniel Smith. When her father forbade the match, Andrew was one of the men who assisted in the elopement. In fact, rumor had it that he had flung the rope ladder up to young Polly's window.

Later his aide, Richard Keith Call, had courted Mary Letitia Kirkman of Nashville. One of the major obstacles to their relationship was her family's threat to disinherit her if she married Call. Eventually the young couple eloped to the Hermitage. There, under the benign gazes of the Jacksons, they were married. They continued to stay at the Hermitage when visiting Nashville because her parents refused to see her or her husband. Both Andrew and Rachel were fervent supporters of lovers in adversity, welcoming other couples to their home whose parents had opposed their matches.

In 1831, Rachel's limestone tomb was completed. Like a light and airy gazebo in her garden at the Hermitage, the graceful tomb is modeled on a Grecian monument. The inscription on the tombstone was probably written by John Eaton, but it sums up what Andrew felt about Rachel's life and death:

> Here lie the remains of Mrs. Rachel Jackson, wife of President Jackson, who died the 22nd of December, 1828, aged 61. Her face was fair, her person pleasing, her temper amiable, and her heart kind; she was delighted in relieving the wants of her fellow creatures, and cultivated that divine pleasure by the most liberal and unpretending methods; to the poor she was a benefactor; to the rich an example; to the wretched a comforter; to the prosperous an ornament; her piety went hand in hand with her benevolence, and she thanked her Creator for being permitted to do good. A being so gentle and yet so virtuous, slander might wound, but could not dishonor. Even death, when he tore her from the arms of her husband, could but transport her to the bosom of her God.

When Andrew joined her there, his inscription read simply: "General Andrew Jackson/ Born March 15, 1767 / Died June 8, 1845."

The love story of Rachel and Andrew lacked the stormy spectacle of Napoleon and Josephine, Antony and Cleopatra, or other fabled lovers. True, it began dramatically enough with an elopement, but afterward they settled into a long and happy domestic life, neither tempted to roam. Their greatest happiness was being together, and they were miserable when apart. Friends and acquaintances saw their pleasure in close companionship and the congeniality of their minds. As the years destroyed her beauty and tortured them both with ill health and debility, they continued to behave like the lovers they were. Their lives were wrapped up in each other.

Despite her religious conversion and his political troubles, nowhere is there any indication that they regretted their flight or wished it undone. Whatever it took to bring them together was worth it. They supported and adored each other until the day of her death. When they were parted, Andrew never looked at another woman and mourned Rachel every day for the rest of his life.

NOTES

PROLOGUE: THE PEOPLE'S PRESIDENT

1. U.S. Census, 1830.
2. Margaret Bayard Smith, *Forty Years of Washington Society*, ed. Gaillard Hunt (London: T. Fisher Unwin, 1906), 273.
3. Ibid., 257.
4. Ibid., 273; Robert Remini, *Andrew Jackson*, 3 vols. (New York: Harper & Row, 1977–1984), 2:159.
5. Smith, *Forty Years*, 273.
6. Quoted in James Parton, *Life of Andrew Jackson*, 3 vols. (New York: Mason Brothers, 1860), 3:170.
7. Arthur J. Stansbury, *Arthur's Home Gazette (May 1851)*, quoted in ibid., 3:169; Smith, *Forty Years*, 284.
8. Smith, *Forty Years*, 293–294.
9. Ibid., 291–292.
10. Ibid., 294.
11. William Wetmore Story, ed., *The Life and Letters of Joseph Story*, 2 vols. (London: John Chapman, 1851), 1:563.
12. Smith, *Forty Years*, 295–296.

CHAPTER 1: THE TENNESSEE FRONTIER

1. Donelson Journal, Tennessee Historical Society Miscellaneous Files, 1688–1951, Tennessee State Library and Archives. All material on the voyage is taken from this journal.

CHAPTER 2: A MARRIAGE MADE IN HELL

1. Ann Toplovich, "Marriage, Mayhem, and Presidential Politics: The Robards-Jackson Backcountry Scandal," *Ohio Valley History* 5, no. 4 (Winter 2005): 4.
2. Ibid., 4–5.
3. *The Papers of Andrew Jackson*, ed. Sam B. Smith and Harriet Chappell Owsley (Knoxville: University of Tennessee Press, 1980), 1:423.
4. Robert Remini, *Andrew Jackson*, 3 vols. (New York: Harper & Row, 1977–1984), 1:44.

5. *The Papers of Andrew Jackson*, 1:12.
6. James Parton, *Life of Andrew Jackson*, 3 vols. (Boston: Houghton, Mifflin, 1859), 1: 161–162.
7. *Nashville Republican and State Gazette*, June 5, 1827.

CHAPTER 3: THE ELOPEMENT

1. Norma Basch, *Framing American Divorce: From the Revolutionary Generation to the Victorians* (Berkeley: University of California Press, 1999), 23–24, 45–46, 49.
2. *The Papers of Andrew Jackson*, ed. Sam B. Smith and Harriet Chappell Owsley (Knoxville: University of Tennessee Press, 1980–), 1:32, 130.
3. Ibid., 1:21–22.
4. Ann Toplovich, "Marriage, Mayhem, and Presidential Politics: The Robards-Jackson Backcountry Scandal," *Ohio Valley History* 5 (Winter 2005), 9.
5. *The Papers of Andrew Jackson*, 1:424.
6. Ibid.
7. Ibid.
8. Ibid., 1:425–427.
9. Ibid., 1:427.
10. Ibid., 1:428.
11. Ibid.

CHAPTER 4: MAKING A LIFE TOGETHER

1. Bertram Wyatt-Brown, *Southern Honor: Ethics and Behavior in the Old South* (New York: Oxford University Press, 1983), 43–44.
2. *The Papers of Andrew Jackson*, ed. Sam B. Smith and Harriet Chappell Owsley (Knoxville: University of Tennessee Press, 1980), 1:45.
3. Ibid., 1:417–421, 92.
4. Ibid., 1:91–92.
5. Thomas P. Abernethy, *From Frontier to Plantation in Tennessee: A Study in Frontier Democracy* (Chapel Hill: University of North Carolina Press, 1932), 138–139.
6. Ibid., 203.
7. Ibid.,197–201.
8. *The Papers of Andrew Jackson*, 1:455–476.
9. Ibid., 1:240, 230.
10. Ibid., 1:456.
11. Wyatt-Brown, *Southern Honor*, 236.
12. *The Papers of Andrew Jackson*, 1:101, 102, 112.
13. Ibid., 1:152.
14. James Parton, *Life of Andrew Jackson*, 3 vols. (Boston: Houghton, Mifflin, 1859), 1:166–168, 228–229.
15. *The Papers of Andrew Jackson*, 1:232.
16. Ibid., 1:233–234.
17. Robert Remini, *Andrew Jackson*, 3 vols. (New York: Harper & Row, 1977–1984), 1:119.

CHAPTER 5: THE HERMITAGE

1. Amos Kendall, *Life of General Andrew Jackson* (New York, 1843), 105–106.
2. James Parton, *Life of Andrew Jackson*, 3 vols. (Boston: Houghton, Mifflin, 1859), 1:164.
3. Ibid.
4. *The Papers of Andrew Jackson*, ed. Sam B. Smith and Harriet Chappell Owsley (Knoxville: University of Tennessee Press, 1980), 1:367–368.
5. Ibid., 1:368.
6. Ibid., 1:370–371.
7. Ibid., 1:376.
8. Ibid., 1:377.
9. Ibid., 1:378–379.
10. Ibid., 2:7.
11. Ibid., 2:11, 12.
12. Ibid., 2:13.
13. Ibid., 1:305.
14. *The First Hermitage: Restoration at the Hermitage, Home of President Andrew Jackson, Nashville, Davidson County, Tennessee. Historic Structures Report.* Draft, Dec. 2002, Ladies' Hermitage Association, 1–13.
15. *The First Hermitage*, 18–19, appendix D, 4.
16. *The Papers of Andrew Jackson*, 1:37n, 247–248, 252, 274–275.
17. *The First Hermitage*, 14.
18. Ibid., 1:56–58.
19. James Parton, *Life of Andrew Jackson*, 3 vols. (Boston: Houghton, Mifflin, 1859), 1:295.
20. Ibid., 1:299.

CHAPTER 6: GREAT CONVULSIONS

1. Revelation 6:12–17 (King James Version).
2. Numbers 16:31–32 (KJV).
3. Eliza Bryan letter, quoted in *Lorenzo Dow's Journal* (Wheeling, Va.: Joshua Martin, 1848), 344–346, quoted at http://hsv.com/genlintr/newmadrd.
4. George Heinrich Crist journal, quoted at http://hsv.com/genlintr/newmadrd.
5. John H. B. Latrobe, *The First Steamboat on Western Waters* (Baltimore: Maryland Historical Society, 1871), p. 16.
6. Abridged from Carl W. Stover and Jerry L. Coggman, *Seismicity of the United States, 1568–1989* (Washington, D.C.: U.S. Government Printing Office, 1993), 1–2, http://earthquake.usgs.gov/earthquakes.
7. *The Papers of Andrew Jackson*, ed. Sam B. Smith and Harriet Chappell Owsley (Knoxville: University of Tennessee Press, 1980), 2:281, 282.
8. Herman A. Norton, *Religion in Tennessee, 1777–1945* (Knoxville: University of Tennessee Press, 1981), 16–18.
9. Ibid., 21.
10. Ibid., 21–27.
11. Wilbur F. Creighton Jr. and Leland R. Johnson, *The First Presbyterian Church of Nashville: A Documentary History* (Nashville, Tenn.: Williams, 1986), xx–xxi, 2, 7.

12. *The Papers of Andrew Jackson*, 2:361.
13. Ibid., 1:40.
14. Ibid., 2:270.
15. Ibid., 2:271.
16. Robin Jaffee Frank, *Love and Loss: American Portrait and Mourning Miniatures* (New Haven, Conn.: Yale University Press, 2000), 1, 15.
17. *The Papers of Andrew Jackson*, 2:353–355.
18. Ibid., 2:361–362, 365, 371–372, 374–375.
19. Ibid., 2:361–362.
20. Ibid. 2:369, 372, 379.
21. Ibid., 2:385–387.

CHAPTER 7: THE NATION'S HERO

1. *The Papers of Andrew Jackson*, ed. Sam B. Smith and Harriet Chappell Owsley (Knoxville: University of Tennessee Press, 1980), 2:421.
2. James Parton, *Life of Andrew Jackson*, 3 vols. (Boston: Houghton, Mifflin, 1859), 1:394.
3. *The Papers of Andrew Jackson*, 2:427–429.
4. Robert Remini, *Andrew Jackson*, 3 vols. (New York: Harper & Row, 1977–1984), 1:193; *The Papers of Andrew Jackson*, 2:444, 494–495.
5. *The Papers of Andrew Jackson*, 2:516.
6. Ibid., 2:478.
7. Ibid., 2:486–487.
8. Ibid., 2:494.
9. Ibid., 3:20, 23.
10. Ibid., 3:44.
11. Ibid., 3:28–29.
12. Ibid., 3:34.
13. Ibid., 3:59.
14. Remini, *Andrew Jackson*, 1:222.
15. *The Papers of Andrew Jackson*, 3:105.
16. Ibid., 3:200.
17. Ibid., 3:114, 187–188.
18. Ibid., 3:190, 194.
19. Ibid., 3:145, 187.
20. Ibid., 2:217.
21. Vincent Nolte, *Fifty Years in Two Hemispheres* (New York: Redfield, 1854), 209–210.
22. Ibid., 2:221–222.
23. Remini, *Andrew Jackson*, 1:284–285.
24. *The Papers of Andrew Jackson*, 3:222.
25. Ibid., 3:244–245, 260.
26. Ibid., 3:269.
27. Ibid., 3:298.
28. Ibid., 3:297–298.
29. Nolte, *Fifty Years*, 238–239.
30. *The Papers of Andrew Jackson*, 3:297–298.

CHAPTER 8: LIFE IN THE PUBLIC EYE

1. *The Papers of Andrew Jackson*, ed. Sam B. Smith and Harriet Chappell Owsley (Knoxville: University of Tennessee Press, 1980), 3:344–346, 375–377.
2. Ibid., 3:384–385.
3. Ibid., 3:389.
4. Constance McLaughlin Green, *Washington: A History of the Capital, 1800–1950* (Princeton, N.J.: Princeton University Press, 1962), 3, 21.
5. *The Papers of Andrew Jackson*, 3:391–392.
6. Ibid., 392.
7. Ibid., 3:394–95; Robert Remini, *Andrew Jackson*, 3 vols. (New York: Harper & Row, 1977–1984), 1:320.
8. *The Papers of Andrew Jackson*, 3:397.
9. Ibid., 3:357.
10. Ibid., 3:44.
11. Ibid., 2:353–54.
12. Ibid., 3:101.
13. Remini, *Andrew Jackson*, 1:400–401.
14. Ibid., 1:403.
15. *The Papers of Andrew Jackson*, 5:79.
16. Ibid.
17. Ibid., 5:80.
18. Ibid., 5:80–81.
19. 1 Kings 4:25; 2 Kings 18:31; Micah 4:4; Zechariah 3:10 (KJV).

CHAPTER 9: OUT OF THE WEST

1. Katherine W. Cruse, *An Amiable Woman: Rachel Jackson* (Nashville: The Hermitage, 1994), 16–17, 20; The Hermitage website, http://www.thehermitage.com; Doris A. Hamburg, "The In-Situ Conservation Treatment of a Nineteenth-Century French Scenic Wallpaper: *Les Paysages du Telemaque dans l'Ile de Calypso*," *Journal of the American Institute for Conservation* 20, no. 2 (1981):91–99.
2. *The Papers of Andrew Jackson*, ed. Sam B. Smith and Harriet Chappell Owsley (Knoxville: University of Tennessee Press, 1980), 5:99.
3. H. W. Crew, *History of Nashville, Tenn.* (Nashville: Publishing House of the Methodist Episcopal Church, 1890), 101–102, 103, 105, 113, 115, 131.
4. *The Papers of Andrew Jackson*, 1:223.
5. Ibid., 5:213.
6. Ibid., 5:89.
7. Ibid., 5:121.
8. Ibid., 5:141.
9. Ibid., 5:211.
10. Ibid., 6:21.
11. Ibid., 5:212–213.
12. Ibid., 5:290.
13. Ibid., 5:316.

14. Ibid., 5:320.
15. Ibid., 5:342.
16. Ibid., 5:351–352.
17. Ibid., 5:322–323.
18. Ibid., 5:347, 334–335.
19. Ibid., 6:11–12.
20. Patricia Brady, *George Washington's Beautiful Nelly: The Letters of Eleanor Parke Custis Lewis to Elizabeth Bordley Gibson, 1794–1851* (Columbia: University of South Carolina Press, 1991), 145–146.
21. *The Papers of Andrew Jackson*, 5:361, 329.
22. Ibid., 5:371–372.
23. Ibid., 5:353.
24. Ibid., 5:334.
25. Ibid., 5:327–328.
26. Ibid., 5:442.
27. Ibid., 5:323.
28. Ibid. 5:329, 375–376.
29. Ibid., 5:345.
30. Ibid., 5:432.
31. Ibid., 5:440.
32. Ibid., 5:432.
33. Ibid.
34. Ibid., 5:456–457.
35. Ibid.
36. Ibid., 5:457–459.
37. Ibid., 5:456.
38. Ibid., 6:12.
39. Ibid.
40. Charles Francis Adams, ed., *Memoirs of John Quincy Adams*, 12 vols. (repro, New York, AMS Press, 1970), 6:221, 315.
41. Ibid., 6:447.
42. Ibid., 6:469.
43. *The Papers of Andrew Jackson*, 6:18.
44. Brady, *George Washington's Beautiful Nelly*, 162.
45. *The Papers of Andrew Jackson*, 6:18.
46. Ibid., 6:28; Smith, *Forty Years,* 186.
47. Brady, *George Washington's Beautiful Nelly*, 163; Charles Francis Adams, ed., *Memoirs of John Quincy Adams*, 12 vols. (repro, New York, AMS Press, 1970), 6:501.
48. Margaret Bayard Smith, *Forty Years of Washington Society*, ed. Gaillard Hunt (London: T. Fisher Unwin, 1906), 183–84.
49. *The Papers of Andrew Jackson*, 6:29–30.
50. Adams, *Memoirs of John Quincy Adams*, 6:518; Constance McLaughlin Green, *Washington: A History of the Capital, 1800–1950* (Princeton, N.J.: Princeton University Press, 1962), 1:95.
51. Adams, *Memoirs of John Quincy Adams*, 6:525.
52. J. Bennett Nolan, *Lafayette in America Day by Day* (Baltimore: Johns Hopkins Press, 1934), 285–286.

CHAPTER 10: TRIUMPH AND HEARTBREAK

1. *The Papers of Andrew Jackson,* ed. Sam B. Smith and Harriet Chappell Owsley (Knoxville: University of Tennessee Press, 1980), 6:72–73.
2. Lynn Hudson Parsons, *The Birth of Modern Politics: Andrew Jackson, John Quincy Adams, and the Election of 1828* (New York: Oxford University Press, 2009), 152.
3. Ibid., 69, xvii.
4. Charles Francis Adams, ed., *Memoirs of John Quincy Adams*, 12 vols. (repro, New York, AMS Press, 1970), 7:98.
5. Parsons, *The Birth of Modern Politics*, 137–138.
6. Jeffrey L. Pasley, *"The Tyranny of Printers": Newspaper Politics in the Early American Republic* (Charlottesville: University of Virginia Press, 2001), 364–365; Parsons, *The Birth of Modern Politics*, 134.
7. Parsons, *The Birth of Modern Politics*, 134; Robert V. Remini, *The Election of Andrew Jackson* (Westport, Conn.: Greenwood Press, 1980), 80; Adams, *The Memoirs of John Quincy Adams*, 6:113.
8. Samuel Clement, *Truth Is No Slander* (Nashville: Ariel Office, 1827), 34.
9. Remini, *The Election of Andrew Jackson*, 83–86; Parsons, *The Birth of Modern Politics*, 139.
10. *The Papers of Andrew Jackson*, 6:260–261.
11. Ibid., 6:259–260.
12. Ibid., 6:236–238, 245–246.
13. Adams, *The Memoirs of John Quincy Adams*, 6:532.
14. Ibid., 6:367.
15. *The Papers of Andrew Jackson*, 6:240–241.
16. Ibid., 6:314–315.
17. Ibid.
18. Ibid., 6:xxxvi–xxxvii.
19. Ibid., 6:240–241; *A Letter from the Jackson Committee of Nashville...upon the Subject of Ger. Jackson's Marriage* (Nashville, 1827).
20. *The Papers of Andrew Jackson*, 6:344.
21. Ibid., 6:340.
22. Ibid., 6:354–355.
23. Ibid., 6:355–356.
24. Ibid., 6:367.
25. Ibid., 6:368.
26. Adams, *The Memoirs of John Quincy Adams*, 7:479.
27. *Truth's Advocate and Monthly Anti-Jackson Expositor* (Cincinnati: Lodge, L'Hommedieu, and Hammond, 1828), 4–20.
28. *The Papers of Andrew Jackson*, 6:444.
29. Ibid., 6:469.
30. Eliza Chotard Gould diaries, 27, William R. Galt reminiscences, copies, Ladies' Hermitage Association.
31. J. F. H. Claiborne to James H. Piper, Jan. 12, 1827, Southern Historical Collection, University of North Carolina, copy, Ladies' Hermitage Association.
32. M. T. Simpson, letters, July 16, 1827, copy, Ladies' Hermitage Association.
33. *The Papers of Andrew Jackson*, 6:536–537.
34. Ibid., 6:537.

35. Ibid., 6:537–538.
36. www.u-s-history.com; Parsons, *The Birth of Modern Politics*, xiii.
37. *The Papers of Andrew Jackson*, 6:543.
38. Ibid.
39. Margaret Bayard Smith, *Forty Years of Washington Society*, ed. Gaillard Hunt (London: T. Fisher Unwin, 1906), 252–253.
40. *The Papers of Andrew Jackson*, 6:546.
41. Robert Remini, *Andrew Jackson*, 3 vols. (New York: Harper & Row, 1977–1984), 2:151.
42. Ibid.; *The Papers of Andrew Jackson*, 6:517.
43. Ibid., 6:546–547.
44. James Parton, *Life of Andrew Jackson*, 3 vols. (New York: Mason Brothers, 1860), 3:156.
45. Cyrus Brady, *The True Andrew Jackson* (Philadelphia: J. B. Lippincott, 1906), 175.
46. *The Papers of Andrew Jackson,* 6: 547; Remini, *Andrew Jackson,* 2:156.

EPILOGUE: THE PRESIDENT ALONE

1. Margaret Bayard Smith, *Forty Years of Washington Society*, ed. Gaillard Hunt (London: T. Fisher Unwin, 1906), 299.
2. *The Papers of Andrew Jackson*, ed. Sam B. Smith and Harriet Chappell Owsley (Knoxville: University of Tennessee Press, 1980), 5:366.
3. Smith, *Forty Years*, 252.
4. Ibid., 252–253.
5. Ibid., 259–260.
6. James Parton, *Life of Andrew Jackson*, 3 vols. (New York: Mason Brothers, 1860), 3:204.
7. For further information on the Eaton affair, see John F. Marszalek, *Petticoat Affair: Manners, Mutiny, and Sex in Andrew Jackson's White House* (Baton Rouge: Louisiana State University Press, 1997), and Catherine Allgor, *Parlor Politics: In Which the Ladies of Washington Help Build a City and a Government* (Charlottesville: University Press of Virginia, 2000).

BIBLIOGRAPHY

For more than fifty years, the National Historical Publications and Records Commission, the grant-making affiliate of the National Archives and Records Administration, has supported and set standards for the collection, editing, and publication of modern editions of the papers of the early presidents. Exemplary editions of these fundamental records are now available to scholars, students, and general readers, allowing widespread access to the thoughts and words of the nation's leaders.

The Papers of Andrew Jackson were the fundamental source of information about the romance of Rachel and Andrew Jackson. The first volume of this fine series, edited by Sam B. Smith and Harriet Chappell Owsley, was published in 1980. Since then, under the guidance of Editor-in-Chief Harold D. Moser, five subsequent volumes appeared. Now under the able leadership of Daniel Feller, the publication of volume seven completed the series through the death of Rachel Jackson and its aftermath. Since the inception of the Jackson Papers, the Ladies' Hermitage Association and the University of Tennessee have been essential partners in this project.

Beginning during his lifetime, Andrew Jackson has been the subject of multiple biographies. Since the 1970s, Robert V. Remini, recently retired as historian of the House of Representatives, has published numerous studies of Jackson, including a three-volume biography noted for the depth of its scholarship and the verve of its prose. No one can write about Jackson, pro or con, without consulting his work.

Robert Remini also began the process of unraveling the tangle of half-truths and exaggerations, charges and countercharges, surrounding the Jacksons' marriage. Ann Toplovich, executive director of the Tennessee Historical Society, has continued that quest, teasing out truths that seemed beyond recovery in her research for the first scholarly biography of Rachel Jackson.

MANUSCRIPT COLLECTIONS

Ladies' Hermitage Association, The Hermitage
Tennessee State Library and Archives
Williams Research Center, The Historic New Orleans Collection

Selected Sources

Abernethy, Thomas Perkins. *From Frontier to Plantation in Tennessee: A Study in Frontier Democracy.* Chapel Hill: University of North Carolina Press, 1932.

Adams, Charles Francis, ed. *Memoirs of John Quincy Adams.* Reprint ed. New York: AMS Press, 1970.

Allen, Thomas M. *A Republic in Time: Temporality & Social Imagination in Nineteenth-Century America.* Chapel Hill: University of North Carolina Press, 2008.

Allgor, Catherine. *A Perfect Union: Dolley Madison and the Creation of the American Nation.* New York: Henry Holt, 2006.

———. *Parlor Politics: In Which the Ladies of Washington Help Build a City and a Government.* Charlottesville: University of Virginia Press, 2000.

Arnow, Harriette Simpson. *Seedtime on the Cumberland.* New York: Macmillan, 1960.

Basch, Norma. *Framing American Divorce: From the Revolutionary Generation to the Victorians.* Berkeley: University of California Press, 1999.

Bassett, John S. *The Life of Andrew Jackson*, vol. 1. New York: Macmillan, 1916.

Borneman, Walter R. *1812: The War that Forged a Nation.* New York: Harper, 2005.

Brady, Patricia. *George Washington's Beautiful Nelly: The Letters of Eleanor Parke Custis Lewis to Elizabeth Bordley Gibson, 1794–1851.* Columbia: University of South Carolina Press, 1991.

Brands, H. W. *Andrew Jackson: His Life and Times.* New York: Doubleday, 2005.

Brown, Samuel R. *The Western Gazetteer.* 1817. Reprint ed.: New York: Arno Press, 1971.

Buckley, Thomas E., S.J. *The Great Catastrophe of My Life: Divorce in the Old Dominion.* Chapel Hill: University of North Carolina Press, 2002.

Burstein, Andrew. *The Passions of Andrew Jackson.* New York: Alfred A. Knopf, 2003.

———. *Sentimental Democracy: The Evolution of America's Romantic Self-Image.* New York: Hill and Wang, 1999.

Clark, Thomas D., and John D. W. Guice. *The Old Southwest, 1795–1830.* Norman: University of Oklahoma Press, 1989.

Clement, Samuel. *Truth Is No Slander.* Natchez: Ariel Office, 1827.

Corlew, Robert E. *Tennessee: A Short History.* Knoxville: University of Tennessee Press, 1981.

Cott, Nancy. *Public Vows: A History of Marriage and the Nation.* Cambridge, Mass.: Harvard University Press, 2002.

Creighton, Wilbur F., and Leland R. Johnson. *The First Presbyterian Church of Nashville.* Nashville, Tenn.: Williams, 1986.

Crew, H. W. *History of Nashville, Tenn.*, 2 vols. Nashville: Methodist Episcopal Church, South, 1890.

Crist, George Heinrich. Journal. Quoted at http://hsv.com/genlintr/newmadrd.

Cruse, Katherine W. *An Amiable Woman: Rachel Jackson.* Nashville: The Hermitage, 1994.

Daniels, Jonathan. *The Devil's Backbone: The Story of the Natchez Trace.* Gretna, La.: Pelican, 1990.

Davis, William C. *A Way Through the Wilderness: The Natchez Trace and the Civilization of the Southern Frontier.* New York: HarperCollins, 1995.

Donelson, John. *Journal of a voyage intended by God's permission in the good boat Adventure, from Fort Patrick Henry on Holston River to the French Salt Springs on Cumberland River Kept by John Donelson, December 22, 1779.* Tennessee Historical Society Miscellaneous Files, 1688–1951, Tennessee State Library and Archives.

Drake, Daniel. *Pioneer Life in Kentucky, 1785-1800.* New York: Henry Schuman, 1948.

Eslinger, Ellen. *Running Mad for Kentucky.* Lexington: University Press of Kentucky, 2004.

Faragher, John Mack. *Daniel Boone: The Life and Legend of an American Pioneer.* New York: Henry Holt, 1992.

Frank, Robin Jaffee. *Love and Loss: American Portrait and Mourning Miniatures.* New Haven, Conn.: Yale University Press, 2000.

Green, Constance McLaughlin. *Washington: A History of the Capital, 1800-1950.* Princeton, N.J.: Princeton University Press, 1962.

Hall, Basil. *Forty Etchings, from Sketches Made with the Camera Lucida in North America, in 1827 and 1828.* Edinburgh: Cadell, 1830.

———. *Travels in North America, in the Years 1827 and 1828.* Edinburgh: Cadell, 1829.

Hall, Florence Howe. *Social Usages at Washington.* New York: Harper & Bros., 1906.

Hall, Margaret. *The Aristocratic Journey,* ed. Una Pope-Hennessy. New York: Putnam's, 1931.

Hamburg, Doris A. "The In-Situ Conservation Treatment of a Nineteenth-Century French Scenic Wallpaper: *Les Paysages du Telemaque dans l'Ile de Calypso,*" *Journal of the American Institute for Conservation* 20, (1981).

Hardog, Hendrik. *Man and Wife in America: A History.* Cambridge, Mass.: Harvard University Press, 2000.

Haywood, John. *The Civil and Political History of the State of Tennessee from the Earliest Settlement to the Year 1796 including the Boundaries of the State.* Nashville: W. H. Haywood, 1891 reprint of 1823 ed.

Hermitage, The. website at http://www.thehermitage.com.

Heyrman, Christine Leigh. *Southern Cross: The Beginnings of the Bible Belt.* New York: Alfred A. Knopf, 1997.

Howe, Daniel Walker. *What Hath God Wrought: The Transformation of America, 1815-1848.* New York: Oxford University Press, 2007.

Hunt, Louise L., ed., *The Memoirs of Mrs. Edward Livingston.* New York: Harper, 1886.

Isenberg, Nancy. *Fallen Founder: The Life of Aaron Burr.* New York: Penguin, 2007.

———. *Sex and Citizenship in Antebellum America.* Chapel Hill: University of North Carolina Press, 1998.

Jackson, Andrew. *Papers of Andrew Jackson,* 7 vols. Sam B. Smith and Harriet Chappell Owsley, eds., 1940–

James, Marquis. *The Border Captain.* New York: Grosset & Dunlap, 1971.

Jones, Robbie. *The First Hermitage Restoration at the Hermitage, Home of President Andrew Jackson, Nashville, Davidson County, Tennessee. Historic Structure Report.* Draft. Nashville: Ladies' Hermitage Association, December 2002.

Kendall, Amos. *The Life of General Andrew Jackson.* New York, 1843.

Latrobe, John H. B. *The First Steamboat on Western Waters.* Baltimore: Maryland Historical Society, 1871.

Marszalek, John F. *The Petticoat Affair: Manners, Mutiny, and Sex in Andrew Jackson's White House.* Baton Rouge: Louisiana State University, 1997.

Martin, Joshua. *Lorenzo Dow's Journal.* Quoted at http://hsv.com/genlintr/newmadrd.

Nolan, J. Bennett. *Lafayette in America Day by Day.* Baltimore: Johns Hopkins Press, 1934.

Nolte, Vincent. *Fifty Years in Both Hemispheres.* New York: Redfield, 1854.

Norton, Herman A. *Religion in Tennessee, 1777-1945.* Knoxville: The University of Tennessee Press, 1981.

Pasley, Jeffrey L. *"The Tyranny of Printers": Newspaper Politics in the Early American Republic.* Charlottesville: University of Virginia Press, 2001.

Parsons, Lynn Hudson. *The Birth of Modern Politics: Andrew Jackson, John Quincy Adams, and the Election of 1828.* New York: Oxford University Press, 2009.

Parton, James. *Life of Andrew Jackson,* 3 vols. New York: Mason Brothers, 1860.

Payne, Dale. *Frontier Memories, as Taken from the Shane Interviews. Rev. John Dabney Shane of the Draper Manuscripts.* North Kansas City, Missouri: The author, 2002.

————. *Narratives of Pioneer Life and Border Warfare: Personal Recollections, Memoirs and Reminiscences of Indian Campaigns, Captivities and Pioneer Life on the Eastern Frontier.* North Kansas City, Missouri: The author, 2004.

Putnam, Albigence W. *History of Middle Tennessee or Life and Times of Gen. James Robertson.* Nashville: The author, 1859.

Remini, Robert V. *The Battle of New Orleans: Andrew Jackson and America's First Military Victory.* New York: Viking, 1999.

————. *The Election of Andrew Jackson.* Westport, Conn.: Greenwood Press, 1980.

————. *The Legacy of Andrew Jackson: Essays on Democracy, Indian Removal, and Slavery.* Baton Rouge: Louisiana State University Press, 1988.

————. *The Life of Andrew Jackson*, 3 vols. New York: Harper & Row, 1977–1984.

Smith, Margaret Bayard. *Forty Years of Washington Society*, ed. Gaillard Hunt. London: T. Fisher Unwin, 1906.

Story, William Wetmore, ed. *The Life and Letters of Joseph Story*, vol. 1. London: John Chapman, 1851.

Stover, Carl W., and Jerry L. Coggman. *Seismicity of the United States, 1568–1989.* Washington, D.C.: U.S. Government Printing Office, 1993. Abridged at gttp://earthquake.usgs.gov/earthquakes.

Toplovich, Ann. "Marriage, Mayhem, and Presidential Politics: The Robards-Jackson Backcountry Scandal," *Ohio Valley History* 5 (Winter 2005): 3–22.

Truth's Advocate and Monthly Anti-Jackson Expositor. Cincinnati: Lodge, L'Hommedieu, and Hammond, 1828.

Wilentz, Sean. *Andrew Jackson.* New York: Henry Holt, 2005.

Williams, Samuel Cole. *Early Travels in the Tennessee Country, 1540–1800.* Johnson City, Tennessee: Watauga Press, 1928.

Wyatt-Brown, Bertram. *Southern Honor: Ethics and Behavior in the Old South.* New York: Oxford University Press, 1982.

Zibart, Carl F. *Yesterday's Nashville.* Miami, FL: E. A. Seemann, 1976.

INDEX